With countless examples from across the arts, [...]
of diverse recommendations for Christians who appreciate the arts. [...]
spectacles to constantly amuse us, Glaspey helps readers cut through the clutter and meaning [...]
attend to the good, true, and beautiful. For over-mediated souls whose senses are dulled by the barrage of stimuli before them, a book like this is an absolute gift.

> **BRETT MCCRACKEN,** senior editor at The Gospel Coalition and author of *The Wisdom Pyramid: Feeding Your Soul in a Post-Truth World*

In *Discovering God through the Arts*, Terry Glaspey writes, "Experiencing art is like falling in love. It demands vulnerability at the start and often takes a lot of work." Reading Glaspey's beautiful, rich, and profound new book felt a lot like falling in love. From J. S. Bach to William Blake, from Dante to Dylan, from Caravaggio to Flannery O'Connor, Glaspey explains how artists through the ages have pointed us to God. Glaspey's writing is engaging and winsome, and his insights dazzling and rich. it's a survival manual for the radically changing world we live in. Whether we admit it or not, our artists, musicians, filmmakers, poets, and writers have become our soul's ministers in a time when traditional religious institutions seem to be losing their way. Glaspey's book teaches us how art comforts us; reinvigorates our faith, our empathy, and our prayers; and revives our much-neglected sense of wonder. Read it for the joy it contains—and also for your own soul's sake.

> **ROBERT HUDSON,** author, *The Poet and the Fly, Kiss the Earth When You Pray*, and *The Monk's Record Player*

When we begin to see God as Creator—as artist, as poet, as musician, as novelist, as sculptor, as architect—we find ourselves continually overwhelmed by his loving presence. Not since Brennan Manning has there been a more endearing voice urging us to seek the God of all creation.

> **KAREN SPEARS ZACHARIAS,** award-winning author and speaker.

"Beauty will save the world." So wrote Dostoevsky. No truer statement was ever made. Despite this, we are a people who at best often ignore it, or at worst sometimes outright despise it—and do so to our peril, not least as followers of Jesus. With prose that is as beautiful as the subject matter into which our author bids us come and dine, Terry Glaspey has, with *Discovering God through the Arts*, given us a treasure. Read it and live. Read it and flourish. And by all means, read it and become the very beauty that God envisions you to be.

> **CURT THOMPSON,** psychiatrist and author of *The Soul of Shame* and *Anatomy of the Soul*

Reading this goldmine of insight is like joining Glaspey—a born teacher—on a global art walk. I listen with gratitude as he reveals treasure within pictures, poems, and music. He writes just as he speaks, just as he lives: with generosity, enthusiasm, and a keen eye for recognizing God's glory in unexpected places. He leads us, by example, into a deeper and more dazzling communion with our Creator.

> **JEFFREY OVERSTREET,** assistant professor of English and writing at Seattle Pacific University, and author of *Auralia's Colors* and *Through a Screen Darkly*

Brimming with insight, information, and invitation, *Discovering God through the Arts* reads like a travelogue of Terry's own heart's pilgrimage through the arts to an authentic encounter with God, with others, and with "the teeming profusion of beauty and mystery in this world of ours."

> **STEVE BELL,** award-winning singer/songwriter and author

In *Discovering God through the Arts*, Terry reminds us that art can be a channel through which we experience the Divine. If you long for artistic depth in a superficial age, then you've come to the right place.

> **BEN COURSON,** founder of Hope Generation, and author of *Optimisfits* and *Flirting with Darkness*.

I was a college grad before Francis Schaeffer and Hans Rookmaaker mentored me in the ways of imagination through their books. Terry Glaspey continues down their same path but makes the journey even more accessible in his beautiful book, *Discovering God through the Arts*. You'll be inspired and comforted. And, most importantly, as the arts help you draw near to God through both your reason and imagination, you will enjoy your beautiful God.

LAEL ARRINGTON, coauthor/editor, *Faith and Culture: The Guide to a Culture Shaped by Faith*

I was a college grad before Francis Schaeffer and Hans Rookmaaker mentored me in the ways of *Discovering God through the Arts* is a compelling work that commands the minds and hearts of those with a faith heritage; and those seeking ways in which to engage with the challenging and controversial aspects of the arts. It is a thought-provoking and pivotal work that enlarges one's sense of how art can foster a deeper relationship with God.

MARIE TEILHARD, conceptual portrait photographer and Arts Advocate

In my circles, Terry Glaspey is an institution in himself. In *Discovering God through the Arts*, Glaspey takes us on a whimsical and illuminating journey of appreciating God's gifts of creativity as they are scattered through history. A must read from an unquestionably transformative author.

A.J. SWOBODA, assistant professor of Bible, Theology, and World Christianity at Bushnell University and the author of *After Doubt*

In *Discovering God through the Arts*, Terry Glaspey serves as a skilled and informative tour guide who personally introduces us to his "friends": a myriad of artisans who have profoundly impacted his life by helping him relate to God and the Bible with more openness, wonder, and curiosity. This book will enhance the spiritual life of anyone who desires to be awakened to the multi-faceted nature of God as reflected through poetry, music, film, photography, paintings, and much more.

MICHELLE WATSON CANFIELD, author of *Let's Talk: Conversation Starters for Dads and Daughters*, and radio/podcast host of *The Dad Whisperer*

Terry Glaspey is an incisive and artful craftsman of words who has spent decades paying attention to art in all its forms, and thinking deeply about the ways in which they express and shape the life of faith. Whether you are a long-term kindred spirit in that appreciation or new to contemplating the notion of the arts and spiritual disciplines as vital and intertwined paths to faith, join Glaspey as a fellow pilgrim through the careful, leisurely reading of this warm and winsome book.

JEFF CROSBY, publishing executive, and compiler of *Days of Grace through the Year*

In *Discovering God through the Arts*, Terry Glaspey gives us a perfect pairing for his award-winning *75 Masterpieces Every Christian Should Know*. Thoughtfully written, this book explores the mysteries of how we can meet God in deeper ways through our encounters with art, and how that knowledge can enrich our faith. Glaspey leads us step-by-step through the journey of discovery of art's power not only to inspire but also to heal, and with the honed skill of a good teacher, he offers us a wonderful resource to further our journeying. I heartily recommend it to you!

LANCIA E. SMITH, founder and executive director, *Cultivating* and The Cultivating Project

Discovering God through the Arts is a truly fabulous book, full of profound thoughts and clear-eyed stories, background information into poetry and the visual arts, film, and music—from classical to rock and gospel. With delightful excursions into important art pieces and solid teaching about how paying attention to the arts can help us pray and deepen our discipleship, Glaspey brings his breath-taking knowledge to ordinary folks. This book will make you a better Christian and, happily, a better human being. Don't miss it!

BYRON BORGER, owner of Hearts & Minds Bookstore

(continued on page 271)

DISCOVERING
GOD THROUGH
the Arts

How We Can Grow Closer to God
by Appreciating Beauty & Creativity

TERRY GLASPEY

MOODY PUBLISHERS

CHICAGO

© 2021 by
TERRY GLASPEY

All rights reserved. No part of this book may be reproduced in any form without permission in writing from the publisher, except in the case of brief quotations embodied in critical articles or reviews.

All Scripture quotations, unless otherwise indicated, are taken from the Holy Bible, New International Version®, NIV®. Copyright © 1973, 1978, 1984, 2011 by Biblica, Inc.™ Used by permission of Zondervan. All rights reserved worldwide. www.zondervan.com The "NIV" and "New International Version" are trademarks registered in the United States Patent and Trademark Office by Biblica, Inc.™

Scripture quotations marked ESV are from the ESV® Bible (The Holy Bible, English Standard Version®), copyright © 2001 by Crossway, a publishing ministry of Good News Publishers. Used by permission. All rights reserved.

Scripture quotations marked MSG are taken from THE MESSAGE, copyright © 1993, 2002, 2018 by Eugene H. Peterson. Used by permission of NavPress. All rights reserved. Represented by Tyndale House Publishers, a Division of Tyndale House Ministries.

Scripture quotations marked NASB are taken from the New American Standard Bible®, Copyright © 1960, 1962, 1963, 1968, 1971, 1972, 1973, 1975, 1977, 1995 by The Lockman Foundation. Used by permission. www.Lockman.org

Scripture quotations marked NKJV are taken from the New King James Version. Copyright © 1982 by Thomas Nelson. Used by permission. All rights reserved.

Scripture quotations marked KJV are taken from the King James Version.

Names and details of some stories have been changed to protect the privacy of individuals.

Edited by Mackenzie Conway
Interior and cover design: Erik M. Peterson
Cover painting: Green Wheat Fields, Auvers (1890) by Vincent van Gogh, The National Gallery of Art. Public domain.

All websites and phone numbers listed herein are accurate at the time of publication but may change in the future or cease to exist. The listing of website references and resources does not imply publisher endorsement of the site's entire contents. Groups and organizations are listed for informational purposes, and listing does not imply publisher endorsement of their activities.

Library of Congress Cataloging-in-Publication Data

Names: Glaspey, Terry W., author.
Title: Discovering God through the arts : how every Christians can grow
    closer to God by appreciating beauty & creativity / Terry Glaspey.
Description: Chicago : Moody Publishers, [2020] | Includes bibliographical
    references. | Summary: "What does art have to do with faith? For many
    Christians, paintings, films, music, and other forms of art are simply
    used for wall decoration, entertaining distraction, or worshipful
    devotion. But what if the arts played a more prominent role in the
    Christian life? In The Arts and Our Spiritual Journey, discover how the
    arts can be tools for faith-building, life-changing spiritual formation
    for all Christians. Terry Glaspey, author of 75 Masterpieces Every
    Christian Should Know, examines: How the arts assist us in prayer and
    contemplation How the arts help us rediscover a sense of wonder How the
    arts help us deal with emotions How the arts aid theological reflection
    and so much more. Let your faith be enriched, and discover how beauty
    and creativity can draw you nearer to the ultimate Creator"-- Provided
    by publisher.
Identifiers: LCCN 2020039585 (print) | LCCN 2020039586 (ebook) | ISBN
    9780802419972 | ISBN 9780802498885 (ebook)
Subjects: LCSH: Christianity and the arts.
Classification: LCC BR115.A8 G53 2020 (print) | LCC BR115.A8 (ebook) |
    DDC 261.5/7--dc23
LC record available at https://lccn.loc.gov/2020039585
LC ebook record available at https://lccn.loc.gov/2020039586

Originally delivered by fleets of horse-drawn wagons, the affordable paperbacks from D. L. Moody's publishing house resourced the church and served everyday people. Now, after more than 125 years of publishing and ministry, Moody Publishers' mission remains the same—even if our delivery systems have changed a bit. For more information on other books (and resources) created from a biblical perspective, go to www.moodypublishers.com or write to:

Moody Publishers
820 N. LaSalle Boulevard
Chicago, IL 60610

1 3 5 7 9 10 8 6 4 2

Printed in the United States of America

CONTENTS

Discovering the Power of the Arts

TWO YEARS AGO, I WAS IN VENICE all by myself. The tour of Italy I had joined was moving on to the next city on their itinerary, but I still had several things I wanted to see, so I stayed behind. Venice is a city of almost indescribable beauty—though it is laid out like a maze. One of the joys is purposely getting lost and allowing yourself the luxury of discovery, which is what I did the first day. But on the second day I knew I needed to do a little planning so I didn't miss anything important. As I mapped out my day, I included one of the places that was near the top of my list, though it is often not one that gets much attention from the popular travel guides—the Scuola Grande di San Rocco. When I showed up and paid my entrance fee, I found that I had the place mostly to myself.

The Scuola Grande di San Rocco is an underappreciated treasure of Venice, a building that doesn't look like anything special from the outside, but when you make your way inside you discover an ornately baroque design and walls that contain over sixty paintings by Jacopo Tintoretto, a great late-Renaissance painter who was a very committed Christian. The leaders of the organization who made the building their home asked him to paint a series of pictures illustrating events from the life of Christ. What he created from that commission was a visual retelling of the Gospels, illustrating nearly every major incident of Jesus' life.

I toured the first floor, taking in Tintoretto's exquisite vision of the life of Christ, then climbed the ornate staircase to the second floor, where I turned a corner and entered a side room, a place where meetings were once held for members of this religious confraternity. There I came face-to-face with an image of the crucifixion that extended across the entire back wall of the room. I literally gasped aloud at the power of this triumphant image of the crucifixion.

The Crucifixion by Jacopo Tintoretto, Scuola Grande di San Rocco, Venice

I stood in front of it, taking it all in slowly, and letting my eyes wander across the teeming bustle of activity that surrounds the cross upon which Jesus is hanging. Yet, despite everything that is going on in the painting, Tintoretto has organized the composition so that it always brings your eyes back to the central figure who hangs there against the sky. This unusual image of the crucifixion is more triumphant than somber. Jesus' body is surrounded by a bright halo that almost resembles outstretched wings. It almost appears as though He is about to burst off the cross in a display of power and splendor. His supernatural strength can be seen even in this moment of greatest weakness.

I paused for a long time in front of this painting, letting its power wash over me. Then I found myself praying. I hadn't planned to stop and pray in front of this masterpiece, but it seemed the only natural response.

The rest of the day I was haunted by this image as I toured the splendors of Venice. It made real to me again what had happened on the cross. Jesus' sacrifice was no mere theological abstraction. The painting reminded me of the reality of what Jesus suffered on my behalf and sparked an undefinable, but immensely resonant, emotional response.

There have been so many times when I have experienced something akin to what I felt during those inspiring moments in Venice. I have heard the voice of God whispering to me during a performance of the *Messiah* by Handel, felt my preconceptions challenged while listening to a Bob Dylan album, been left speechlessly exalted by films like *The Tree of Life* and *Of Gods and Men*, and sent into rapturous revelry as I slowly pored over T. S. Eliot's *Four Quartets*. I have gained a new appreciation of Christ's work on my behalf as I read *The Lion, the Witch, and the Wardrobe*, understood the hugeness of God's mercy anew as I pondered Rembrandt's *The Prodigal Son*, and had my breath taken away by the cavernous holiness of Ely Cathedral in England. As I have traveled through my life, I have learned to pay attention to how the arts can open my heart, and how they can draw me closer to God. Sometimes I just sit and enjoy a poem or a song in the presence of God, experiencing the intimacy of His company as we enjoy the beauty together.

Whenever I visit a new city, I search out the art museums. I have collected a library of films and compact discs so that I will be able to re-watch and re-visit those works that have moved me in the past and seek out new adventures in listening and viewing. My bookshelves groan under the weight of the books of poetry and literature that I have collected and set alongside books on history, theology, and the spiritual life. A life of engaging with the arts has changed me, taught me new things, given me amazing vicarious experiences, and been a means for nourishing my spiritual life and growing in my faith. Alongside the more usual spiritual practices—prayer, reading the Bible and meditating upon it, finding time for silence and solitude, and engaging every Sunday morning with fellow believers—I have found the arts to be a way of deepening my experience with God. Again, and again, the arts have become a tool for transforming my heart and mind and spirit.

Many Christians, I have discovered, have a limited vision of the place the arts hold and are content with using them for simple purposes. For them, the arts are often used as decoration, as a distraction from life's stresses, or as a sign of devotion. My argument in this book is that they can do so much more. When we ask little from the arts, we will likely receive little in return. But if we allow them to do so, they can enrich our walk with God in life-changing ways.

For many, art is used for little more than ***decoration***; a way to add a bit of much-needed beauty to their life. Some, for example, choose to surround themselves with visual art that does little more than match the color of their drapes or look good with their couch. Likewise, the music they listen to is often meant simply to create a pleasing backdrop for the activities of their days. They don't really listen to it with any attention. It is essentially musical wallpaper. Of course, art can prettify our environment, and most of us need more beauty in our lives, but the arts can do so much more than that.

> **The arts want to take us on a journey deeper into reality.**

The arts can also do more than provide a *distraction*. Many use the arts to divert themselves from the stress and pressure of life. The arts can be used as a retreat from reality when the world seems too much for us, or just a way to kill some time and keep boredom at bay. Honestly, many popular movies, books, and songs don't really have much of significance to say, but they are useful for keeping us diverted. And what they offer is not so much real life, but a formulaic approach to the complexities of life. They may temporarily make life feel safer or happier as they use their formulaic approaches to avoid life's harsher realities. The usual romantic comedy or action flick generally doesn't ask much from us, nor does it offer much of lasting value for the time we have invested. God knows we all need some distraction now and then. The occasional action adventure movie or romantic comedy can serve their purposes, but these purposes are less than the fulness of what the arts have to offer. The arts want to take us on a journey deeper into reality.

Finally, the arts can be used as a sign of *devotion*. Both in the context of our worship services and our daily lives, the arts can make a statement about who we are and what we believe. Some Christians tend, therefore, to limit their intake of the arts only to those that are useful in this endeavor. They listen only to "Christian" music, only read "Christian" books, and only have an interest in art that makes a clear religious statement. They might even fear the influence of so-called "secular" art. Of course, the arts that we use in our liturgies are things we treasure—our hymns, worship songs, stained glass, and inspiring images. All these are helpful for expanding and enriching the emotional and spiritual impact of our worship experience, which is why they are a part of most worship traditions. But we need not limit engagement with the arts to these purposes. As we will explore in this book, the arts can impact us in powerful ways beyond their pragmatic usefulness or as an adornment for the serious business of worship. They can be everyday tools for growth and transformation in our lives.

Many of my most transformative spiritual experiences have been in the company of the arts. Books, poems, music, and films have been constant companions on my spiritual journey and played a part in defining moments along that path. I'll share a few of my stories in the course of this book.

I am not alone in finding engagement with the arts to be a way of deepening my connection with God. Over the years I've heard a lot of stories. I know of a woman who started attending church again after several years away as a direct result of attending a performance of Bach's *St. Matthew Passion*. Another had his interest in Jesus Christ ignited by watching the mini-series *Jesus of Nazareth* on television. It transformed formerly abstract ideas about religion into a focus on the incarnation of God in Christ. It made the stories in the Gospels feel more like real history. Another person I know marks the beginning of his serious exploration of faith with reading a collection of the poems of Mary Oliver. Her vision of the natural world awakened something within him. Yet another friend tells of joining a gospel choir because she enjoyed singing, but then slowly beginning to comprehend the hope contained in the songs, which caused her to revisit her spiritual questions. Singing the lyrics caused her to begin to feel in her heart what she sang off the page. I know others who say that listening to Mozart or Bach gets them in the right frame of mind to pray. And still others use poetry to ignite their contemplation of spiritual things.

Most of us, if we think about it even for a moment, can recall childhood experiences with art that first oriented us toward the spiritual life: hearing a dramatic telling of a Bible story (or a rhyming children's *Arch Book* version of it), or being taken with the words of a favorite hymn or gospel song, or maybe being enraptured by the way the light slanted in through a stained glass window and caused colored light to dance among the pews, or possibly a beloved painting that hung in a Sunday school or a sanctuary, or maybe the soul-stirring vibrations of an organ prelude that seemed to rouse something deep down inside. And such experiences have continued to be a part of our spiritual journey. Again and again the arts have been companions along our spiritual path, though many of us may not have thought much about their impact. In this book, we are going to do just that.

CHAPTER ONE

The Arts and the Spiritual Disciplines:

Two Paths to a Deeper Faith

ONE DAY I WAS SITTING IN THE LUNCHROOM where I worked, and I was thoroughly engaged in reading a novel by Kurt Vonnegut. His books have always made me laugh even as they challenged my thinking, and it must have been the snort of mirth I released that made Carl determine that this would be a good time to interrupt me. "Whatcha reading?" he asked, gently closing the Bible that sat on the table in front of him as a sign he wanted to chat. Honestly, I didn't want to talk right then, as I was kind of lost in my book, but I knew the polite response would be to answer him. So, I did.

"It's a really great novel by Kurt Vonnegut," I answered, holding it up so he could see the cover.

"Hmmm," was his only response, and I detected a disapproving tone in it.

"Yeah, Vonnegut is so creative and such a great cultural critic," I offered.

"Oh."

"Have you read any of his books?" I asked, thinking it likely that he had at least been assigned *Cat's Cradle* or *Slaughterhouse-Five* at some point.

"Nope. I don't really have time for reading fiction," he explained. "I mostly just want to read books that will help me in my life or help me grow closer to God. Life is too short to read about things that never really happened. I figure that if I mostly just read the Bible, I am going to learn everything I need to know." He knew that I was a Christian, so I imagine he thought I would find this convicting somehow.

As we chatted further, I learned that he also didn't go see movies unless they had a strong Christian message (or at least no swearing or dirty bits), that he rarely listened to anything other than worship music, and that, outside the Bible, his reading was pretty much limited to popular faith-based books about how he could be a better Christian or how he could overcome certain sinful tendencies that he struggled with. Carl felt that it was dangerous to pay too much attention to art and culture, as it might cause a person to doubt or your choices might cause others to stumble.

He was completely sincere, and I knew him to be a person who tried to walk out the implications of his faith. I understood his passion to place every area of his life under the lordship of Jesus. But I found his thoughts to be a little short-sighted and actually not in line with what the Bible teaches or with what Christians have believed down through time. Such thinking, I suggested, could actually cut him off from tools that God might want to use to help him in his spiritual growth.

After some back and forth, I could tell he had decided I was a lost cause on this issue, at least until he could gather some more ammunition for arguing his views. So, he suggested we agree to disagree, and he let me go back to wasting my time with my book. I gladly did so.

There have always been Christians who were suspicious about the value of the arts. It is a conversation that Christians have been having since the early days of the church. Some early leaders suggested that any focus on the *visual* instead of the *verbal* or *written* was potentially dangerous, and, quoting the second commandment, they warned against making any "graven images" (Ex. 20:4–5 KJV). While that passage is focused on forbidding idolatry, some were concerned that a revered piece of art might easily become an idol. Such fears arose again during the Reformation, based on a concern about the excesses of previous centuries; their artistic creations may have, at times, brought people perilously close to confusing the divine with a human creation.

In some cases, these artistic artifacts were believed to have spiritual powers as direct connections with the divine. Some thought, for example, that touching a statue of the virgin or of a revered saint could heal them of their diseases. In response, some of the Reformers took a hard line and stripped their churches of all adornments, even busting statues, whitewashing over frescoes, melting down gold furnishings, and destroying religious paintings. Luther, however, suggested a different approach. He was open to the arts as long as it was clear that they were only symbols of divine truth, and not actually direct channels of any divine power. He saw that art and music could help people understand the new Reformation theology. He even collaborated with his friend, the painter Lucas Cranach the Elder, to create new altarpieces with a more distinctly Protestant message to replace the previous Catholic ones.

And outside the walls of the church buildings, Reformation

polemics on all sides were often carried out by the popular media of broadsheets, paintings, and prints, made possible by the new technology of printing and distributed to the common folk as visual tracts. Or such art could be useful for explaining the meaning of the new Protestant theology in simple terms, as in this wonderfully didactic picture by Lucas Cranach. Such work was art as instruction.

Allegory of Law and Grace by Lucas Cranach, Alte Pinakothek, Munich

Art as a helpful tool. Art as a dangerous temptation. Both views of art survive into our own time. While some remain cautious, others have seen the great power of the arts to move the human soul and assist believers along their spiritual journey.

The Bible does not forbid using art as part of religious practice. In fact, it encourages it. The prohibition against graven images, writes Francis

Schaeffer, "does not forbid the *making* of representational art, but rather the *worship* of it."[1] The artist is free to exercise their creativity, but must never confuse the work of art with that which it points toward.

The Tabernacle, and then later the Temple, were places where worship took place for the ancient Israelites. As we read their descriptions in the pages of the Old Testament, we discover that each was a work of architectural artistry and each was embellished with elaborate ornamentation. When God gave directions for what He wanted these buildings to look like, He did not order up a straightforward or simple design, nor did He instruct the craftspeople to only create the expected religious imagery, but instead had them use images of natural objects such as flowers, trees, and animals. When building God's temple, King Solomon called for the walls to be encrusted with precious stones. The purpose of such ornamentation was not utilitarian. Its purpose was that it be beautiful (2 Chron. 3:6).

The designs for the Tabernacle and the Temple are a good reminder that God, the One who created everything, delights in creativity, and sees it as a way of pointing toward His truth. And God takes art so seriously that He handpicked a man named Bezalel to undertake this work of creativity and filled him "with the Spirit of God, with wisdom, with understanding, with knowledge and with all kinds of skills—to make artistic designs for work in gold, silver and bronze, to cut and set stones, to work in wood, and to engage in all kinds of crafts" (Ex. 31:3–5). It was not enough, in God's eyes, to create something functional; He wanted something that was exquisitely artful.

Art has been part of the Christian heritage from the earliest days. Deep in the catacombs of Rome, early believers left behind images that reflected their faith and their struggles against persecution. It is really a miracle that any early Christian art still exists today, but some has survived the intense persecution of the faith, the ravages of time, and the suspicion of some early church leaders about the appropriateness of representing the sacred in a visual form. In the early days, there were no public places (no church buildings) to display art and, for the first few centuries, scant financial resources in the churches to patronize artists. With all the challenges, art went underground. Literally. Creative believers left behind their pictures in these burial chambers to celebrate the new faith.

Many of these images focused on Old Testament stories of deliverance, such as the three Hebrews in the fiery furnace, the story of Noah and the ark, Daniel in the lion's den, and Jonah, whose three days in the belly of a whale was seen as a prefiguration of the three days Jesus spent in the tomb before His resurrection. Other images illustrate stories of Jesus' miraculous healings or celebrate Him as the Good Shepherd. There are, in fact, more than 120 instances of the Good Shepherd image in the catacombs. This image was never intended to be a literal portrait of Jesus, but it was a potent symbol of His love and care.

WikiCommons

The Good Shepherd, Catacombs of Priscilla, Rome.

As early as 215 AD, the church father Hippolytus allowed new believers to become or remain artists as long as they didn't make idols.

By the time of Gregory the Great (600 AD), a tradition of valuing the arts as a way of communicating truth had become generally accepted, though there would still be a drawn-out iconoclastic controversy, which ultimately had as much to do with political motivations as religious ones. Finally, when the rhetoric cooled and the dust settled, the church came down on the side of embracing the value of images.

Gregory famously wrote, "Pictorial representation is made use of in churches for this reason: that such as are ignorant of letters may at least read by looking at the walls what they cannot read in books."[2] He saw the arts as a way to educate the largely illiterate population of his time in theology and spirituality. This perspective

Art helps us understand the complexities of theology and of life and awakens our spirits to the wonder of God's Word and God's world.

was responsible for an explosion of visual art, sculpture, mosaics, and church architecture in the centuries that followed. The views of such thinkers might be encapsulated in this quote from Robin Margaret Jensen, a prominent historian of early church art:

> Art crystalizes, or perhaps materializes, certain points of
> doctrine which, while based on scripture, are sometimes
> more often encountered in theological arguments than
> in ordinary daily experience. Images can make the bridge
> between the material and the intellectual. . . . Visual images
> also speak directly and clearly, even to the simplest believer.[3]

So artistic images continue to speak to us today, as well as other art forms that comment on the Scripture text, reinforcing Scripture's power and bringing it to life with dramatic effect. They help us understand the complexities of theology and of life and awaken our spirits to the wonder of God's Word and God's world.

Music found an easier acceptance in the church because of its connection with worship in ancient Israel. From the song of Moses (Ex. 15) to the poetic expression of the Psalms, there is a strong tradition of valuing music in the Bible. The New Testament records that Jesus and the apostles sang a hymn after celebrating the last supper (Mark 14:26), Paul and Silas sang in prison (Acts 16:25), and singing was part of the early gatherings of the church (Acts 2:46–47). In Ephesians 5:19, Paul celebrates the value of "psalms and hymns and spiritual songs" (ESV). Many scholars even suggest that several Pauline passages may be quotes from the hymns of his day, such as 1 Timothy 3:16 and 2 Timothy 2:11–13, which were used as quick summaries of key doctrinal beliefs. Then there is the book of Revelation, which is filled with instances of worship and singing. Singing, it seems to imply, is nothing less than a foretaste of heaven.

Martin Luther was a proponent of the great value of music in the church. He recognized its ability to communicate the truths of Scripture in a way that could stir the hearts of every man and woman. In fact, he wrote that "next to the Word of God, the noble art of music is the greatest treasure in the world."[4] He wrote at least thirty-six hymns and made music and singing a centerpiece of worship. He reveled in the joy that music could bring to the human heart, and memorably said:

> This precious gift has been bestowed on men to remind
> them that they are created to praise and magnify the Lord
> . . . one begins to see with amazement the great and perfect
> wisdom of God in this wonderful work of music, where
> one voice takes a simple part and round it sing three,
> four, or five other voices, leaping, springing round about,

marvelously gracing the simple part, like a folk dance in heaven with friendly bows, embracing, and hearty swinging of partners. He who does not find this an inexpressible miracle of the Lord is truly a clod.[5]

Each of the artistic disciplines we'll be exploring in this book—visual art, music, literature, poetry, architecture, filmmaking, photography, and more—cannot only be a source of enjoyment but also a tool for spiritual growth and formation. The arts can change and transform us within, which is why they are indispensable for our lives. And hey, you don't want to be a "clod," do you?

Spiritual growth, as most of us can personally testify, doesn't just happen. It requires that we make some choices and some commitments. It requires that we engage with spiritual practices or spiritual disciplines to guide us along the path to spiritual maturity. Our salvation may not be primarily concerned with how diligently we pursue our life with God, but our actual spiritual maturity is most definitely connected to it. Spiritual disciplines are what we do that encourages growth. That's why, when we talk about our relationship with God, we often use metaphors of progression, words and

> **We practice our faith so we might become more adept as disciples of Jesus Christ.**

phrases that speak of our spiritual maturity as a walk, a journey, running a race, or moving through stages. When we stand still, we aren't going forward. We practice our faith so we might become more adept as disciples of Jesus Christ.

If we want to become a better piano player, we must practice in order to improve, and it's the same for playing golf, cooking, painting, or any number of skills at which we want to become more adept. We get better by focusing on the skill at which we want to excel. Similarly, the spiritual life also contains practices that will help us deepen our connection with God and become the kind of people we really want to be. Prayer, reading the Scriptures, meditating on God's Word, and fellowshipping with other believers are just a few of the practices that keep us moving forward on the spiritual path.

Whereas *religion* is often concerned with structures, institutions, and dogmas, growing spiritually is about deepening our beliefs, becoming more aware of God's presence, surrendering to His will, searching for a more profound understanding, finding inner peace, discovering greater freedom and contentment. And, ultimately, it is about transformation. To move forward in the spiritual life is, as Paul writes in 2 Corinthians 3:18, to be "transformed into his image with ever-increasing glory" into a reflection of Christ's likeness. God wants to do the necessary interior work in our hearts that will manifest itself in outward change. When the inner life is strengthened, the outer life changes for the better. Our relationship with God is not just about "getting saved," but about "being remade" in the likeness of Jesus. Salvation is the event that begins the journey. True spirituality is not about just believing the right things about God, but about living out those truths in our daily lives.

> **Discipline isn't meant to lead to guilt, but to a life of more intense devotion.**

Whether you are an artist trying to perfect your craft, or a believer seeking a more perfect life reflecting Christ (Matt. 5:48), you must show up every day and do what needs to be done. Even when you don't feel like it. And you must do most of the work yourself. You can't rely on your family, your pastor, or your counselor. No one else can do it for you. And spiritual growth takes time and patience. You can't get good at playing the violin, for example, if you only put in half an hour a week. Can you really expect to find more intimacy with God if you just check-in with Him for a few minutes each week? Spiritual growth requires some discipline. Discipline doesn't mean getting caught up in a long menu of shoulds. Discipline isn't meant to lead to guilt, but to a life of more intense devotion. At the start it may feel like hard work, but the end result is worth the energy expended.

To be clear, God doesn't love us more when we are disciplined. Our goal in a disciplined life is not about earning salvation or gaining His attention. It is about a desire to draw closer to Him, to deepen our experience with Him, and above all, to change. When you show up through the disciplines, things start to happen. Not all the time and every day, but increasingly so when intimacy with God becomes a focus for your life.

Discipline is also a critical part of the making of art. Artists must master all the technical aspects of their work before a creative break-through can occur. They must learn about line and color and composition, as well as shapes and shades. They must gather their supplies and make certain they have the right tools at hand. Only then can they create a beautiful work of art. So, in the spiritual life, you might need to learn some basics so that your spiritual breakthrough can happen. You might recite some great prayers from Scripture or from believers through the centuries in order to give you the language you need to express your heart to God. You might need to learn how to deal with distractions that rob you of focus. You might want to learn some breathing techniques that help calm and focus your mind.

These are all tools that you can use in a natural way once they become part of your spiritual toolbox. The reason golfers spend a lot of time swinging a golf club in practice is so that when they are standing over the ball and getting ready to hit it, they don't have to even think about the details. It has become ingrained. Second nature. Spontaneity can occur because of all the preparation.

And it requires a commitment to stay patient and keep moving forward. "Spirituality," writes Robert Wuthnow, "is less like a water-color that can be finished quickly and more like a sculpture that requires a long, slow process of chipping away without seeing any immediate results."[6]

But spiritual growth is not only about spiritual practices, for which the arts can sometimes be a great companion and encourager, but it is also about renewing our spiritual vision and passion, which is precisely where the arts can have the most impact and influence.

The arts are, for most of us, already an important element of our journey of faith. We may not, however, always be conscious of this fact. The architecture of the places and spaces where we worship, along with their stained-glass windows and the vessels for celebrating the Lord's Supper. The music we sing together or listen to a choir per-form—hymns, gospel songs, worship choruses, anthems, and musical interludes that occur during key parts of the service. The cross that adorns most sanctuaries. In some traditions, the vestments worn by clergy. The floral arrangements on the altar. Even the creative designs of the bulletins we use are a reflection of our creativity. But we generally don't give much thought to any of these. We take them for granted. They are, however, some of the ways that the arts influence our experience every Sunday.

All these elements may inspire us, move us, and delight us. Or they may disappoint us or cause bafflement, boredom, or tears. But they *will* have an impact.

Whether in a worship service or in our daily lives, beauty often catches us by surprise. We don't expect to be bowled over by it. Other times, though, we intentionally seek it out. We might put on a favor-ite record, attend a concert, visit an art exhibit, or tour a natural site famed for its beauty. The act of seeing, hearing, and feeling leaves a mark on us, and adds a memory that we can revisit later, or stirs something inside our soul.

Experiencing art is like fall-ing in love. It demands vulner-ability at the start, and it often takes a lot of work to keep it alive and growing.

Learning to appreciate great art often takes time. One of the signs of lesser art is that it can be accessed more immediately,

Martyrs' Window, Freiburg Minster

and you can pretty much grasp everything it has to offer very quickly. Such art makes little lasting impact. It generally doesn't stay with us or haunt our thoughts like a more complex work of art might. Such art is often created for propaganda purposes—to sell a product, arouse us to political or social action, convince us of a religious commitment or make us feel more comfortable about holding it. We glance and then forget. We listen and then move on. But the best art, the kind of art we will explore in this book, tends to take its time in impacting us, just as spiritual formation does. It is a worthy goal to learn to discriminate between the "just ok" and the "truly great," to recognize what is of lasting value, to probe more deeply into the ideas that gave rise to it. This can involve a bit of study and reflection rather than just expecting an immediate pleasurable response. Similarly, a sermon that stirs up an audience through rhetorical flourish may not produce the lasting results of one that causes us to have to question and ponder what we already think we believe.

The arts want to create a conversation with you. Are you ready to engage with them and see what they have to say?

QUESTIONS AND SPIRITUAL EXERCISES

1. When have you found the arts to be a useful companion to your spiritual journey?

2. Ponder the way that you engage with the arts in your own life. How often is it for distraction, decoration, and devotion? When are such uses valuable and when are they not?

3. In what ways might the arts become a detriment to your spiritual journey?

4. Which spiritual disciplines are a regular part of your walk with God? How might the arts be a useful companion for them?

CHAPTER TWO

Coming Awake:

Teaching Us to Pay Attention

TWO SUMMERS AGO, I HAD THE JOY of spending time in London, Oxford, Cambridge, Rome, Florence, and Venice. It was a summer of fulfilling some of the highest-ranking items on my personal bucket list. I got to spend time looking at iconic paintings and sculptures at some of the world's great art museums, to explore the ruins of ancient Rome, to stand in awe inside historic cathedrals, to view some of the most beautiful architecture anywhere, to go punting on the river in Cambridge and ride a gondola amid the twisting canals of Venice, and to experience both the glories of Britain and the wonders of the Italian Renaissance. This traveling was one of those rare times in life when something lived up to—and even surpassed—my expectations. It was all just amazing, and I'm ready to repack my suitcase as soon as I can.

I love to travel, and I'm convinced it can be one of the great joys of life, an opportunity to expand your understanding of the world and your place in it. But not everyone travels in the same way. It seems to me that there are two kinds of travelers, two different approaches to how we approach the opportunity to visit different places. They are the *pilgrim* and the *tourist.*

The pilgrim knows that traveling can be part of their spiritual education, so the pilgrim commits to fully experiencing the culture where they are a visitor, immersing themselves in the food, the rituals, and the pace of life of the country in which they consider themselves honored to be a guest. They are pleased to join in, to fit in, to take part in the ebb and flow of normal life in a place that isn't normal for them, and they know this can expand their perception of what is normal. They can learn new things and have unexpected experiences. Part of the joy in being a pilgrim is in the unplanned surprises or unexpected diversions from the itinerary. Customs and sights that might initially seem a bit unusual or weird or uncomfortable become part of the pilgrim's fund of life experiences. Just another step on the lifetime journey and moments to savor forever. And the pilgrim is changed by it all.

The tourist, on the other hand, is more concerned about traveling with a very specific agenda, attempting to check off as many of the "must see" sights as they can. The tourist brings their own world with them, hoping not to be stretched too much by the habits of the locals. They complain about the inconveniences as they rush from one "important" site to the next. Tourism is exhausting, but it can be satisfying to think that you have done everything that was listed in the travel guide. You can always spot the tourist in the art museum. They are the ones who move quickly from one iconic painting to the next, making sure they saw the most significant paintings by van Gogh, Picasso, and Rembrandt, so they can say that they "did" the museum. The tourist is rarely surprised by what they see, unless they know ahead of time that they are *supposed* to be surprised . . .

I try to be a pilgrim as much as possible when I jump on a plane to go visiting distant places. But I have found that it is all too easy to become a tourist in my own day-to-day life. I get so engaged with the things that simply must get done that I pass by a thousand little wonders and surprises every day. I can move through the museum of my life without taking time to stop, ponder, enjoy, and be inspired by what is around me. There is so much coming at me from minute to minute that I often can't be bothered by the details. And the outer chaos of my life is often just a mirror of the inner chaos. I find myself missing out on some of the little pleasures and beauties of my life because I am acting like a tourist when it comes to living my life on any given day.

When we live our lives in this way, we'll often find ourselves falling back upon "stock responses" to the world around us, as well as to our inner life and our relationship with God. We respond to the stimuli around us with our first instinct or with the way we have been trained to respond (by our culture, our parents, our religious education). Instead of a full-hearted, soulful response from the deepest part of ourselves, we respond in the totally expected manner. We settle for living by shorthand when God wants to write a new chapter in our lives in His own flowing cursive.

The arts can be one of the most effective tools for helping us overcome the stock responses of the spiritual tourist and embrace the world as a pilgrim. They can give us new ways of seeing and open us to new ways of responding—to the world around us, and to God.

The arts can teach us to slow down and pay attention. If you really want to fully experience, for example, what a great painting has to offer, you can't just glance at it as you pass by. You must stop and really take a closer look. You need to "sit" with it. Maybe literally sitting down so you can study it and let it do its work on you.

I remember visiting the Art Institute of Chicago with a friend.

© 1998 Kate Rothko Prizel & Christopher Rothko / Artists Rights Society (ARS), New York

Untitled 1969 by Mark Rothko, Art Institute, Chicago

When we found ourselves in front of one of Mark Rothko's mysterious canvases, one where blocks of color float indistinctly above one another against a light background, she looked at me quizzically. "I just don't get it. What is this even about?" Although I was tempted to offer a mini-lecture on how the artist built up multiple layers of paint that seep through to create an effect where the pigments vibrate and to explain that his intentions were to create an emotional connection through its colors, I thought better of it. My pontifications would likely get in the way of experiencing the painting as Rothko intended.

"Just stand in front of it for three minutes," I recommended. "Give it your full attention and surrender to it." She did as I asked, though her body language denoted impatience and the look in her eyes a bit of suspicion. Then, about two and a half minutes in, a gasp escaped from her mouth.

"Oh, my goodness. I can *feel* the colors and see them moving." She experienced what the artist had intended. I cannot guarantee that will happen for everyone with every work of art, but there is little chance it will happen if you don't slow down and give a painting your full attention. When you consider how much time the artist invested in creating the work, surely, we can spare a little extra time to engage with it.

I think of another friend, to whom I had raved about how much I was moved by Henryk Gorecki's masterful Third Symphony, *The Symphony of Sorrowful Songs*. When we sat down together to listen, he initially was a bit frustrated by the slow, repetitive fugue-like theme at the beginning of the piece, which builds so languidly. But there is an amazing moment midway through when this work completely comes to life. When we got to that point, my friend sighed and gazed upward, utterly captured by this soaring piece of transcendent music. Later he told me it had become a favorite. Sometimes, he said, he would just lie on the carpet in his home as the music played, letting it wash over him. A careful listen had made a convert.

Sometimes it takes time to fully appreciate a piece of art. When I first heard one of his records, I decided Bob Dylan needed singing lessons. But I stayed with it, listening a second and third time to the

album I'd been given. I eventually came to see that he has an unusu-
ally potent gift for phrasing and has one of the most emotionally
resonant voices in music. He has become one of my very favorites.

When I was first introduced to jazz, I couldn't really understand
what was going on. Sometimes it sounded like the cacophony of
everybody doing their own thing, and I was always waiting for the
neat musical resolution that never seemed to arrive. But now, thanks
to watching the Ken Burns documentary series and, more than that,
through hours of careful listening, I love jazz. Albums like Miles
Davis's *Kind of Blue*, John Coltrane's *A Love Supreme*, or Charles
Mingus's *Mingus Ah Um* are frequent visitors to my CD player, and I
have found it to be great music to write to. Its rhythms and its impro-
visations seem to keep my thinking flexible and active.

One learns by listening, by looking, by reading, by watching . . .
music, art, film, books, poems, dance, and opera . . . all have something to say to us. Are we willing to stop and listen?

Art, in all its forms, has the power to awaken us. We so often sleepwalk
through our lives, missing the many little wonders spread out before
us each and every day. The arts can function as an alarm clock to
jolt us into wakefulness, keeping us from
bumbling inattentively through our lives.

At every moment there is usually so
much noise, so much visual stimuli, and
so many smells that we would probably
be overwhelmed if we took it all in at the
same time. Our brain makes the necessary

> **The arts can function as
> an alarm clock to jolt
> us into wakefulness,
> keeping us from
> bumbling inattentively
> through our lives.**

decisions about which things need to be ignored so that, frankly, we aren't overcome with all that is happening around us at any single moment. We need our brain to do its job of filtering and focusing or we might just go crazy. But while this important process keeps us sane, it can sometimes do the job *too well* and filter out too much. It can cause us to quit paying attention and ignore the ordinary things happening in our vicinity. It can cause us to miss so much of what is right in front of us. Our mind often works more like the tourist than the pilgrim as it helps us move effectively and efficiently through life.

Sometimes we need to take control of this filtering process and not let our brain automatically sort things out for us. We must slow down, pay attention, feel fully, and experience the unexpected in our daily lives.

The arts help us learn how to do this. They teach us how to open our eyes and our ears. They retrain us about what is worth attending to. They re-sensitize us when life has desensitized us. They bring to the foreground the things that we might otherwise miss: the sights, the sounds, and the emotional responses that we might otherwise have ignored, except that the artist brings them to our attention.

Ansel Adams was one of the greatest American photographers, most famous for his breathtaking black and white images of the scenic majesty of our national wonders, especially our National Parks, and particularly Yosemite, where his camera captured the otherworldly symphony of granite rock faces, plunging waterfalls, and a valley filled with evergreens. I find it calming to page through my book of these images.

But the image by Ansel Adams that I treasure the most is a photograph simply named "Leaves, Mount Rainier National Park." In it he has captured a closeup image of leaves. They are photographed in

© The Ansel Adams Publishing Rights Trust

Leaves, Mount Rainier National Park, Washington, c. 1942. Photograph by Ansel Adams

high definition; alive and intricate and covered with gem-like droplets of water.

The man who could see the glory in the majestic expanse of a mountain range or a tree-filled valley could also see that same glory in rain-covered leaves or rocks at the edge of a stream or in the shifting patterns of a sand dune. One would have to be blind to miss the bigger beauties that Adams photographed so memorably, but he also helps us notice the smaller beauties that we could so easily just pass right by.

In a sense, what the arts do is to provide a frame around a moment, highlighting it so that we might fully appreciate it. They foreground what we might otherwise have missed.

That is one of the ways an artist can help us to see.

In teaching us to attend to what is around us, the artist reminds us not only of the beauty to be found in the glorious, but also in the ordinary, in the sacredness of everyday objects.

Vincent van Gogh made several paintings of the well-worn boots of the peasants whom he had once served as a missionary. There is a beauty that is hidden in these paintings, hidden behind our first response, which is probably: Why would you spend time painting something as mundane as a pair of old boots? And his probable answer would be that there is nothing in the least bit mundane about these boots. Behind them is a story—a story of hard work, of a life lived in communion with the earth, of some pain and suffering. When we stop and listen to what the boots are saying we will find them fascinating and beautiful and surprising. And van Gogh gives us the gift of bringing them to our attention.

Or consider one of the still life paintings of the Spanish painter,

WikiCommons

A Pair of Shoes by Vincent van Gogh, Van Gogh Museum, Amsterdam

Francisco de Zurbarán. Set against a black backdrop—which serves to push the objects in the painting forward and demand our attention—is a cup, a bowl, and some fruit. During his career, Zurbarán painted a number of unforgettable images of religious subject matter (the crucified Christ, saints, martyrs, and a sacrificial lamb), but he invests the same sort of holiness in this straightforward still life. These

Still Life with Lemons, Oranges, and Rose by Francisco de Zurbaran, Norton Simon Museum, Pasadena

too are symbols of purity and the grace of God.

The poet Samuel Coleridge believed that the purpose of his poetry was to "disimprison the 'wonder' in the 'familiar.'"[1] Many poets have followed in his footsteps, illuminating something beautiful, mysterious, and wondrous in the ordinary things that surround us. Among others, I think of his companion, William Wordsworth, the mystical poetic priest Gerard Manley Hopkins, and one of our best current observers of the ordinary, Mary Oliver. At your nearest opportunity read her wonderful poem "The Summer Day,"[2] and let it be an impetus for slowing down and paying attention.

Poetry, painting, photography, film, and other forms of art can help us see the revelation of God that is evident in the world around us.

Psalm 19 uses the metaphor of nature *speaking* to us, an experience that probably most of us have shared with the psalmist:

The heavens declare the glory of God;
    the skies proclaim the work of his hands.
Day after day they pour forth speech;

night after night they reveal knowledge. (19:1–2)

In other words, the beauties of nature, whether seen in their native state or captured by a work of art, aren't just beautiful—they are trying to tell us something.

Art helps us to notice the aura of significance that surrounds an otherwise seemingly ordinary object. It is an aura that normal words are often too weak to describe, so the poet gives us new words and a fresh vision, just as visual artists do. They help us pay attention to what we ordinarily would have missed. As Alain de Botton and John Armstrong have suggested, "Good artwork pins down the core of significance."[3] It helps us discern what matters and what needs our attention.

With the rise of the smartphone, photography has become the most democratic of art forms. In the past, to take a good picture, you needed an expensive camera, you needed to know how to focus it properly, and you had to process your photos at a lab to get them into a sharable form. Photography could be a tricky business. Now, everyone can take respectable shots of beautiful scenery, fascinating objects, or of friends, family, and even themselves. Often we use our cameras to take photos that prove that we and our loved ones visited an interesting site: "Here we are at the Grand Canyon; here we are in Hawaii; here we are posing with Mickey Mouse at Disney World." Such photos can be a useful remembrance of past vacations and pilgrimages.

But there is another possible approach to photography—the contemplative. This is when we search for and shoot objects that strike us as beautiful, fascinating, or mysterious, like the snapshot of leaves by Ansel Adams, a curious cloud formation, or an extremely close-up examination of a flower. The very adventure of seeking out such things to photograph can be an act of contemplation and attention. To take a good picture is to focus intently on what is in front of you, to give it your full attention. You need to think about the light that surrounds the object or person, how you will compose the picture, what angle of approach should be used, and how the colors interact with the background. This means that you must look closely. And to look that closely means paying close attention.

Dirk deVries, who calls himself a "contemplative photographer," writes about it this way:

> Photography . . . offers a means of meditation and
> reflection, a method of prayer, a key to open the
> imagination, a doorway into stillness, depth, and meaning.
> For those who pursue it, contemplative photography
> invites us to slow down and notice, to heighten awareness,
> to see the extraordinary in the ordinary. Photography
> can be a form of contemplation, a spiritual discipline,
> motivated, not by the desire to produce something, but
> the desire to be in process, open and present, ready to be
> refreshed, to receive insight.[4]

Clearly deVries is arguing for photography as a way to prepare your heart for prayer and meditation, a tool for mindfulness. It would be a good spiritual exercise to take your own digital camera with you on a walk around your neighborhood and pause often to examine and photograph the intriguing textures, splendid colors, and curious forms that you encounter. Stop and spend enough time to investigate the beauty you discover, allowing it to deliver a message about the God who

Cotswold Sheep. Photograph by Lancia E. Smith

created it. What does the intricacy of a fallen leaf or patterns of the bark of a tree or the colorful explosion of a wildflower tell you about Him? If you ever think to yourself that there is "nothing here to photograph," it only means you aren't really looking closely enough.

Of course, you can pursue this kind of contemplative vision even without a camera. Your eyes can serve the same purpose. The principles that you'd use in setting up a shot are principles that can help you slow down and really look at things with your naked eye. Having a photograph to show off when you are done isn't the point of the exercise but training yourself to look as closely as a photographer would. To pay attention to what is right in front of you, right now. To be truly present.

As Mary Oliver, whose poetry often has the precision of a photograph, reminds us, "Attention is the beginning of devotion."[5]

It isn't just photography that can be our teacher; all the arts can instruct us on how to be truly aware and be truly present.

We expend much of our energy mulling over the past and worrying about the future. In the process, we often lose touch with *now*, with the present moment. Art can help us learn to be *immersively present* in the moment. Not just kind of there, but totally there. Some refer to this as mindfulness. In the Christian tradition it is also seen as a critical part of the act of contemplation.

For the spiritual writer Jean-Pierre de Caussade, this sense of living in the present is also a sense of living in the Presence. He calls this attitude of awareness "the sacrament of the present moment."[6] He believed that God is at work in each of our personal histories, and that God is speaking to us at all times through the things we see and hear, as well as through our experiences. The present moment is one in which we can experience the presence of God if we are paying attention, and all the smallest things of our lives are potential mouthpieces for Him to communicate with us.

I think of Brother Lawrence, the monk who wrote about practicing the presence of God. His goal was to attain an awareness of God at work in his life every moment, never losing sight of His presence. Although he had the humble job of working in the monastery kitchen, there amidst the clamor and clatter of the pots and pans and the dishes, he learned to hear God. (Maybe he could help me change the way I think about doing the dishes . . .)

Both of these great writers remind us that we don't have to look for overpowering spiritual experiences. We can find God in the mundane and the ordinary, and we can discern His direction for our lives by attending to what He is revealing to us in the present moment.

But we must be paying attention.

As C. S. Lewis memorably wrote:

We can ignore, but we can nowhere evade, the presence of God. The world is crowded with Him. He walks everywhere *incognito*. And the *incognito* is not always hard to penetrate. The real labour is to remember, to attend. In fact, to come awake. Still more, to remain awake.[7]

The great artists and the great spiritual writers have the same goal: to teach us to remain awake.

We can slow down. We can quiet the inner chaos inside us. We can focus. We can fully attend. We might need to put aside our tendency to analyze and evaluate everything, and just be fully present. Just let things be. And let them speak to us. Whether it be a pair of worn boots, a simple white bowl, rain-speckled leaves, a sunrise, or the song of a bird.

The great artists and the great spiritual writers have the same goal: to teach us to remain awake.

The arts can help us learn how to pay attention. I've discovered that looking at art, listening to music or a poem, reading a descriptive passage in a novel, or viewing a film can force me to slow down, quiet my restless thoughts, and open myself to a moment of revelation. A moment when I can see the wonder in the ordinary.

Because, in a very real sense, nothing is ordinary.

The great Russian filmmaker Andrei Tarkovsky believed that sometimes true seeing comes on the other side of boredom. In his quiet, slow-moving, and deeply contemplative films, he would often let the camera stay focused on something mundane or pan very slowly over something that was seemingly insignificant. He believed that when he did this, his audience would at first grow impatient and maybe even bored. But if he held the camera on an object long enough, he believed that something would happen for the viewer. On the other side of boredom, they would begin to *really see* what they were looking at. He knew that we are trained to look and to move on, but if we simply stop and attend to what is around us we can see afresh . . . and maybe for the first time.

Prayer can be like that. Prayer is a way of being attentive to your life. It is a way of bringing God into what you are seeing, feeling, and experiencing. At times it may be hard to stay focused with your prayers. But if you attend in prayer, you'll begin to experience something beyond the boredom that might first arise from sitting quietly with God.

Sometimes we just need to pass through the boredom to find revelation on the other side of it.

This is how many of us experience prayer. We sit down to pray, and it goes well for a short period of time. Then we start to get tired and bored and our mind races to things we need to do, conversations we need to have, and to just about anything except staying focused on prayer. But if we just continue to pray and keep focused on the act of communicating with God, we will pass into a state where prayer feels more intimate and more connected. Sometimes we just need to pass through the boredom to find revelation on the other side of it. Like sitting with a piece of art while you wait for it to do its work upon you, so sitting patiently in prayer will eventually open up into a deeper spiritual connection with God.

Attentiveness is at the foundation of spiritual growth and

transformation. We must learn to pay attention if we are going to change. Not just to sights and sounds and smells around us, but to what is happening within us. As Frederick Buechner suggests, we need to listen to our own lives:

> Listen to your life. See it for the fathomless mystery it is. In the boredom and pain of it no less than in the excitement and gladness: touch, taste, smell your way to the holy and hidden heart of it because in the last analysis all moments are key moments, and life itself is grace.[8]

Sometimes the first step on your journey is just to look down and see exactly where you are on the path before you spend too much time looking down the road. Such is the way of the pilgrim traveler.

QUESTIONS AND SPIRITUAL EXERCISES

1. What does it mean to become more awake in terms of your awareness?

2. Take a nature walk, even if it is just around your neighborhood. Walk slowly, taking in all that you see. Stop occasionally and take a close look at something you might normally just pass by—a flower, a leaf, or even a crack in the sidewalk. Listen to what you might hear. The breeze, the song of a bird, the leaves rattling in the wind, or the sizzle of tires passing by on the wet street. Lift a prayer of gratitude for the small beauties in your world.

3. Grab a sketchbook or notebook and position yourself in front of something you find interesting, or beautiful, or unusual. Now, with pencil in hand, make a sketch or drawing of the thing you have chosen. Don't worry about your

artistic talent or lack of it. That isn't the point. This kind of sketching teaches a person how to see with new eyes and pay attention to the small things.

4. Visit an art museum. Pick one painting that somehow moves you and sit in front of it for at least five minutes. Let your eyes wander over the canvas and take in the details. Look. Feel. Experience it. What does it have to say to you?

5. Go exploring your neighborhood or a local park with your camera. Keep your eyes open for things you might have missed if you weren't paying attention. Find a fascinating or beautiful object and take several pictures of it—from different angles, as an intense close-up, or experiment with the different filters on your camera to get a unique perspective on the object.

CHAPTER THREE

The Eyes of a Child:

Rediscovering a Sense of Wonder

LET'S BEGIN THIS CHAPTER WITH A LITTLE THOUGHT EXPERIMENT.

Imagine, if you will, that there was only a single red rose in the whole world, a unique and fragrant unfolding of scarlet beauty. If only one red rose existed, wouldn't it be considered one of the world's great treasures? It would probably be exhibited at the world's finest museums, where patrons would line up around the block so they might get a look at it—paying their admission for even a brief glimpse of such startling beauty. Wouldn't people marvel at its exquisite form, its lovely scent, and its rare perfection? That single red rose would be something that

WikiCommons

Red Rose. Photograph by Shahzaib D. Cruze

everyone would cherish and long to see.

Yet our world is filled with such wondrous sights. There are unnumbered roses growing on rose bushes all over the world. You might have some in your own backyard. But our world has such marvels aplenty. From the fragile architecture of a single snowflake to the ever-shifting colors in an evening sky as the sun sets; from the shimmering feathers of a hummingbird kept aloft by the furious beating of his tiny wings to the sleek splendor of a jungle cat on the prowl; from the Grand Canyon to far-flung galaxies. And then there is one of the greatest of all wonders—the miraculous innocence shining from the face of a newborn.

In the face of such wonders we may simply fall silent, or we are overcome with awe, or maybe we gasp in astonishment. The novelist Barbara Kingsolver, a writer who knows how to evoke the world's beauties, reminds her readers how simple it is to miss the wonders that are right in front of us if we are not paying attention: "A great many people will live out their days without seeing such sights, or if they do, never *gasping*. My parents taught me this—to gasp, and feel lucky. They gave me the gift of making mountains out of nature's exquisite molehills."[1] I think she is right. If we are really paying attention, we will often find ourselves gasping at the beauty and mystery of life.

Our response to such things is one of the things that sets us apart from the animal kingdom: I marvel at the delicate beauty of the rose. My dog relieves himself on the rose bush.

Maybe we can learn something about wonder from children.

Think back to when you were a child. How did you experience the world then? As a child, didn't you get easily distracted by the sheer wonderfulness of the things around you? Didn't you approach life with a sense of immediacy, excited and intrigued by all wonderful little details of the world? As a child, weren't you and I generally more open-hearted, fascinated, and constantly curious? Didn't we see all things about us as interesting, as though they seemed to have just freshly sprung into existence before our eyes?

When I was small, I used to visit my grandmother's house for a week every summer. She lived in a little house at the end of a winding gravel road, perched up on top of a hill, just off the highway, overlooking the blue expanse of Dexter Lake. When I stayed with her, I played with the batch of old toys she stored in an old wooden apple crate. These toys largely consisted of those my mother had played with as a child, and they exhibited the signs of their use. As I remember, there were blocks, an old top that you could set spinning by pushing down on its handle, as well as a toy telephone.

When I wasn't invading the toy box, I was listening to the radio with my grandmother or singing along to an old plastic yellow record of "The Eensy Weensy Spider." (You know, the one whose climb up the water spout was repeatedly cut short when "the rains came tumbling down.") At lunchtime we would often feast on sandwiches fashioned of white bread, bologna, Velveeta cheese slices, and an almost transparently thin layer of mayonnaise.

We'd normally take our sandwiches out onto the back porch, where there was evidently a nest of little black ants living nearby. As a child, I was fascinated by these little ants, and I loved to watch them scurry around hurriedly, seemingly in a big rush to get no place in particular. Grandma and I would take pity on the little critters and tear off little pieces of our sandwiches to share with them, dropping them on the ground, and then watching the ants rush to gather them. Clearly their goal was to hustle them all back to the nest for later ingestion. It was amazing to watch one of them hoist a bit of food that was almost as large as itself and quite handily make off with it.

When the small chunks of bread and condiments were too large for any one ant to carry by itself, they would organize into a team of bread-haulers and wrestle the pieces of sandwich away as a group. Sometimes I'd squat down so I could see them at eye level and could size up these little creatures, intrigued by their multiple legs and their twitchy little antennae. It was not unusual for me to be entranced for a very long time at the industry of these little fellows. It's no wonder that one of Solomon's proverbs suggests that spending a little time contemplating an anthill could be a very valuable use of time, as it had much to teach the observer (Prov. 6:6).

These days, I don't generally spend much time watching the ants, and I am quite certain that my life is the poorer for it. But when I take the time for even a short walk in my neighborhood, I am flabbergasted at all the surging life going on around me that I never notice when I am behind the wheel of my car. The patterns of leaves casting shadows on the sidewalk, the low, barely discernable hiss of insects in the grass, the sound of birds celebrating in the trees, and the way that the sun glints and shimmers off everything. These are some of the things a child will notice, which is why, if you take the time to let them explore along the way, a short walk can take a very long time. Which probably isn't a bad thing at all. Because as we grow older, we tend to become dulled to the world around us.

We become indifferent: "So what?"
We become cynical: "Yeah, right . . ."
We become world-weary: "Whatever . . ."
We become complacent: "Seen it."
We become jaded: *Yawn.*

Jesus warned that this could happen to us. One time, He pulled a little child to His side as a living illustration and spoke these words to His disciples, "I'm telling you, once and for all, that unless you return to square one and start over like children, you're not even going to get a look at the kingdom, let alone get in. Whoever becomes simple and elemental again, like this child, will rank high in God's kingdom" (Matt. 18:3–4 MSG).

This is, I suppose, what G. K. Chesterton had in mind when he reveled in the joy of childlikeness:

> Because children have abounding vitality, because they
> are in spirit fierce and free, therefore they want things
> repeated and unchanged. They always say, "Do it again";
> and the grown-up person does it again until he is nearly
> dead. For grown-up people are not strong enough to exult
> in monotony. But perhaps God is strong enough to exult
> in monotony. It is possible that God says every morning,
> "Do it again" to the sun; and every evening, "Do it again"
> to the moon. It may not be automatic necessity that makes
> all daisies alike; it may be that God makes every daisy
> separately, but has never got tired of making them. It may
> be that He has the eternal appetite of infancy; for we have
> sinned and grown old, and our Father is younger than we.[2]

Wonder is our response to a world crowded with miracles and mysteries. It is an emotional reaction of astonishment and surprise, of admiration and reverence, as well as acceptance and embrace. It is a reminder that there is more to life than our small philosophies and understandings can contain. It is the basis for so much of our greatest art; the bright shining shadow thrown over all of creation by the glory of God.

Wonder is the place where our words often fail us. It moves us to a place that speech can only hint at but can't fully comprehend or expound upon. It is about an experience we might call "Grand Canyon theology."

If you asked me to describe the Grand Canyon, I could easily provide the vital facts about it: It stretches over 1,904 square miles at a depth of about one mile. The canyon is 277 miles long, and its walls are multicolored, made up of various layers of sediment and minerals, which blaze in different shades and hues as the sun rises and sets on the walls of the canyon.

But if you have ever actually visited the Grand Canyon, you know how inadequate such a description is. Standing there on its rim evokes a feeling that none of my descriptions can adequately do justice to. Perhaps that is why a common response for many people visiting is simply a hushed silence.

The many beautiful photographs and paintings that have been made of the Grand Canyon come a little closer than my list of its attributes, but until you see it in person, you don't really know the Grand Canyon. The sense of overpowering awe, of your own smallness in the larger scheme of things, the ever-changing visual exuberance before you, and the silent stillness of awe are just something that must be experienced. What you are experiencing is wonder.

The Bible is a book of wonders. It is filled with stories where people come face-to-face with things that are too big to explain. And as it tells these stories it uses the vocabulary of wonder. The word "wonder" itself is used 109 times. There are 53 references to "awe," 22 to "astonishment," and 38 to "reverence." Often the Scriptures talk about such an experience without even using these words.

Perhaps just a few examples will suffice:

The whole earth is filled with awe at your wonders;
   where morning dawns, where evening fades,
   you call forth songs of joy. (Ps. 65:8)

"Listen to this, Job;
   stop and consider God's wonders." (Job 37:14)

"You will go out in joy
      and be led forth in peace;
the mountains and hills
      will burst into song before you,
and all the trees of the field
      will clap their hands." (Isa. 55:12)

Wonder is a way of talking about our response both to the mystery of life and to our experience of God in the context of His creation. Wonder is that which takes our breath away.

But it is possible to look at the world and not see wonder; to be bored and unengaged and unmoved. When that happens, it is a sign of a disorder in our soul that needs to be healed.

Wonder is not an emotion we can manufacture, or strive after, or pursue. In fact, it will likely prove elusive if we focus too much on

> **We'll never experience awe and wonder if we are sleepwalking through our lives.**

trying to experience it. It can't be forced or faked. Wonder tends to come unbidden, a response that catches us by surprise. If we want to respond to life with an attitude of wonder, it will come because we have made ourselves open to it.

So, how do we open ourselves to more fully experience wonder?

In the previous chapter we discussed the need to become more fully awake. We'll never experience awe and wonder if we are sleepwalking through our lives—if our senses are partially asleep. Becoming awake is important if we are to take notice of the wonders around us. In one of his poems, Antonio Machado asks himself, "Is my soul asleep?" and he rouses himself to be wide awake and to listen "at the shores of the great silence."[3]

I sometimes enjoy taking a walk around my neighborhood and playing a little game of attentiveness. I'll keep my eyes open for something that I might normally not pay attention to, then I'll stop and give it a long, focused look. Maybe it is a single leaf that is clinging to a branch as fall approaches, or a wildflower sprouting in an unexpected place, or the texture of bark on a tree, or veins of color in a smooth stone. For anyone who is a writer, this kind of exercise is an especially helpful discipline. It'll teach you to become better at finding the small details that make writing come alive, and it will add a greater depth of beauty and feeling to your words. You'll write your best when you write with all your senses attuned, because that is what engages the senses of your readers.

We can widen our peripheral vision and take in more of the world and see the sacred beauties that glimmer at the boundaries of our experience, but only if we stop rushing through life and slow down.

The biblical phrase that the angelic messengers used for calling some-one to pay full attention was "Behold!" Perhaps we need to let the angels whisper that word into our own ears.

The great writers, painters, and sculptors are also addressing us with such a cry: *Behold! See what I have noticed about the world that I take joy in sharing with you!* The task of every creative artist is to see things with fresh eyes, and then to usher others into the presence of what they have perceived themselves. At their best, they hold up what is sacred and holy for our inspection.

Are you open for an epiphany? Are you prepared for a moment where God might break through all the clutter of your everyday events and capture your attention? It might happen with a hike in the light-dappled forest, a saunter along the sandy boundary of the sea, or even an evening stroll in your neighborhood.

Or it might come through a work of art—through a painting, a piece of music, or a poem.

A few days after Jesus was crucified, two men who had been His fol-lowers were on a road trip from Jerusalem, where all the tragic events of the Passion week had occurred, headed to the small town of Emmaus. As they walked along a stranger caught up with them and a conversation ensued. That conversation quickly turned to the events of the recent days, and when the two travelers expressed confusion about what it all meant, their new companion offered an explanation, pointing to how the whole story of the Scriptures was leading to this very event. The two men were flabbergasted by the knowledge and insight of this stranger, and they plied Him with questions as the dust rose around them and the hours passed. When they came to a stop for the night, they invited their new friend to share a meal with them. They arranged themselves around the table and the food was served. As the stranger leaned over and broke the bread, they suddenly knew Him to be the very One around whom the day's conversation had focused. Here, at the table with them, was the resurrected Jesus Himself (Luke 24:13–35).

One of my favorite paintings by Caravaggio captures this very moment so unforgettably. In his version of the story, we see Jesus raising His hand in blessing as His two road-weary companions suddenly become aware of the identity of their dining partner. One of them starts out of his seat, gripping the arms of his chair as he begins to lift himself up out of it. The other throws his hands out wide in complete astonishment, his left hand almost breaking out of the space of the picture. The third observer, perhaps the innkeeper, seems less agitated. Perhaps the moment of revelation is making little impact on him, for one must be open-hearted and seeking if one is to be a recipient of the truth.

Caravaggio, who specialized in unidealized depictions of Bible stories, has portrayed this moment as one that was very ordinary until the

Supper at Emmaus by Caravaggio, National Gallery, London

moment when Jesus unveils Himself to His dining companions. There is a gritty realism to Caravaggio's depiction of the event. The travelers' clothes are worn and patched, the meal before them a humble one, and the basket of fruit is perched precariously on the edge of the table. It is into such an ordinary moment that something very sacred occurs.

One of the things this story suggests to us is that sometimes God comes to us incognito. That we might not even realize at first the import of what we are experiencing at the moment we are experiencing it. God sometimes enters our lives when we least expect it. He might appear as an ordinary traveler on the dusty road we travel, and we may travel quite a distance unaware of the presence of our Companion on the journey. But He is there with us every step. The wonder of God-with-us is present to those who are open to the moments when revelation breaks through the ordinary and awakens us to the extraordinary. To live in wonder is to be on the lookout for the instants when we might get a glimpse of God revealed in the commonplace.

The Irish Saint Brendan of Birr once wrote, "If you become Christ's you will stumble upon wonder upon wonder and every one of them true."[4]

One of the things that can keep us from living in a state of wonder is our tendency, especially in our scientifically informed modern world, to immediately seek to categorize, label, judge, evaluate, and control whatever we see or experience. Such an overly rationalistic approach to existence will quickly rob it of the mystery that is so closely related to wonder.

There is often more going on than what can be encircled by our five senses. If we are not in a rush to explain everything . . . or explain it away . . . we might be surprised by how much we stand to experience if we stand humbly before life's mysteries. I am convinced that it is in these mysteries that we will often encounter God in a fresh way.

So, slow down. Take it all in. Sit with the experience. Honestly, isn't this even what real scientists do before they finally draw their conclusions about whatever they are observing? They take the time to be fully ignorant before they can become fully informed. A rush to judgment will lead to scientific error, and a rush to judgment in the spiritual realm might likely lead away from the truth.

As is so often the case, perhaps G. K. Chesterton said it best:

> One of the deeper and strangest of all human moods is the mood which will suddenly strike us perhaps in a garden at night, or deep in sloping meadows, the feeling that every flower and leaf has just uttered something stupendously direct and important, and that we have by a prodigy of imbecility not heard or understood it. There is a certain poetic value, and that a genuine one, in this sense of having missed the full meaning of things. There is beauty, not only in wisdom, but in this dazed and dramatic ignorance.[5]

In the ancient world, people tended to see the divine in everything. They lived in an enchanted world of gods, spirits, fairies, and phantoms. Though, from a Christian perspective, they wrongly labeled the sources of the mysterious things they encountered, at least they were seeing a world that was filled with meaning and significance. Our modern culture has largely gone in the opposite direction. We have emptied out the mystery and wonder and have found ourselves losing the feeling of being at home in our universe. Our modern world has become disenchanted.

I am not suggesting that we should embrace again the pantheism of old. Neither, however, do I think we should be resigned to the spiritual barrenness of a world emptied of its mysteries. Instead, we can recognize that an incarnational God has brought the natural and supernatural spheres together by His act of personally entering our sphere, and He has left His fingerprints over all of His creation. Even the most ordinary sights and sounds and smells are telling a deeper story than just their own. This is the message of William Carlos William's famous short poem, "The Red Wheelbarrow," where he reminds us that "so much depends" upon noticing the simple beauties all around us. Ordinary things have extraordinary things to tell us.

Great poetry, painting, and literature are often concerned with helping us see what we might otherwise have missed. Engaging with the arts can be a workshop for training us how to slow down, pay attention, and see—maybe for the first time. One of the things I treasure about the paintings of Jan Vermeer is his ability to arrest a perfectly normal moment in time and invest it with a deeper and more profound meaning.

In this painting, *The Milkmaid*, we are given access to a very private moment as a young woman fills a bowl by pouring milk from a jug that is heavy enough that she has to place one hand underneath it to steady to a slow stream the thick, white liquid. The table on which the bowl sits is partially covered by a rumpled blue cloth that matches the blue in her skirt. There is a loaf of bread in a wicker basket, as well as some broken pieces on the table. Her face is all quiet intensity, and the light that floods in through the window (a common Vermeer touch) casts its illumination over the scene. The moment Vermeer portrays strikes me as completely ordinary, and yet somehow invested with an otherworldly quiet. I feel

WikiCommons

The Milkmaid by Johannes Vermeer, Rijksmuseum, Amsterdam

more at peace when I look at a painting like this, as it enquires about stillness within my own soul. This is surely wonder in its gentlest guise.

Wonder is very often accompanied by awe, which arises as we are overwhelmed by the presence of something beautiful and glorious and much bigger than we are. It embraces our own smallness and finitude in the larger scheme of things and awakens a sense of humility before the great and glorious God and the amazing world He created.

The Hudson River School is the name given to a group of

American landscape painters who lived and worked in the vicinity of the Hudson River. They were not an actual school or an institutional movement, but a collection of like-minded artists. What their work held in common was a predisposition for grand scenic vistas. Human beings are usually either absent from their paintings or dwarfed by their natural surroundings. The two foundational passions for these artists were a strong commitment to their Christian faith and their love for the unspoiled American wilderness. They celebrated America as a New Eden and were deeply concerned that progress and civilization would damage its pristine beauty. This wilderness, they believed, could be a spiritual refuge from a materialistic culture.

These artists embraced the message of Psalm 19, that "the heavens declare the glory of God," and they sought to reveal God as the ultimate artist, whose canvas was the natural world. One of their number, Asher Durand, laid out their artistic program: "The whole province of art is the representation of the work of God in the visible creation, independent of man."[6] Jasper Cropsey reveled in the poetry he found in nature: "The voice of God came to me through every motionless leaf—on every blade of grass—in every breath of air . . . in all things I could see the beauties of holiness and the greatness of the Lord."[7]

What the artists of the Hudson River School were seeking to evoke in their paintings was a feeling of awe, which might be considered a second cousin to wonder. The best definition I've heard for awe comes from psychologist Dacher Keltner at the University of California, Berkeley, who once defined it as: "Awe is the feeling of being in the presence of something vast or beyond human scale, that transcends our current understanding of things."[8] Whereas one might feel a simple sense of wonder at the sight of wildflowers growing in a field, awe works on a different scale, causing us to be overwhelmed at a vision of something that dwarfs our understanding; something so spectacular that it leaves us without an adequate way to express our experience of it; something that makes us recognize our smallness at the same time as it invites us into a feeling of being part of something bigger than us.

Producing awe was the stock in trade of this group of landscape artists. Their founder, Thomas Cole, was also a poet, and he viewed the world through a poetic lens. His paintings are both beautiful and mysterious, and often invested with subtle spiritual symbols. His *View from Mount Holyoke: The Oxbow* is an early example of his work. One of the first things you notice about the painting are the light effects of the passing storm, which perhaps stands as a symbol for changes occuring in his time. The wilderness is giving way to cultivation, as he, in a tiny self-portrait in the bottom right of the image, attempts to capture the loss on canvas. Carved into the side of the mountain in the center of the painting are Hebrew letters, hidden upside-down

The Oxbow by Thomas Cole, Metropolitan Museum of Art, New York

but still readable: *Shaddai* (the Hebrew word for Almighty).

The reality of change was a common theme for Cole, whose series of paintings include *The Voyage of Life* and *The Course of Empire*. The paintings of these series mourn the loss that comes in life, but look beyond that loss toward an eternal and immortal reality.

Twilight in the Wilderness by Frederic Church, Cleveland Museum of Art

Frederic Church, who was a student of Cole, sought to unveil the mysterious presence of God in nature through his works and was fascinated by the effects of light, which he saw as both a natural and spiritual phenomenon. For him, light was the spiritual aura that surrounds the natural world, and he captured the beauty of its effects. *Twilight in the Wilderness* could be viewed as simply as an almost photographic representation of the sun setting over a lake with the corresponding effects in the sky. But Church intended us to see something more, and I think most viewers of his painting experience an uncanny sense of awe at his glorious riot of color and the pronounced emphasis on light as a form of revelation. Church was capturing a sense of the transcendence he felt, as he always saw a spiritual quality in light itself.

These artists believed that the contemplation of beauty could direct the heart of the viewer toward God. For them, the landscape is a grand, natural cathedral, and everywhere we look within it, we can see a manifestation of the glory of God. And our natural response is awe.

Wivenhoe Park, Essex by John Constable, National Gallery of Art, Washington, DC

The great British landscape painter John Constable was a man of deep faith. A devout Anglican, he seriously considered becoming a priest early in his life, but his great love for drawing and painting caused him to take the artistic path instead. But he followed that path as a believer, convinced that God's glory was manifest in the beauty of the English countryside. He painted only a few explicitly religious paintings, mostly as commissions for churches. But these paintings, such as *Christ Blessing the Bread and Wine* and *The Ascension* are unremarkable, emotionally flat, and somewhat derivative. His forte was in capturing the beauties around him as he prowled and painted the farms and ancient churches of his homeland. Here he saw traces of divinity. He wrote:

> The landscape painter must walk in the fields with an humble mind. No arrogant man was ever permitted to see nature in all her beauty. If I may be allowed to use a very solemn quotation, I would say most emphatically . . . "Remember now thy Creator in the days of thy youth." . . . The art of seeing nature is a thing almost as much to be acquired as the art of reading the Egyptian hieroglyphics.[9]

One friend wrote of Constable, "I have seen him admire a fine tree with an ecstasy of delight like that with which he would catch up a beautiful child in his arms."[10] This embrace of nature led him to find the tranquility present in his rural paintings. One of my favorites is an early work called *Wivenhoe Park, Essex*, where one sees not the spectacular vistas of the Hudson River School painters, but a quiet and peaceful contemplation of a perfectly ordinary, but nonetheless perfectly wondrous scene.

WikiCommons

Starry Night by Vincent van Gogh, Museum of Modern Art, New York

Vincent van Gogh had a less photo-realistic vision of the created world, but it was also spiritually charged. In *Starry Night*, van Gogh produces a mystical vision of the eternal realities that lay behind the earthly beauties. "When I have a terrible need of—shall I say the word —religion, then I go out and paint the stars."[11] Here van Gogh has attempted to peer beneath the curtain of the natural world and reveal something infinite that emerges from the churning night skies. He believed that God could be found in such a vision: "If one feels the need of something grand, something infinite, something that makes one feel aware of God, one need not go far to find it."[12] In his iconic painting the modern viewer can see the pulsing night skies, alive with a supernatural message of praise to the One who created them.

"Glory be to God for dappled things," begins a poem by Gerard Manley Hopkins called "Pied Beauty." In it he reflects on how the variety of the world sings the praises of God—both the elegant and the earthy. The words and phrases almost trip over one another as he breathlessly gushes about God's greatness as experienced in the things He has made; the grandeur and splendor of the Creator revealed in His creation. A humble Catholic priest whose poetry was mostly unknown until after his death, Hopkins found fresh approaches to rhyme and unusual rhythms in his attempt to express the glory of God:

> Glory be to God for dappled things—
> For skies of couple-colour as a brinded cow;
> For rose-moles in all stipple upon trout that swim;
> Fresh-firecoal chestnut-falls; finches' wings;
> Landscape plotted and pieced—fold, fallow, and plough;
> And all trades, their gear and tackle and trim.
> All things counter, original, spare, strange;
> Whatever is fickle, freckled (who knows how?)

With swift, slow; sweet, sour; adazzle, dim;
He fathers-forth whose beauty is past change: Praise him.[13]

The awe Hopkins feels as he considers all the variety and dazzling life of the world leads him to praise—his poem, an inventory of wonders that results in a response of worship.

As it did with Hopkins, awe can arouse a sense of gratitude within us, and give rise, if we are experiencing it fully, to a response of worship. Perhaps that is why the arts are such an important part of the worship experience when we gather together in community. Hymns, worship choruses, readings, visual art, and symbolism are all designed to help us draw close to a place where our heart is lifted in worship. These art forms can be powerful engines for igniting wonder in our hearts and minds.

WikiCommons

Several years ago, I had the opportunity of touring Paris, and among the primary destinations on my all-too-short visit were the famous cathedrals in that city. I will never forget stepping out of the crisp Paris sunshine into the dark and vast interior of Notre Dame cathedral and

Interior, Sainte-Chapelle. Photograph by Pierre Poschadel

being instantly overcome by its immensity. I understood that this was a place where serious transactions with God might occur or where one might stumble upon some deeper truths about existence. I also visited the chapel of Sainte-Chappelle, just down the street from Notre Dame, which, though much smaller and more intimate, also left my mouth agape in astonishment. It was a space surrounded by walls whose only apparent support seemed to be the panes of patterned colored glass. The jeweled light that slanted down through the walls of stained glass made the very air vibrate with color and luminosity. I lingered there long, breathless at the beauty.

When we gather in our own churches every Sunday, though most of them considerably less spectacular in their architecture than the grand cathedrals, we nevertheless may invite the same kind of awe as we participate in wonder through the art and architecture, and especially through the music. The greatest of our hymns give a lyrical voice to the powerful truths of Scripture. In some churches, the echoing notes of an organ resonate through the sanctuary, making it seem even more like a holy place.

I've had this same kind of experience in a concert hall, where glorious sounds enter my ears and, thereby, my heart. Whenever I listen to the solemn gravity of Bach's sacred choral music, or the roaring celebration of Beethoven's Ninth, or the delicacy of Mozart's *Eine Kleine Nachtmusik*, I feel lifted out of myself and into another realm of experience.

The experience of wonder can add a deeper dimension to our spiritual practices. And, conversely, our spiritual practices can help open us up to wonder.

The great Jewish theologian Abraham Heschel once wrote that "To pray is to take notice of the wonder, to regain a sense of the mystery that animates all beings, the divine margin in all attainments."[14] Wonder prepares us for praying, and it teaches us a way of seeing that makes prayer more central to our lives. When we learn to pray, we learn to live with our eyes wide open. Prayer changes our perspective because it brings God's perspective into focus.

The best way to experience more wonder in your life is to place yourself in the path of beauty. Make decisions that provide opportunities to engage with beauty. Fyodor Dostoevsky suggested that beauty is the battlefield where God and Satan contend with each other for the human heart. If he is correct, and I believe he is, then to experience more beauty is to experience more spiritual freedom.

When we learn to pray, we learn to live with our eyes wide open.

So, explore the wonders of the created world all around you. Get out into nature whenever you can, even if it is just your own backyard, a walk around the neighborhood, or a visit to a quiet corner of the nearby park. Let all your senses come alive and see . . . and smell . . . and hear the beauty of the Divine creation. Take it all in. Breathe deeply, listen closely, look intensely. There might just be a message in the birdsong. That humble rhododendron might just become a burning bush.

Embrace opportunities to expose yourself also to the work of great writers, painters, musicians, filmmakers, and photographers. These fruits of human creativity are another powerful way to invite beauty into your life. Visit a museum. Buy pieces of art and photography that inspire you and find a place for them in your home. Go to a concert. See an artistic film. Base your choices upon something more than just what will entertain, distract, or divert you. Look for beauty. Be ready for beauty to find you.

Wonder can become a way of living if we train ourselves to begin to pay attention, to take more notice of the gifts that come our way every day from the hand of God.

1. Listen to the song "Holy as a Day Is Spent" by Carrie Newcomer and reflect on how she sees the ordinary experiences of life as moments to engage with wonder.

2. Visit an art museum and take note of which paintings evoke in you a sense of wonder or awe. Stand or sit in front of the work for at least a couple minutes, first taking in the work as a whole, then looking closely at the details that are revealed when you begin to spend a little more time with it. What might the work have to teach you?

3. Get outside. If possible, take a hike or a long walk and pay attention to everything around you—all the sights and sounds and smells. Then respond with a series of simple prayers of gratitude.

4. Read the poem "I Wandered Lonely as a Cloud" by William Wordsworth and meditate upon the idea that beauty can be a consoling way of coping with the struggles of life.

5. What are some ways that you can add a little wonder to your own life?

CHAPTER FOUR

The Mystery Dance:

Digging for Deeper Meanings

I BELIEVE THAT THE BIBLE HAS A CLEAR and life-changing message for all human beings.

And yet, I also believe that the Bible is full of mystery, poetry, and riches that I have yet to discover despite years of study. I'm always discovering more than I had previously seen in its pages.

I used to think that if I only studied the Scriptures diligently that I would be able to answer any objection to faith and have a response to every question someone might raise. I spent hours poring over books on apologetics, which attempted to build a rational argument for the truth of the Christian faith. They helped me to understand that my faith was not irrational or unhistorical, and they buttressed my confidence in what I believed. However, I eventually discovered that there are a lot of questions that can't be answered with a single Bible verse or a logical syllogism. That life is too big, too mysterious, too complicated to allow us to boil everything down to doctrinal statements or reduced to simple formulas. This doesn't mean that we can't have a lot of certainty about what we believe, but it means that our certainty requires a dose of humility to keep it honest.

Poetry and mystery are two categories that make some Christians a little nervous, as though saying we can't have *everything* nailed down means that we can't have *anything* nailed down. No, not at all. I still enjoy reading books of apologetics and I have a few friends who've made that the focus of their studies. We have great conversations, and I learn a lot from them. I leave these conversations with a greater confidence that I have made good decisions about what I believe.

But just learning a series of propositional statements of faith or knowing how to build a convincing defense of your faith may not be enough. For the Bible itself, the book that lays claim to being God's primary form of communication to human beings, is not a book of clear philosophical or theological statements. A lot of the Bible is made up of narrative and storytelling, and when the biblical authors talk about theological ideas, their writing is filled with word pictures and poetry. Much of Paul's thoughts are not delivered in simple, easy-to-understand statements, but is beautifully poetic in its expression and makes room for mystery. And Jesus taught by using parables and word pictures more than any other means of communication. He often resorted to the kind of mysterious verbal zingers that left His hearers scratching their heads—probably because He wanted them to continue thinking about what He was saying even after He was gone.

The point is, we should not be afraid of the categories of poetry and mystery, of those things not written or spoken in simple prose and not easily understood without a little wrestling. For it is in wrestling with the biblical texts, and in wrestling with God, that we are sometimes, like Jacob, given a clearer vision of the deepest truths.

Climbing Jacob's ladder may require a little openness to poetry and mystery. The arts can help us begin to think more poetically and be more open to mystery.

What good is poetry if you are searching for the truth? If you want to learn what a tiger is, for example, you can get a basic definition and description from a dictionary. It might read something like this: "A large carnivorous feline mammal (Panthera tigris,) of Asia, having a tawny coat with transverse black stripes."[1] Or you could seek out a zookeeper and learn of the tiger's habits and way of life. Another option, one that might not immediately come to mind, is to read what a great poet has written about this fearsome beast. William Blake, the great English poet, wrote a poem about the "tyger," which provides a perspective beyond the merely scientific:

WikiCommons

Illustration from *Songs of Innocence and Experience* by William Blake

Tyger Tyger. burning bright,
In the forests of the night;
What immortal hand or eye,
Could frame thy fearful symmetry?[2]

Granted, you aren't going to learn anything about the mating habits of the tiger from this poem. Nor will you gain much insight into its diet. But you will come to understand more clearly about how even this most fearsome of beasts is a creation of God; that the Creator is responsible not only for the sweet and comforting things in this world (as in Blake's companion poem, "The Lamb," which offers a picture of God as seen through the gentleness of a lamb), but also for that which inspires "dread" and even terror.

As is so often the case with poetry, the poet tells us not only what something *is*, but what it *means*. Perhaps to truly understand the tiger you require both ways of knowing. You need both scientific observation and you need a poetic eye. In our time, the poetic perspective is often neglected or seen as less important. But to see most clearly demands finding the balance. And it is even more true when it comes to spiritual matters. Poetic thinking can be an important asset in our search for deeper spiritual insight, truths that are simply not available to reason alone.

One of the common mistakes people make is thinking that poetry is only about the subjective feelings of the poet, only a reflection of the inner life of the one who has composed the poem. Certainly, subjective experience is an element of poetry, but poetry is more than just that. Poetry is a way of communicating, using tools like metaphor, simile, ambiguity, and indirection to express concepts and realizations. Poetry relies on intuition, tacit knowledge, and images rather than straightforward didactic statements.

Poetic thinking rejects the Enlightenment idea, put forward by thinkers such as Francis Bacon, that only logic and reason and scientific experimentation can help us arrive at the truth. Such thinkers ignored the wisdom that was embraced by the ancients, who saw great value in poetic and imaginative thinking. The ancients understood that stories and myths and epic songs could embody some of life's most profound truths—many of them truths about which science would have little to say.

A scientist can only tell us about the chemical reactions we experience when we feel affection for another person. A psychiatrist or psychologist can only help us deal with the emotional states that such affection may create within us. A philosopher can only theorize about how love works within a particular system of thought. A poet, however, will delve deep into the mystery of love. Poetry can help us experience that mystery vicariously, and perhaps be reminded and

Poetry is a window beyond this world that sheds a light that transforms and transfigures everything on which it falls.

reconnected with our own experiences of love and its attendant feelings.

One of William Shakespeare's characters says that poetry is "holding a mirror up to nature;"[3] merely a reflection of ourselves and our world. Throughout his plays and poems, however, poetry is clearly something more than that. Poetry is a window beyond this world that sheds a light that transforms and transfigures everything on that it falls. Poetry reminds us that there is a mystery deep down in things. It struggles against the reductive tendencies of scientism, an approach that dissects what is before it, in order to understand and therefore control it. Scientism suggests that reality is only that which can be measured, weighed, and recorded. The arts remind us again and again that life is never that simple. There is so much more going on.

The spiritual person recognizes that there is a realm beyond our own that cannot be ignored, but that is essential for a richer understanding. In his autobiography, *Surprised by Joy*, C. S. Lewis recalls the tension he felt when he was a thoroughgoing rationalist and not yet a Christian, but somehow was still attracted to things that could not be explained in purely rational terms. He felt a tension between his rational explanations and mysteries that he could see were best probed by an intelligence that makes room for poetic, mythic, or imaginative truths. He found the explanations that relied on rationalism alone to be ultimately unsatisfactory:

> Such, then, was the state of my imaginative life;
> over against it stood the life of my intellect. The two
> hemispheres of my mind were in the sharpest contrast. On
> the one side a many-islanded sea of poetry and myth; on
> the other a glib and shallow "rationalism." Nearly all that I
> loved I believed to be imaginary; nearly all that I believed
> to be real I thought grim and meaningless.[4]

Lewis understood that the realm of imagination—the realm of the poetic—could be the very thing that would help him integrate, and make sense of, the facts that he discovered through science and reason.

Poetry can help us see below the surface of things. Our senses only perceive the *outside* of objects, but the poetic eye sees *through* things. English poet John Davies suggested that our senses can

Oxford Windows. Photograph by Lancia E. Smith

only see the bark of the tree, but the soul can glimpse the very life of a tree.[5] As the contemporary English poet Malcolm Guite has written: "The poet's task is to allow the vision of the soul to underlie the vision of the senses so that for a moment we see both the outside and the essence."[6]

This is essential because things are almost always more than they appear to be—more complex and more multivalent. Objects and people alike contain more layers of meaning than what we might first perceive. There are deeper realities and meanings hidden within them. In a wonderful scene from C. S. Lewis's *The Voyage of the Dawn Treader*, one of the newcomers to Narnia, Eustace Scrubb, is intent on showing off his knowledge, so he spouts off what scientists understand about the nature of a star. "In our world," he says, "a star is a huge ball of flaming gas." To which the wise old man he is addressing sagely answers, "Even in your world, my son, that is not what a star is but only what it is made of."[7]

Part of our spiritual quest, and indeed our human quest, is not only to know what things are, but what they mean. Imagine a tea kettle that has come to a boil and is whistling shrilly on the stovetop. If you ask the question, "Why is the tea kettle boiling?" there is a perfectly good scientific explanation: It is sitting on an element on the stovetop that has reached 212 degrees Fahrenheit, which has agitated the water within the pot and caused the water to boil, releasing some particles as steam, which creates a whistling noise as it escapes the kettle.

Or, you could answer the question about why the kettle is boiling by saying that it is because you wanted some tea! The scientific approach provides valuable information, but it doesn't usually reveal purpose. For that, we must explore on another level. As C. S. Lewis suggested, "In science we are only reading the notes to a poem; in Christianity we find the poem itself."[8]

The poetic imagination is, thus, a way of broadening our way of seeing. We do not need to be afraid of it, as if it will somehow lead us astray; we can embrace it for the way it equips us to dig deeper for meaning. It is not a replacement for our intellectual endeavors, but a companion on our quest to understand.

Some readers might get a bit nervous when we transition to talking about how reading poetically might help us be better readers of the Bible. Such nervousness is unnecessary. To say something is poetic is not the same as saying that it is fictitious or untrue. "Truth-bearing language," writes Malcolm Guite, "does not have to be purged of ambiguity in order to be truthful."[9] In fact, when it comes to the Bible, that very ambiguity can sometimes be very helpful for understanding the many nuanced layers of meaning in the Scriptures.

Poetry is not a replacement for our intellectual endeavors, but a companion on our quest to understand.

Reading poetry has taught me to read the Bible with an expanded set of lenses, and thereby gain a fuller understanding of what it has to say. That may sound like a bit of a stretch to some readers. Why in the world would we need poetry? After all, we live in a culture where poetry (outside of the lyrics to songs) doesn't get much attention at all. You'll rarely see a book of poetry on the bestseller list, and there seems to be an ever-decreasing number of people who pay much attention to it at all.

To begin with, reading poetry teaches you a lot about how language works. Language is a complicated business. We all know that words can have a variety of meanings, depending upon their context. But poetic expression makes things even more complicated than that, for sometimes in a poem there is not just one intended meaning in play. The meanings are multivalent, purposely intending more than just one idea to be communicated at the same time. Sometimes all the various meanings of a word are working together to invent a phrase with several shades of meaning.

Many Christians put a great deal of emphasis on taking the Bible literally. They see this as the only way of reading that does justice to the divine authority of God's Word. Taking the words of the Bible at face value, they would assert, is fundamental to an orthodox faith. There is much to commend in this kind of respectful approach to the Bible. But even the most ardent supporter of literalism must admit that such a reading isn't always called for. When Jesus refers to Himself as "the Door," for example, no one is looking for His hinges. When He calls Himself "the Good Shepherd,"

WikiCommons CC-BY-SA photo by Toby Hudson

The Good Shepherd stained glass window by Alfred Handel, St. John's Ashfield

we aren't thinking that His literal occupation was watching over a flock of wooly, white sheep. These statements are metaphors, which have connotations that are larger than their simple literal meanings.

When we consider the meaning of these and other biblical metaphors, symbols, and word pictures, we understand that they work simultaneously on more than one level. They expand our horizons of understanding and interpretation. Consider Jesus' parable about the shepherd going out to search for the lost sheep. One of the obvious things this parable teaches is that God has a deep concern for each and every one of us as an individual. So much that He will seek us out when we have strayed. That is a comforting truth. But there are more layers at work. By using this metaphor, Jesus also indicates the burden that God takes on Himself by going in search of the lost sheep. That lost and soiled and frightened sheep must be picked up, cared for, and carried across the hills to safety.

The simple literal statement that "God cares for each one of us" can be significantly deepened when expressed poetically and meta-phorically through a metaphor that more fully illustrates the extent to which God is willing to go on our behalf. When we think of Christ as a Shepherd, the whole concept of being cared for is invested with a new richness. The metaphor adds layers of meaning that cannot be fully captured in a simple statement of fact. As Sallie McFague has written, "The poet mounts many metaphors, many ways of seeing 'this' as 'that,' many attempts to 'say' what cannot be said directly. The poet sets one metaphor against another, and hopes that the sparks set off by the juxtapositions will ignite something in the mind as well."[10]

That's why an overly literalistic reading of the Bible that fails to appreciate the power of metaphors and word pictures can restrict or even limit our understanding and application. If we do not appreciate the poetic nature of so much of Scripture, then we may well fail to interpret it correctly or at least fail to comprehend the complex mean-ings that are there for those who will look for them.

Some form of poetic expression can be found on many of the pages of Scripture. This doesn't mean that there aren't lots of passages that are meant to be understood at face value—for surely there are—but we need to remember that sometimes it is only in pondering the symbolism and metaphor that we can come closest to understanding what the original authors had in mind. Let's not make the mistake of thinking that the biblical writers were ignorant of how poetic and metaphorical expression work. Their writing is full of such expression.

There is not only poetry in the so-called "poetic books" of the Old Testament, but it is also abundant in many historical and narrative passages, in the parables and sayings of Jesus, in the theological reflections of Paul (many of his letters contain passages of soaring and mysterious poetic expression), and in the book

An openness to the poetry of Scripture calls us to more careful study.

of Revelation, which is poetic at its core, and whose primary message can be missed by those trying to interpret it in some literalistic scheme. We open ourselves to all kinds of misunderstandings if we don't appreciate the poetic sense in the pages of the Bible and restrict ourselves to what it "clearly says." An openness to the poetry of Scripture calls us to more careful study. Often, because poetry is suggestive rather than definitive, it demands some serious thinking if we are to unpack all it has to say.

Poetic writing makes use of ambiguity and the multiple meanings of words. And it doesn't flinch from a bit of mystery. It evokes something that not only engages the mind, but also touches the heart and the soul. When, for example, we consider the death of Jesus on the cross, it is easy to miss the mythic power inherent in the language of sacrifice when we either (as some more liberal theologians tend to do) recoil in disgust from the images of blood that are evoked, or when we (as the more fundamentalist theologians tend to do) reduce what happened at the cross to some kind of legal transaction. When Paul uses the language of the law courts to illustrate what happened at the cross, he is using a poetic image—a metaphor. While there may well be a legal transaction of some sort involved (a debt being paid to restore another to a state of freedom from sin and guilt), there is more than that going on.

The meaning of Christ's crucifixion is so much richer, and the stakes are so much greater than any of our tidy little theories of the atonement can contain. Fleming Rutledge's magisterial study *The Crucifixion: Understanding the Death of Jesus* searches out numerous biblical word-pictures for what was accomplished at the cross, each of them drawing on different biblical passages and different metaphors— a court of law, a cosmic battle, a ransom, a substitution, a reenact-ment of the exodus, a sacrifice, etc.[11] As Rutledge explores the power of each of these images, she exposes how they accumulate to form a much richer understanding of what the Bible is saying than those who settle for only one image drawn from a simplistic reading of any one particular passage. She shows how a deeper understanding emerges from the combined poetry of all the various images, each of which are, at heart, a poetic image to express something that is grand and glorious beyond what words can fully communicate.

That which is clearly literal should be read in that way. But we should always have an eye to the truths imbedded in the metaphors and symbols that are so very prevalent in the Bible. The truth is larger than literalism. And it is bigger than any theological or philosophical system that we use to try to comprehend it. Ultimately, even the theological systems themselves cannot avoid trading in the coin of metaphor.

For some, this kind of openness to metaphor and poetry might seem to make interpretation too difficult to attempt—or even dangerous.

Such an approach can be seen, though, as just another tool in our toolbox for understanding the Bible, and one that is within everyone's reach. We can begin to develop a more poetic eye by exposing ourselves to the arts. Nothing will help us become more *poetic* in our thinking than to spend time not only with poetry, but also with literature, the visual arts, film, and music. These forms of art can teach us by example important concepts about how language works, how visual images are used, and how a richer understanding can be achieved. They will help us become better readers and interpreters of the Bible.

> **The Bible is filled with poetry meant to take us deeper into our understanding of the mystery of God's grace to us.**

The great painter Marc Chagall was an artist who commonly used biblical images in his works. He embraced the poetic beauty of the Bible. "For me, painting the Bible is like a bouquet of flowers. The Bible for me is absolutely pure poetry, a human tragedy. The prophets inspire me. It is a committed poetry."[12] That is a wonderful phrase: "committed poetry." The Bible is filled with poetry meant to take us deeper into our understanding of the mystery of God's grace to us. When we read poetically, we remain committed to truth, but we understand that sometimes truth comes packaged in poetry and image.

Consider the parables of Jesus. Why did He not simply state the ideas and ideals He wanted to communicate? Why was He not more straightforward in His approach to teaching? Why did He cloak so much of it in stories and images? Honestly, even the Sermon on the Mount is delivered less like a sermon and more like a poem. It is full of word pictures and statements that He clearly intends us to puzzle over. His teaching is filled with such moments when He was more poetic than straightforward.

One example might be, "Very truly I tell you, unless a kernel of wheat falls to the ground and dies, it remains only a single seed. But if it dies, it produces many seeds" (John 12:24). Another might be, "For whoever wants to save their life will lose it, but whoever loses their life for me will find it" (Matt. 16:25). In His teaching, Jesus often couched the truth in little stories or in puzzling statements that clearly contain several layers of meaning that He waits for us to unwrap. They demand we give them more than just cursory attention. We must ponder them. Was this perhaps because He recognized that reality itself contains layers of meaning?

The ancient Zen masters would sometimes offer their listeners a puzzling statement called a *koan*. The idea behind the *koan* was that one would hear it, and initially be somewhat puzzled by it. The famous question, "What is the sound of one hand clapping?" is an example of such a *koan*. The listener would be puzzled at first, but upon pondering it further, and continuing to ponder it, the full meaning of the truth behind it begins to fully emerge.

I think some of Jesus' teaching works a little like that. He is often seeking to not just offer an immediate truth but put it forward in such a way that necessitates a process of puzzled pondering, which often awakens further truths. Often His disciples would be debating His meaning after He was no longer present. That wasn't because of an incompetent teaching style. It's because He was planting a "truth bomb" in their mind that would later explode, blowing away all their previous incorrect ideas about themselves and about God.

Because there are layers of meaning in the texts, the discipline of prayerful meditation on Bible passages is an important element of spiritual growth. The Bible is an inexhaustible source for insight and growth. Though I've read most of it literally hundreds of times, I still keep discovering hidden gems within it—things I never noticed before that cause me to awaken to deeper truths.

A poetic way of thinking about my faith has changed the way I live it out. Through it I discover again that belief is more than just intellectual assent to a spiritual ideology or a set of doctrines. Faith involves a trusting embrace of the living God with my whole self. The arts can be helpful for reminding me that my spiritual life isn't just about the thoughts bumping around in my brain. It is existential and experiential as well. Growth in faith includes being transformed at the level of my heart and emotions, as well as in my thinking.

At its root, faith is a mystery. Not like a murder mystery story where everything gets satisfactorily explained in the end, but more like the kind of mystery where the deeper you delve, the more questions you discover. As Frederick Buechner writes, "The more you try to fathom it, the more fathomless it is revealed to be."[13] If you want to settle for a simple faith, then it becomes dangerous to ask too many questions of life and faith. But if you want a rich, full, and authentic faith, then you are going to have to be willing to live with the mysteries and only partially answered questions that are embedded in Christian belief. You must make some room for uncertainty, for those things that you can't figure out, can't make sense of, and are still asking questions about. The poet John Keats called this kind of attitude "negative capability," the willingness to live with some doubts, some uncertainties, and without fully satisfying answers to all your questions.

This openness to what you can't prove doesn't mean giving up the search for understanding. It's just that you are willing to admit that you don't have it all figured out and are still on that humble journey toward God, who is the greatest mystery. If you think you have God all figured out, well, then I am happy for you, but I'm also convinced that just around the corner you are certain to encounter, or the unavoidable tragedies of life will force upon you, some new realizations that will poke a sizeable hole in your neat and tidy theology. Life has a way of doing that. As Frederick Buechner wrote, "To say that God is a mystery is to say that you can never nail him down. Even on Christ the nails proved ultimately ineffective."[14]

When it comes to exploring the mysteries of life and faith, the arts are among our greatest assets. The arts are all about living the questions, letting them guide us toward truths that are richer and deeper than rationality alone has the ability to explore. As the German poet, Rainer Maria Rilke wrote in his *Letters to a Young Poet:*

> I would like to beg of you, dear friend, as well as I can,
> to have patience with everything that remains unsolved
> in your heart. Try to love the questions themselves, like
> locked rooms and like books written in a foreign language.
> Do not now look for the answers. They cannot now be
> given to you because you could not live them. It is a
> question of experiencing everything. At present you need
> to live the questions. Perhaps you will gradually, without
> even noticing it, find yourself experiencing the answer,
> some distant day.[15]

I've learned that art can sometimes reach into places deep inside me where my brain simply cannot go. Art can bypass my many intellectual objections and rationalizations, striking more directly at my heart and my intuition. Art doesn't normally begin with making an argument as much as with creating an experience. It generates insight through an experience that the artist, writer, musician, or filmmaker has created. After our initial engagement with the artistic work, we can begin to flesh out that insight with our intellect. Often the experiential knowing precedes the cognitive knowing.

The weakness and ineffectuality of much of today's popular "Christian art," whether visual art, music, movies, or novels, is that it focuses more upon creating either a shallow and predictable emotional response, or upon trying to prove a theological truth through the manipulations of a story. Those who create such art are usually so busy trying to convince you of some truth or the other that they rarely reach down into that deeper part of your soul. They miss what is essentially human, with all its complexity, and rely instead upon a sort of theological shorthand that is already assumed by the one who reads their book, listens to their music, or watches their film.

However well-meaning or sincere, such work is little more than propaganda for the gospel, and because it often fails to be honest about our human condition, it rarely convinces anyone of anything. Such art might prove comforting in that it confirms what someone already believes, but it doesn't stretch them to ponder the deeper implications of that belief.

At its best, art brings the right brain and the left brain together to create a more wholistic understanding of our lives. Great art weds thinking and feeling in the context of creating an experience, but that experience usually begins with honest human feeling. In that way, art can help us feel our way toward the truth.

Appreciating the poetry of faith opens us to accepting its mystery. The arts remind us that life isn't simple, but that it is deeply (and satisfyingly) mysterious.

Sometimes that mystery can feel like a challenge we need to over-come by arguments. But this is seldom effective. In his fascinating study, *When Art Disrupts Religion,*[16] sociologist Phillip Francis recounts his research into what happened to the students of several fundamentalist Bible colleges when they became aware of art outside the comfort zone of their tradition. The book offers many individual stories of how exposure to great art, music, and literature changed, broadened, and reshaped the thinking of these students and widened their vision of the world through its complexity, ambiguity, and mystery.

The arts remind us that life isn't simple, but that it is deeply (and satisfyingly) mysterious.

For many of these students, a widened exposure to the arts led to a rethinking of their beliefs, opening them to a more nuanced and complex way of seeing themselves, their world, and their faith. It permanently immunized them against a belief system that was simplistic in its attitudes and approach toward life. The arts disrupted their formerly triumphant certainty of having everything all figured out. It raised questions that didn't have easy answers . . . or maybe any answers at all.

The experience of many of these students whom Francis interviewed has a close parallel with my own spiritual journey toward finding God in the complexity of life rather than just being satisfied with simple answers to what are actually very complicated human questions. It was, more than anything else, my exposure to the arts that made me realize I'd have to learn to live with limitations in my understanding and without the ability to provide a nifty scriptural quotation to answer every question. I also found that the Christian apologetics writers did not have a completely satisfying answer to the increasingly complicated questions that were arising in me.

I began to have more questions. I felt some intellectual uncertainty, but eventually came to realize that I didn't need to be able to explain everything. It didn't stop me from searching, but it did free me from the tendency to latch onto whatever "evidence" I could find that might confirm my belief system. I became okay with embracing a faith I couldn't prove by the normal rational or philosophical methods. I wanted my faith to be intellectually responsible and reasonable, but not at the cost of deluding myself with overly simple answers from religious authorities. This path has been painful at times, as I had to let go of the security I had in my old way of thinking, but it has been a path that has led me into an even deeper love for God, even if I am no longer as confident that I have Him all figured out.

For some of the students in Francis's study, their engagement with the arts led them to make a complete break from their former faith. Such is the power of art. It can provoke new ways of thinking and feeling and understanding. It can be dangerous. It might just shake things up. But it also might initiate a search for deeper and more fulfilling answers.

Though the arts have the potential to create an earthquake of insecurity, this is often a very good thing. For it leads to searching. It leads to trying to "live the questions." Frankly, the arts can have the same sort of effect on non-believers. Often the experience of a work of art can disrupt unbelief just as profoundly, revealing that there is more to life than a secularist vision can account for. Through interaction with the arts the unbeliever will come to understand the wisdom of Shakespeare's Hamlet: "There are more things in heaven and earth, Horatio, than are dreamt of in your philosophy."[17] It is often a novel, a piece of music, a poem, or a film that first sets people on the path of questioning their unbelief, that gets them doubting their doubts. And they might just find that such a disruption brings them right to the door of faith.

Peter Berger has suggested that our culture's problem with faith isn't so much that our arguments are less cogent and effective than those of secularism, but that they have been rendered ineffective because modernism has created an intellectual environment in which the gospel message no longer seems *plausible* for many people.[18]

We cannot even get to the question of whether the Christian religion is true or false when faith doesn't even seem like a plausible option for modern folks. But because the arts can take us inside the experiences of others, they can help us to rethink what is plausible as they expand our worldview and our fund of experiences. As, for example, we read the pages of Marilyn Robinson's novel, *Gilead*, a faith lived in integrity and honesty seems a little more plausible for an unbeliever than it might have when they first opened its pages. Art can work vicariously to remind us that there is something more to life than the empty and meaningless march of events that some would have us believe is all it amounts to. The arts have the power to call out not only to our reason, but also to our feelings, our intuitions, and our passions. Art helps us dare to dream, to imagine, to embrace realities that we cannot see—in short, to believe.

In C. S. Lewis's *The Great Divorce*, the heavenly guide promises: "Hitherto you have experienced truth only with the abstract intellect. I will bring you where you can taste it like honey and be embraced by it as a bridegroom. Your thirst shall be quenched."[19]

We need not fear mystery. We can embrace mystery, for we know we will find God there.

The arts remind us that we live in a world that is haunted by things beyond it. They help us see that our world is suffused with supernatural realities that science and reason cannot account for, realities that are beyond our five senses, toward which our senses can only point.

There are two primary philosophical approaches for understanding the world in which we live: immanence and transcendence. *Immanence* is focused on what we can see and experience; it asserts that the only truth is what can be discovered in the context of this world and directly accessed through our five senses. *Transcendence*, on the other hand, suggests that there is a realm beyond this earthly one, a realm revealed only in glimpses and intuitions, a world outside of what our senses can account for.

> **The arts remind us that we live in a world that is haunted by things beyond it.**

Charles Taylor, in his epic study of modernity *A Secular Age*, suggests that most modern people, whatever they say they believe, actually share what he calls an "immanent frame" for understanding reality. For all practical purposes, most of us pretty much limit to the category of reality what we can taste, touch, hear, and smell. Even most religious people, he says, tend to think in the limited terms of immanence.

Yet, at the same time, this immanent worldview remains unsatisfying for most people. They remain unsettled by an innate sense that we live in a world that is haunted by realities outside of it. For most people, Taylor asserts, there is still an abiding sense of a mysterious otherness that surrounds their lives, which is inexplicable in terms of that immanent frame.[20] Such spiritual realities cannot be so easily evaded. This common sense of realities that lay beyond us creates the kind of tension we see when the members of a secular society are so fascinated by ESP, angels, psychospiritual techniques, and horror films. Even the most ardent secularists seem unable to escape the allure of a "something more," even if they don't want to assign it any connection to traditional religion.

It just isn't that easy for members of our secularized culture to dismiss the reality of God or of some sort of spiritual realm beyond our present existence. Try as hard as some might, our modern minds cannot seem to get away from trying to make sense of the transcendent experiences in the world around us, especially such experiences as awe, wonder, love, and mystery. One of the values of the arts is that they can serve as a way of awakening us to such realities or reminding us that our lives consist of more than simply existing on the treadmill of day-to-day experience.

This is our contemporary reality: one where it is not always easy for us to believe, nor is it easy to disbelieve. Belief and doubt exist alongside one another. In a sense, we are all Thomases now.

Flannery O'Connor expressed it well in a letter she penned. There is, she said, "always the conflict between an attraction for the Holy and the disbelief in it that we breathe in with the air of the times."[21] Or as contemporary novelist Julian Barnes wistfully opines in the first line of one of his non-fiction books, "I don't believe in God, but I miss Him."[22] He understands the immense loss we experience that jettisoning such a belief entails, and admits to sometimes being haunted by the hypothetical possibility that it just might be true.

One of the implications of this internal struggle within the modern soul is that when we communicate with people locked inside the immanent frame, it is not enough simply to offer a counter argument. The problem for unbelievers isn't simply a lack of information but actually a lack of vision and a lack of imagination. We can help them make a connection to that something more, and the arts might be one of the best ways to achieve that.

The arts give us a new and richer window into the world, whether through a novel by Dostoyevsky or Jane Austen, a painting by Rembrandt or Chagall, a poem by Emily Dickinson or T. S. Eliot, a symphony by Mozart or Mendelssohn, or a song by Bob Dylan or Van Morrison. These creative artists, and countless others like them, help us understand that the world is bigger, more complicated, more morally nuanced, and much more mysterious than we'd imagined before partaking of their art. We need the kind of experiences of ecstasy, of connection, and of fellow feeling with others that they can provide. We need to somehow make sense of the complex business of being a human being, a creature part angel and part beast. And the arts are one of the best ways to begin to explore such realities.

As the poster that hangs on the wall of Fox Mulder's office on *The X-Files* confidently proclaims: The truth is out there. The difficulty is that the truth is, in a very real sense, hidden in plain sight. It is there, but it is so very easy to miss or misunderstand. It might just take the kind of fresh perspective an artist provides to help us really see it.

For the arts help us see the world differently. They can help us imagine another way of thinking than our own as they offer their unique vision of the world. They can help us feel a connection with the transcendent that simply isn't possible with arguments alone. They can question the certainties of the non-believer by giving them a new way of seeing and by helping them feel their way into the compelling truth of the Christian perspective on reality. They can offer experiences that reflect or create those moments where transcendence shines through our world; those inklings of *something more*.

Such transcendent experiences are not irrational, but they *are* something that is more than merely rational. They are needed to complement rationality if we are to see more fully and communicate our faith more effectively and winsomely. When you begin a discussion with shared experiences of transcendence instead of an argument, you have a touch point for a real conversation. In such a scenario, you aren't trying to communicate a series of doctrinal presuppositions from scratch but instead are beginning from a vantage point you can both agree upon. Then, the task becomes finding a winsome way to communicate your interpretation of the experience you hold in common. This is so much more effective than taking the salesman's approach of offering a "product" that you must badger and cajole the listener into "purchasing."

The purpose of the arts is not so much found in giving tidy answers to the big questions about life, but about provoking the right kinds of questions. Art isn't primarily a means for the delivery of information as it is an invitation to experience something of what its creator has seen and experienced. In doing so, it can move you deeply and change the way you see your life and your world, as well as the way you feel about it.

Perhaps that is why I sometimes find a tear forming in my eye when I listen to Mozart's *Requiem* or Gorecki's Third Symphony, why a Rouault canvas can often leave me speechless and weak in the knees, or why the paintings of the Hudson River School often spark a longing within me for an eternal home, or why the whole world looks different when I emerge from a dark theater after watching a film by Terrence Malick, or why a novel by Walker Percy or Marilynn

Robinson lets me simply become lost in the alternative world that they create with their words and discover truths I never suspected.

The arts can open you to the realities of the spiritual world and help you see how spiritual realities penetrate and suffuse *this* world in which you live. If you follow the clues strewn like breadcrumbs along the path of life by the greatest artists, you'll discover that they can guide you toward a higher truth and a bigger story. So, live with your heart and mind open to the mystery. And don't be afraid to develop a more poetic approach to your life and your faith.

QUESTIONS AND SPIRITUAL EXERCISES

1. Explore the world of poetry. In the appendix I've provided a list of some of my favorite poets. If you aren't familiar with many poets, see which ones in my list especially speak to you.

2. Write your own poem about a spiritual experience, something that fascinates you in nature, or on a biblical theme.

3. Explore one of Jesus' parables, with a special emphasis on how He tells the story and why He chooses story as the method for delivering this truth. You might start with the parable of the prodigal son (Luke 15:11–32).

4. Frederick Buechner suggests that you "listen to your life." Take a few minutes and write down your thoughts on what life seems to be teaching you right now.

5. Ponder what it means to "live the questions." How might you begin to practice this?

CHAPTER FIVE

A Bigger Picture:

Bringing the Scriptures to Life

A COUPLE YEARS AGO, while shuffling through the Uffizi Gallery in Florence and amazed at how many iconic masterpieces had been gathered together in one place, I was struck afresh with the realization of how many of them were based upon biblical themes. As I slowly wandered among the galleries, I saw masterwork after masterwork that attempted to illustrate key events from the pages of the Scriptures—the annunciation, the nativity of Christ, the Last Supper, and the crucifixion, as well as the stories of Noah, Adam and Eve, David, and others from the pages of the Old Testament. Moving slowly from painting to painting, taking it all in, I was privileged to experience many diverse interpretations and unique evocations of these mostly familiar stories. In the process, some of these biblical narratives came to life for me in a new way. I hadn't come to the museum with that purpose in mind, but that was one of the things I took away from my visit.

I thought to myself: What if all the paintings on biblical themes were to suddenly vanish from our museums? What would be left? How many gallery walls would be left mostly blank? So many of the most treasured works of art in any museum are based upon Bible stories. They are an important part of our Christian heritage, not only our entire Western artistic tradition. That's one of the reasons why my frequent visits to art museums are so inspiring. Through the works hanging on their walls I see these sacred stories come to life, and it leaves me thinking about them in new ways. Then, as I read these scriptural texts later, some of these images will come flooding back to me, helping me experience all the emotion and insight they offer. They become a sort of visual commentary on God's Word. Frankly, learning to "read" these paintings has made me a better reader of Scripture.

As modern Christians, we face two major hurdles as we read the Scriptures, and they confront us with something of a paradox. Our problem with the Bible is that its world is so *unfamiliar* to us . . . and, at the same time, the stories themselves might possibly have become too *familiar* to us.

In the pages of the Bible we read the record of ancient events, and will, at times, find ourselves unable to easily understand or identify with what we see recorded there. The original text of the Bible was written in languages with which few of us are familiar and which none of us use in our ordinary daily lives. The settings of the stories can be a problem too, taking place during historical periods that can only be partially reconstructed through the few remaining artifacts that have survived. Then there are the ancient customs, which often seem strange and puzzling. And even troubling at times. It can be hard to relate to the heroes of the faith and what makes them tick.

We live at such a distance from the world of the Bible that it can be difficult to make sense of the stories it tells. The result of the strangeness is that it can become all too easy for the contemporary reader to import their own prejudices into these pages in the quest for understanding them, imagining the Bible to say things that it almost certainly isn't saying. Or we might be tempted to simply dismiss this ancient book as irrelevant for someone living centuries later.

How can we overcome this distance?

On the other hand, to those of us who have been surrounded by these stories for much of our lives, they may well have become overly familiar. We've heard them taught in Sunday schools, preached in sermons, or written about in devotional literature. And because of their familiarity, we are in danger of becoming numb to them. They lose their ability to shock or surprise us. "We've heard it all before," we think, so we don't wince at the strangeness of the story of Abraham being asked to sacrifice his son or admit into our minds the horror of King David, "the man after God's own heart," orchestrating a killing so that he could cover up his misdeeds. Nor do we seriously ponder what it might mean for God to destroy all living things in a flood, except for one family and their boatful of animals. All these stories might have become so familiar to us that they may no longer make much emotional impact upon us or cause us to ask any of the obvious questions they should provoke. Perhaps, in the process, we have de-fanged and de-clawed the Bible, making it safe reading for any age group, but at the cost of missing much of its dramatic power and staggering implications.

How can we overcome this over-familiarity?

One answer to these questions, of course, is to immerse oneself in a careful study of the Bible—to read the commentaries, to grapple with original languages in search of the fuller meaning of the words, to consult the theologians, and to engage with the archaeology and geography and history of the Holy Lands. This is an important task for opening new avenues of understanding and revealing the fuller context of the scriptural text. We should not settle for simplistic interpretations that fail to challenge us, but look for the best and most accurate interpretation possible. We should read the Scriptures carefully, not just searching for verses that confirm our own theological predispositions, or verses that can be pulled out of their context and used for inspirational purposes or promises to claim, or verses that can serve as fuel for our side in theological disagreements. Instead, we should read with our eyes and our minds wide open, as well as our hearts. This takes effort, but if we believe God reveals Himself through these pages, it would be foolish for us not to make that effort. When we do, we might be surprised by what we'll find. And if we don't find anything that surprises or discomforts us, we probably just aren't reading very carefully.

So, where do the arts come into all of this?

Like Bible study, the arts can be a way of engaging with the Bible and gaining new perspectives. Their impact can help us reach beyond mere intellectual comprehension into a fuller emotional engagement. Great art can help us to better imagine ourselves into the stories of

> **Perhaps, in the process, we have de-fanged and de-clawed the Bible, making it safe reading for any age group, but at the cost of missing much of its dramatic power and staggering implications.**

the Bible, conveying them in sharper focus and, in a sense, bringing them to life, much as a high-quality historical film can help the viewer better understand what it would have been like to have "been there" when the events unfolded. The arts can reveal deeper meanings and fresh perceptions through their attempt to engage with the sacred texts. They can also help us to feel the impact of the stories—what was at stake, the emotional effects upon the characters, and their complex motivations. The arts can cause the biblical stories to leap off the pages and into our hearts. They become more real to us on a number of levels and do more than just impart information or offer a literal rendering of the events portrayed. They give dimension to the storytelling and amplify its truths. They give us a new point of view for comprehending them. And while no replacement for careful biblical study, they are an additional tool for understanding—intellectually, emotionally, and spiritually.

There is a long tradition with our Judeo-Christian heritage of engaging with the Scriptures in an imaginative way, and it might be worth a brief consideration of a traditional Hebrew approach to reading and contemplating the Scriptures that has emphasized making it more relevant and spiritually nourishing to its readers—the tradition of Midrash. What these rabbis of the past were attempting to do with Midrash is similar to what artists of all kinds do today.

The *Midrash* is a collection of reflections on the Hebrew Scriptures based upon a method of biblical interpretation developed by rabbis in the post-biblical era. Exegetical in nature, these writings attempt to find revelation not only in the text itself, but in alternative readings that might stand alongside to illuminate—though never replace—the original sacred texts. Their goal was primarily "pastoral," aimed at making the Scriptures more relevant and vital to their time.

Since the Bible was written in a rather spare style and is often lacking in specific details, these rabbis sought to explore its stories by adding the "missing" information and offering imaginative interpretations and applications. Some of what they came up with is stunning and insightful, and the best of it was recorded for posterity. These rabbinic scholars, who were careful and passionate students of the text, knew it well enough to generally not stray into heretical areas. They believed that they weren't "making up" their new additions to the text, as much as uncovering what was already implicit in the text. They saw themselves as continuing a conversation that had begun at Sinai.

These biblical scholars would take a passage and interrogate it closely, looking to fill in the gaps where details are omitted, reading closely to gain a better understanding. Rabbi Ben Bag-Bag defined how this method worked: "Turn it [the biblical text] and turn it again, for all is in it, and contemplate it, and grow gray and old over it."[1] He, and other writers of the *Midrash*, saw the Scriptures as a diamond whose every facet reflected light.

These rabbis would engage with text imaginatively by searching out not only the text in front of them, but also the text behind the text, and even the text in the cracks and crevices between the lines and between the letters. Such an approach allowed them to stop and ask questions of the biblical text, to imaginatively fill in the blanks, and to puzzle out the motivations and backstory of biblical characters.

In such an approach, the tensions and questions that are sometimes raised by an intensive reading of the Scriptures aren't seen as a problem, but as an opportunity—a challenge to wrestle and explore, and to mine the text for more meaning. This way of approaching Scripture is not intended to end a conversation with firm answers, but to continue an ongoing conversation.

Too often Christians today go to the Bible for ammunition to support their own pet theological ideas, or to dig up some nice inspirational thoughts to encourage them, or to hunt down a "promise" that they can "claim." Those who practice *Midrash* are challenging us to a closer kind of reading. Francis Wade compares this approach to the process of fracking, whereby oil and natural gas are extracted "from the cracks and crevices of deep rock formations by applying pressurized liquid to fracture the rock."[2] This process, explains Wade, uncovers hidden reserves of petroleum. He proposes that serious Bible readers can use "biblical fracking" to get more out of the biblical texts.

Because it is largely an imaginative endeavor, there is always the danger that we might begin to read things into the text that aren't there. Our own ideas and prejudices can easily enter the process of interpretation. (Though, to be fair, this is always a temptation for *everyone* who reads the Bible, even those who would attempt to read it as literally as they can.) That's why this methodology was only undertaken by those who knew the original texts most intimately, for they could square any new insights with "the whole counsel" of the Bible. The better you know the text, the better will be the results of such a deep imaginative dive into it.

When approaching Scripture in this way, these rabbis weren't looking for new truths, but rather for a fleshing out of the emotional and psychological and theological truths that underlie the simpler stories of the Bible.

> **The Bible is a book that confronts us with mysteries and then invites us to participate in them.**

Midrash reminds us that the Bible is not a simple static deposit of truth, but an invitation for us to explore and wrestle and be perplexed and be challenged, and ultimately to be transformed by what we discover. The Bible is unlike any other book in that it is a *living* book (Heb. 4:12). It isn't a book that can be tamed or conquered intellectually. It isn't a book of well-organized propositions to memorize and parrot. It is a book that confronts us with mysteries and then invites us to participate in them.

Rachel Held Evans captured this sense of the Bible being a *living* book when she wrote: "The ancient rabbis likened Scripture to a palace, alive and bustling, full of grand halls, banquet rooms, secret passages, and locked doors."[3]

A similar approach to the biblical stories that we see practiced in the *Midrash* is at work when creative artists attempt to portray biblical events in their work. They provide a reading that engages not only the mind, but also the imagination. Thus, great art can provide fuel for contemplation as it offers a sort of visual commentary, literary commentary, or a musical commentary on the Scriptures, bringing the stories of the Bible to life for us in a fresh way.

Since, as we noted earlier, the biblical writers were usually quite spare in their details and descriptions, the artists who reflect on these stories can exercise their imaginations in an attempt to recreate what it might have been like to have been present as these events unfolded, or to provide new insights into what they have to say to us today. Our eyes and ears can become the portals for a fresh interpretation that may bring these truths alive in a new way.

We might think about it in terms of *immersion*.

When the lights dim in a movie theater, I prepare to give myself over to the story that is about to unfold on the big screen. There in the darkness, my entire focus shifts to the tale being told. And when the film is a good one, I tend to lose all track of time. As the film winds to its conclusion, I am often surprised by how quickly the time has passed because I was so entirely involved with what was being projected on the screen. I find myself experiencing emotions—fear, sadness, exhilaration, peace—that are connected to what I am viewing. I am immersed in the story. I am "all in."

So, when I experience an effective retelling of a story from the Bible, I am fully immersed in the story and moved in ways that go beyond mere reading of words on a page. Now, it must be admitted that effective adaptations of the biblical text are notoriously hard to create in the world of cinema. One could reference dozens of Bible movies that are rigid and lifeless, pious in a sentimental and implausible sort of way, overly romanticized, and ultimately dull and boring and unconvincing. Whatever the good intentions of their creators might have been, the result is a film that is not believable and not engaging, and that will not be of interest to anyone beyond those who are looking for a tidy cinematic sermon on celluloid.

From the very dawn of moviemaking, filmmakers could see the potential of telling the story of Jesus through the medium of film. These early films of the silent era did so mostly in a rather wooden manner, but one imagines they still had a powerful effect on their original audiences. After all, audience members could see Jesus move and act with their own eyes. The stories were incarnated in the flesh right before them. Some of the better of these early films are D. W. Griffith's *The King of Kings* (1927) and Cecil B. DeMille's *The Ten Commandments* (1956).

During the 1950s and '60s there were a flurry of biblical films, though most were of questionable artistic merit and usually were filled with overwrought acting and distracting non-biblical elements. Closer to our own time there have been several noteworthy filmic adaptations of the Jesus story. In 1964, Pier Paolo Pasolini directed *The Gospel According to St. Matthew*, a spare but very moving black-and-white production that grounded the gospel story in very human terms and emphasized the social justice aspect of Matthew's Gospel. Pasolini's personal vision focused on some elements that are normally not emphasized in most Jesus films.

Jesus of Nazareth was a high-budget TV mini-series from 1977 that stretched over six hours. It is very effective storytelling: a strong script, well-acted, and visually stunning cinematography. Mel Gibson's *The Passion of the Christ* (2004) is also gorgeously mounted, with many of its scenes shot to resemble classic Renaissance paintings. Some would argue that it is marred by its emphasis on the violence of the Passion narrative, the camera unblinking in the face of torture that just seems to go on and on. One cannot help but wonder if some judicious editing would have made such scenes more effective, as the unsparing brutality tends to draw too much attention to itself and take viewers out of the immersive experience. Despite this weakness, the film is carefully constructed, and the cinematography is both inventive and beautiful.

In 2016, two more striking films on the same themes were produced. *Risen* tells the story of the resurrection through the eyes of an unbelieving Roman soldier who is tasked with investigating the purported resurrection of Jesus and discovering what really happened. *The Last Days in the Desert* is a more speculative and more artistically driven film, contemplating what might have happened when Jesus emerged from the desert after His forty days of temptation. It is a powerful meditation on the nature of temptation, family conflicts, and dealing with the evil inside ourselves. More recently, *The Chosen* is an episodic series on the life of Jesus that is remarkable for its character development, attention to detail, and cinematic craft. Its fresh approach to telling the story of Jesus demonstrates anew the potential of film to bring the Bible to life. Films like these can draw the viewer into the world of the Bible and offer an emotional and imaginative engagement with the events recorded there. While we view them, we are immersed anew in the power of the stories that the Bible recounts.

———————————

Long before the motion picture camera was invented, visual artists sought to create this same sort of immersive experience in their art.

When investigators are trying to piece together what happened in the aftermath of an accident, they will call upon various witnesses to describe what they saw and heard. Since each witness was usually located in a different spot when the accident occurred, each has a somewhat different story to tell. Each brings a unique perspective, and when all these various perspectives are taken together, the investigators can get a more fully rounded understanding of what really happened.

Perhaps that is why there are four Gospels in the New Testament. Each of the writers tells the story in a different way, with different events included or excluded, and a different overall theme in mind. If we only had one or two or even three of the Gospels, we'd be missing out on important aspects of the story of Jesus Christ. They complement each other. They create certain tensions between each other. They each provide a somewhat different focus on these events. The result is that we do not have a single voice narrating the events of Jesus' life, but a polyphonic collection of four voices. (And to them we can add the various reflections in the letters of Paul and the other apostles on the specific moments of which they write). The result is less a solo than a symphony, or at least a chamber orchestra. Each adds something to the rich recounting of Christ's life that we find in the New Testament.

One of the things that the arts can provide are further voices and further perspectives on the biblical text. They can give us new insights as they round out the view of what took place, deepening our under-standing and giving us a more fleshed-out vision of what transpired.

I was reminded of the power of art to expand our vision when I taught a class on the events of Passion week. Drawing on works from the whole history of art, I shared various important paintings with the class, and we pondered and discussed their significance in rounding out our understanding of what happened at the cross. Since the cruci-fixion has been painted countless times by many artists, we explored a great variety of images of Jesus on the cross and asked these questions: What did this artist want to emphasize about the significance of the Passion? What new light do they throw upon the biblical text?

We looked at a thirteenth century cross by Cimabue, which shows the body of Jesus twisted in pain and exhibiting a facial expression of intense suffering. We considered the famous fresco by Masaccio in the Church of Santa Maria Novella in Florence, which is an early exercise in the

WikiCommons

The Crucifixion by Cimabue, San Domenico, Arezzo

The Trinity by Masaccio, Church of Santa Maria Novella, Florence

use of perspective to create an illusion of depth, as well as a reminder that the entire Trinity played a role in the offering of Christ for our sins. The Father is supporting Jesus as He slumps upon the cross, as well as offering Him to us, as the Spirit subtly hovers between them.

We gazed upon the horrifically scarred and contorted body of Christ in the Isenheim Altarpiece, which reveals the full brutal reality of the crucifixion. This harrowing reminder of what He endured for each of us is especially powerful because this painting originally hung above the altar in a hospital for those suffering with a disfiguring skin disease called "St. Anthony's fire." Surely these inmates would have personally connected with this image of pain and ugliness—of Christ carrying their suffering in His scarred body and empathizing with their pain.

The Isenheim Altarpiece by Matthias Grunewald

And we pondered the mystical image of Christ on the cross by El Greco where He appears almost flame-like in the fluid brushstrokes. This mystical image shows only a dainty drop of blood and a look of resignation . . . almost serenity. You can almost imagine this figure just lifting right off the

WikiCommons

Christ Crucified with Toledo in the Background by El Greco, Fundacion Banco Santander, Salamanca

cross and soaring heavenward. Here is a hint of the resurrection even in the midst of the crucifixion. In all we looked at over a dozen images, and various members of the class shared their own thoughts and feelings about the paintings.

Each of us had each been moved in different ways by the unique depictions of Jesus' death, and we deepened our understanding of what Jesus accomplished on the cross through contemplating these varying versions of the same scene. It is a reminder of another way that the arts can enrich our understanding of the pages of the Bible.

———

One way artists found to approach the Bible through art was to attempt to tell the whole story in one location by painting a series of frescos. Giotto, for example, covered all four walls of the Scrovegni Chapel in Padua with images that present the major events from the life of Jesus. When you enter this small chapel, you'll find yourself surrounded on all four sides with several layers of paintings stacked upon each other. Most of the space is dedicated to the life of Jesus, though the life of Mary, His mother, is also illustrated in this vivid, colorful series of paintings that were painted directly onto the wet plaster of the walls. It is a visual feast.

When you compare Giotto's work with that of earlier artists, the thing that stands out is his gift for emotionally engaging storytelling. His figures do not float in an ethereal spiritual realm like the work of most medieval painters. Instead, they are grounded in simple, but believable, earthly settings with their surrounding architecture and landscape. He reminds us that the story he is telling took place in real earthly settings, and that the story he is telling involved real people with real emotions. Giotto brings emotion, drama, confrontation, tenderness, and humor to his depictions of the biblical text, emphasizing the human relationships within the stories. In the panel representing the lamentation of Christ after His death, for example, we

The Lamentation of Christ by Giotto, Scrovegni Chapel, Padua

grasp the monumental tragedy of the event through the expressions of the onlookers. Their expressions take us into the narrative, and we experience the story alongside them.

In Venice, Tintoretto was commissioned to create paintings for the two floors of the Scoula Grande di San Rocco, and he spent several years painting large scale images of key scenes from the Gospels. They are vivid, highly imaginative, and emotionally resonant. They culminate in one of the most glorious and triumphant visions of the crucifixion that exists in all of art history, one we discussed in the first chapter.

In Florence, Fra Angelico, a monk, painted frescos for each of the monastic cells in the monastery of San Marco. His paintings were smaller and used a bright and colorful palette, and they manifest the sweetness and devotion for which this angelic brother was known. As the modern visitor passes from room to room, they cannot help being touched by his re-telling of these familiar stories.

Closer to modern times, James Tissot took this goal of creating an immersive experience to another level through the research that was the foundation of his painting project: a series of paintings covering virtually every event recorded in the Gospels.

Tissot, who lived and painted in the age of Impressionism and Post-Impressionism, worked in a highly finished realistic style. He was fascinated by elegant clothing and costume and is still best known for his many paintings of fashionable ladies in urban settings. Though born in Paris, Tissot spent an extended amount of time in England, where he not only painted, but fell passionately in love. Sadly, the focus of his passion died after an all-too-brief romance.

Heartbroken, he returned to Paris, and eventually decided on his next series of paintings. He would capture beautiful women in locations all around the city. One of the locations he needed to research for one of these paintings was the Church of Saint-Sulpice. He had decided to use it as a background for a picture of a woman worshipping, so he slipped into a Sunday mass so he could observe a service in action. Tissot had grown up as a Catholic, but by this time in his life any remnants of faith were more in the nature of custom than conviction.

But something happened to Tissot at the moment when the priest raised the host aloft at the height of the mass. He had a vision of Jesus Christ comforting two destitute and despairing urban dwellers. He was so profoundly moved by this vision of the compassionate and caring Christ that he returned to his studio and went without sleep for several nights as he painted a work called "Inward Voices (The Ruins)."

This epiphany led him to a serious study of the Bible, especially the Gospels. Over time he would paint several dozen images of Old Testament stories, but his real focus was upon the stories of Jesus. He was so fascinated by the Gospels that he decided to create an extensive series of paintings that would cover every major occurrence in the life of Christ. When he was done, he had created over 350 paintings in all. It was a ten-year project, and it involved two extended trips to Egypt, Syria, and Palestine, where he interviewed Rabbis, studied Jewish customs, and made extensive sketches of the landscape, plant life, animals, architecture, and landscape of the Holy Land.

Tissot's goal was to achieve a high level of historical and cultural accuracy in his depictions, rather than filling his work with the usual anachronisms of earlier artists. He was striving for an almost journalistic, eyewitness approach in his paintings, and wanted to create a "you are there" experience for the viewers who would look at these works. When they were toured around the world in the early 1900s, the paintings were a sensation. There were reports of deep emotional responses from viewers—of quiet reverence, weeping, and even kneeling in prayer in front of the pictures. They were even gathered together to create an oversized book in which they were accompanied by a harmony of the Gospels and cultural commentary that Tissot penned himself.

The entire collection was eventually purchased by the Brooklyn Museum, who displays one of them now and then. For the most part, they are usually in storage. I had the privilege one rainy fall day of looking through the boxes that currently house them as they await another showing. These watercolors are so intricate and detailed that they seem to spring to life in front of your eyes. The curator who showed them to me remarked that he had never seen them before, and he commented that he was struck by the exquisite detail that Tissot had achieved with the very difficult medium of watercolor.

As would be expected, the paintings are not all uniform in quality or equally imaginative. Some are a bit stiff, and when Tissot tries to depict a supernatural event—angels or the resurrection, for example— it is less convincing than those that seem to capture a more ordinary event, such as Jesus teaching along the shores of the Sea of Galilee or the magi crossing the desert on their camels. But at their best, these paintings provide much to ponder and meditate upon. As a whole, the project is one that can invite deeper understanding of the stories it portrays. Perhaps my favorite of the series is "What Our Lord Saw From the Cross," which manages to depict the crucifixion from an entirely unique perspective. Literally. We see the event of Christ on the cross from *His own perspective*, hanging on the cross, as He gazes down upon those who are His torturers and upon His heartbroken followers. Somehow, in a way that I cannot explain, this image seems to speak of Jesus' mercy and compassion even as these horrifying events are unfolding. It is as though, through His pain, His gaze of love is focused upon each and every individual face in the crowd.

What Our Lord Saw From the Cross by James Tissot, Brooklyn Museum

At some point in their career, nearly every artist of note deployed their talents to explore themes from the Bible—Leonardo, Michelangelo, Manet, Picasso, van Gogh, Andy Warhol, Rubens, and Chagall among them. Others have given more extensive focus to such subjects. Among them was Caravaggio, whose paintings on biblical themes are now recognized as works of genius, but in their own time were considered scandalous by many due to their earthiness and lack of pious tidiness. These paintings, which dramatically cast light upon their figures against a dark background, are full of real human drama and a gritty realism. Perhaps that is because Caravaggio went out onto the streets to find the faces he wanted as models and presented them on canvas in a "warts and all" manner.

The unidealized saints who inhabit his pictures generally wear torn and frayed clothing, and are often caught in movement, rather than being posed solemnly, as was the usual religious convention of painting in his time. He tells stories that feel "lived in," which is the source of their power. He is not afraid to portray what many would consider vulgar or ugly. Take, for example, his startling painting of the moment when the doubting Thomas is finally convinced that Jesus has indeed risen from the dead.

Caravaggio was a master at rendering the psychology of an unfolding spiritual drama, as we can see from the intense and amazed facial

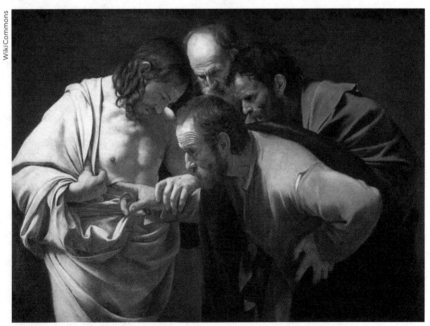

The Incredulity of Thomas by Caravaggio, Sanssouci Picture Gallery, Potsdam

expressions of the disciples as Jesus takes the hand of Thomas and guides it into the open wound in His side. Caravaggio is not engaging in any pious sentimentality here but capturing the physical reality of the resurrection. It is a moment where the spiritual and the physical interact most powerfully. The resurrection, under Caravaggio's brush, is not merely a lovely spiritual idea, but a reflection of the very earthy mystery of incarnation.

Many artists did not attempt the kind of historical veracity that Tissot brought to his task. In fact, many great paintings have many anachronistic elements—clothing that is contemporaneous to their time or architecture that looks like nothing from the Holy Lands. In some cases, this could be the result of historical ignorance. Detailed information about the customs and cultures of the Mideast were simply not available to earlier artists, leaving them to make their best guesses.

For other artists, however, the anachronisms are purposeful, a sort of imaginative exploration of what the biblical stories might have looked like if they had taken place in the artist's own time—a reminder that these stories aren't just ancient history, but that their implications are just as relevant for today as they ever were. The modern British painter Stanley Spencer, for example, created a number of paintings in which he imagined these biblical tales unfolding in his own little English village of Cookham, which he called a "holy suburb of heaven."[4] These purposeful anachronisms are a reminder that the biblical stories aren't just past history. They are timeless, continuing to be relevant to us today. His "The Resurrection in Cookham" is one of the great masterpieces of the twentieth century.[5]

So far, all our visual art examples come from a Western artistic heritage. But much fascinating art has been created by those in other traditions. Space does not allow us to examine this as closely as I'd like, but I can recommend a couple of books worth pursuing to begin such an exploration: *Christ for All People: Celebrating a World of Christian Art*[6] and *The Christian Story: Five Asian Artists Today.*[7]

One of my favorite non-western biblical artists is Sadao Watanabe, a Japanese artist whose creative output consists almost entirely of works on biblical themes, created with a distinctly Japanese visual vocabulary. Watanabe was a Christian living in Japan during a time when only a very small percentage of the population embraced the Christian faith.

One day, while shopping at a Christian bookstore in Tokyo, Watanabe was struck by the realization that the covers of most of the

From the Collection of Anne Pyle

The Last Supper by Sadao Watanabe

books in the shop were decorated with European religious art. His response was to create a fresh artistic approach that used the visual language of Japanese traditions to express his faith. As he said, "I wanted to find a way of expressing my Christianity within a Japanese context instead of just adapting the European tradition."[8] The result was a highly original approach to biblical painting.

In his print, "The Last Supper," Watanabe has reimagined the Last Supper as an event taking place in a Japanese context. The disciples wear kimonos and kneel upon a tatami mat around a low table. There is a Japanese menu for the Last Supper—large-eyed sea bream (a fish usually served at ceremonial occasions), accompanied by sushi rolls and stylized bottles of sake. Jesus presides at the center of the meal, surrounded by His disciples, who look on in wonder as Jesus blesses the meal.

Artists all over the world have followed a path like that of Watanabe in Japan. They have imagined these stories as occurring in their own cultures and thus have communicated the biblical stories in ways that are fresh and relevant for their own audience.

Like painting, the novel has provided another way of retelling these stories. Given the expansiveness of fictional writing, considering that a novel usually takes many hours to devour, the reader is drawn ever more deeply into the inner lives of the characters and more fully experiences the cultural background in which the story takes place. So, it has become another genre for commentary on the text, a modern form of *Midrash*. Sometimes a novel will take a minor or imagined character from the biblical text and tell the story largely through their eyes. One thinks of books such as Lew Wallace's *Ben Hur*, Anita Diamant's *The*

Red Tent, Frederick Buechner's *Son of Laughter*, or the numerous but often uneven books that fall in the category of contemporary biblical fiction. At their best, they open up the text in previously unimagined ways. At their worst, they can sometimes import modern customs and values and religious ideas into stories where they don't belong.

Also deserving of mention is Walter Wangerin's engaging volume, *The Book of God*, which sets out to tell the entire story of Scripture in the form of an epic novel and succeeds in brilliant fashion. Dorothy L. Sayers's radio play, *The Man Born to Be King*, uses the genre of drama to tell the story of Jesus, but without the usual stiffness and pious sentimentality that often weigh down such attempts. She creates real drama with believable characters, and even manages to inject some humor into the proceedings. Which is undoubtedly why her friend, C. S. Lewis, made a habit of reading it every year during Holy Week.

The great poets have also sought to provide comment on biblical stories through their poems. Robert Atwan and Laurance Wieder have provided the service of bringing a great number of these together in their two-volume work, *Chapters into Verse: Poetry in English Inspired by the Bible.*[9] Nearly a thousand pages, this indispensable collection, arranged in biblical order, gathers the work of Emily Dickinson, George Herbert, John Milton, Walt Whitman, Henry Vaughn, G. K. Chesterton, Isaac Watts, Thomas Merton, Thomas Traherne, and countless others. Their reflections on the biblical stories and passages are enlightening and inspiring. D. S. Martin has similarly gathered poetic reflections on biblical events and characters in his poetry anthology, *Adam, Eve, and the Riders of the Apocalypse,*[10] in which the work of thirty-nine contemporary poets is featured, many of them among today's premier Christian poets.

The tradition of classical choral music on biblical themes is expansive, wide-ranging, and profound. The masterworks of Bach and Handel come immediately to mind, but composers such as Mendelssohn, Stravinsky, Arvo Part, and countless others have created musical masterpieces that move the listener deeply as they unfold biblical stories. And in modern times it is worth mentioning the many albums by folk musician Michael Card, who gives musical settings to biblical themes in many of his albums. Card is a serious biblical scholar, and this is evident in the depth he brings to his compositions of the stories and themes of the Old and New Testaments. Especially significant are his two trilogies: *The Ancient Faith*, which covers Old Testament themes, and *The Life*, which reflects on the life of Jesus. I return to these often for fresh inspiration. Andrew Peterson is another Christian musician who brings poetry and rich biblical insight to many of his albums, especially his Christmas album, *Behold the Lamb*, which refreshingly breaks the rules and expectations of a traditional holiday record, and his reflections on the passion story in his *Resurrection Letters Anthology*.

Studies show that children remember things better when images are wedded to words, or when the words are read aloud while their eyes can follow along. That's why most textbooks for kids are filled with pictures, and why the best teachers read aloud to their students. Frankly, the brains of adults aren't much different. We are more likely to retain information and ideas when we not only read them but also see them and hear them. There is a symbiotic relationship at work.

You cannot know the Scriptures in their fulness through the arts alone. These creative images should never *replace* careful study and meditation on the words and stories they depict. Such works of art might be inspired, but they are not divinely inspired in the way the Scriptures are. They can, though, be used as tools for spiritual reflection and enriching our engagement with the Bible. Their imaginative depictions can make the Bible come alive in fresh ways. They can be a companion for reading Scripture, fuel for meditation and contemplation, and material for theological pondering. And they can be a powerful tool for getting more from your reading in God's Word.

QUESTIONS AND SPIRITUAL EXERCISES

1. Choose one of the images from this chapter (or another painting that means something to you) and examine it slowly and at length. Don't overthink or jump to a quick interpretation. Let the image do its work on you. Pause over the details, asking yourself why the artist made the choices that they made. Then go the Scriptures and read about the event that is being portrayed. What impact does the picture have on your reading, or your reading on how you look at the picture?

2. Visit an art museum and pay special attention to the images there that reflect on biblical events. Ponder how some of these works can give you new eyes for understanding that text.

3. Explore one or more of the novels, plays, or musical compositions discussed above. Reflect on how it adds emotional impact to your experience of the stories from the Bible.

4. Create your own short story, song, poem, drawing, or painting about a favorite Bible story.

CHAPTER SIX

The Best Kind of Heartbreak:

Helping Us Deal with Our Emotions

WHEN I WAS GROWING UP it wasn't uncommon on the weekends for my family to load into our cherry red station wagon and head up into the foothills, where my grandparents lived near the crest of a mountain in a rather ragged house warmed by an ever-present fire from a wood-burning stove. I can still remember the smell of that blaze and the warmth it sent out into the room. I can also recall the smell of Grandma's home cooking, prepared on the stove with a cast iron skillet; an aroma of biscuits and gravy and fried chicken and green beans. Grandma was a master chef of comfort food. My grandfather worked as a mechanic in a sawmill and consequently my grandparents never had a lot of money, though you'd never know it from the way they celebrated life.

One of the ways they celebrated was through country music. My grandfather had an old, well-loved violin, though he referred to it as a fiddle. He would often play for the family and occasionally even attend local old-time fiddler events where other fiddlers gathered to swap songs and jam. As a child, I can't say that I loved the music. My feelings were kin to those of their pocket-sized dog, Dino, who would howl as though in pain every time Grandpa rosined up the bow and began to draw it across the strings.

One of the Saturday night traditions in my grandparents' home was to tune in the *Grand Ole Opry*. Since we were often there on Saturday evenings, we couldn't avoid hearing Roy Acuff, Porter Waggoner, Dolly Parton, or the other stars of the Nashville-based program. Frankly, I hated the music of the Opry when I was a kid. I'd often retreat to another part of the house when the TV program started, or when my grandma would put a country album on the turntable and sing along to its words. This wasn't music I could identify with. I was a city kid who liked rock and roll. This was, I thought, music for hicks and hillbillies.

Flash forward to the present. I still like rock music, but my tastes in music have expanded to where I can enjoy just about every genre from classical to jazz to blues . . . and yes, even country. Over the years, my appreciation for country music has grown to the point where I have as much of it on my iPod as I do rock and roll. And I identify with country music, especially in its old-style form, in a way I never would have imagined possible when I was younger. I wonder if the reason for the transformation in taste is a change in me. Country is so often about pain and struggle and loss and loneliness, and as I have grown older, I have experienced my share of all those feelings. The classics of country music, like "He Stopped Loving Her Today" (recorded by George Jones) or "Sunday Morning Comin' Down" (written by Kris Kristofferson and made famous by Johnny Cash) or "The Coat of Many Colors" (by Dolly Parton), are all songs that could only have been written and performed by someone who had experienced a heaping helping of life's pain.

The genius of country music is that it gives such authentic voice to the hardships and difficulties of life. And now, several decades in, I'm more able to identify with some of that struggle. There is an ache in the twang and a sob in the pedal steel that speaks truth to me about what life is often really like. The stories of pain in country music carry an authenticity that resonates at a deep emotional level for me. Often the songs have the power to nudge me to the edge of tears.

Country music is not, of course, the only kind of music that evokes an emotional response. Rock and jazz and pop music are also filled not only with heartbreak, but also with anger and defiance and a cry for freedom or justice. Classical music has that same ability, and often does not need any words to rouse an emotional response from the listener, who can be roused by the soaring sounds of the string section or a weeping piano solo. And then there is opera, a musical form that is really all about the emotions evoked through passionate singing. Often the melodramatic story that a given opera is telling is hardly worthy of attention. The beauty is found in the stirringly passionate sounds escaping from the lips of the singers. The paper-thin narratives are often just an excuse for the singers to emote. And emote they do, gloriously and ardently, and sometimes unforgettably.

As the playwright William Congreve mused: "Music has charms to soothe the savage breast. To soften rocks, or bend a knotted oak."[1] Indeed, music can charm us or disarm us, make us weak or make us weep, stir our hearts or change our mind. Music is not alone in having this kind of power. Indeed, every work of art, whether music or film or literature or visual art, has a primary goal of moving us toward some sort of emotional response.

The arts, in all their forms, reach beyond a purely rational response and seek to move us emotionally. And we love to be moved. Why do we enjoy watching a tear-jerking movie or listening to a sad song? Because we want to be stirred out of our doldrums. We want to feel. We long to have our emotions moved and tears sprout in the corner of our eye.

> The arts, in all their forms, reach beyond a purely rational response and seek to move us emotionally.

Whenever the Christmas season rolls around again, I have several friends who camp out in front of the television for their nightly dose of holiday movies on the Hallmark Channel. These movies are not high art, as my friends will be quick to admit. But that doesn't lessen their enjoyment of the latest "feel good by first feeling bad" films. The stories are usually predictable, but that predictability is precisely what their devoted viewers are looking for. They want to see a simple story that will move them, that will evoke tears and smiles, and then pay-off with a happy ending that the attentive viewer can see coming from a mile away. People watch these kinds of movies because they want to have their emotions roused and then be assured that life is actually okay. They may be sentimental, but they do the job.

Sometimes Christians have been wary of the emotional power of the arts, seeing it as a path that can lead to selfish excess or open us up to various kinds of temptation. Over the years I have sat through more than a few sermons about the dangers posed by our emotions, and to a certain degree these exhortations make sense. When emotions are out of control, they can have frightening consequences for us and for everybody in our general vicinity. It isn't without reason, for example, that James 1:19–20 warns us about what happens when our anger gets out of control. Some will argue that our emotions are not trustworthy, that they really don't tell us anything helpful about the way things actually are. That emotions are just our response to the stimuli, and hence tend to be shallow, unreliable, and unstable. If you remember being thirteen years old, you can probably see the force in such an argument! We can, indeed, get carried away by our emotions and sometimes can make very poor choices on the basis of how we might feel at one particular moment.

Emotions are tricky. They might cause us to feel an elevated rapture in the face of something that is actually quite unremark-able and unoriginal. They might be mostly a response of our hormones and cause us to not see another as an actual person, but

> **While letting our emotions entirely rule us can be a dangerous thing, perhaps it is as equally dangerous to ignore them.**

as an unattainable object of desire or the cause of all our grievances. Emotion can turn a crowd of people into a mob when they get swept up by a moment of shared experience or cause us to react with melo-drama rather than a measured response.

But the problem isn't emotions per se. It is the immature handling of our emotions. While letting our emotions entirely rule us can be a dangerous thing, perhaps it is as equally dangerous to ignore them, to not work at developing more mature emotional responses to what happens in our life. Maturity does not come from suppressing emo-tions or denying them a place in our lives, but from learning to let them take their proper place and letting them enrich our experiences.

This is where the arts can come in. They give us an opportunity to exercise our emotions or acquaint ourselves with our own some-times unexpected emotional responses, but they do it in a safe envi-ronment, one where there is little danger of them harming others or ourselves. The arts present us with various situations and scenarios in a virtual form, and then offer us options for how we will respond to them. Through that we can learn something about ourselves and what makes us tick. They give us the opportunity to ask ourselves, "Why am I responding this way?"

A modern cultural touchpoint on how we deal with our emotions might be found in the *Star Trek* franchise of TV programs and movies. In the original *Star Trek*, one of the three main characters is Spock, the first officer of the starship U.S.S. Enterprise. He is a member of the Vulcan race, who have weaned themselves away from any emotional responses and rely solely on logic and rational thinking. His famous response, when others show emotion, is to intone in a disapproving manner, "Illogical." Spock became arguably the most popular character on the show due to his reliance on thinking over feeling, although there are a few episodes where his half-human heritage bleeds through, revealing that there is actually a simmering caldron of passion existing just below the surface of his placidity. For the most part, though, Spock seems to get by just fine without any dependence upon emotion, which he sees as a way that intellectual activity is subverted.

The follow-up series, *Star Trek: The Next Generation*, offers a more complex meditation on what our emotions might tell us about our humanity. Here the character lacking in an emotional response is Lt. Commander Data, who is not a Vulcan but an android—a creation of scientific genius. Data can compute problems with computer-like efficiency and grasp the logical solution to vexing problems without any interference from emotions. And yet, Data, who has a surprisingly strong self-understanding, sees that the gulf that separates him from the humans on the ship is his lack of feeling and emotion. It is precisely this missing element in his programming that he desires and for which he works, without any final success, to achieve. He is after all, just a sentient machine.

The episodes where he deals with his own longing to be more human are some of the best and certainly most touching of the series. *Star Trek: The Next Generation* offers a much more complex view of emotions that the earlier series, and suggests that, in their place, emotions are one of the primary things that make us human. Emotion is a necessary component in making the correct human decisions.

Sometimes I struggle with my emotions, not really understanding where they come from. Why do I wake up sometimes feeling like my life is empty and fighting against a wave of despair that threatens to engulf me? Why does a little thing, like someone cutting me off when I'm driving, suddenly fill me with a rage that frightens me, an anger all out of proportion to the event that gave rise to it? Or how can I sometimes feel an immediate uprising of love and care for someone I have just met, or do something sacrificial on behalf of someone who might never even know that I was the source of the kindness?

My emotions regularly surprise me, inspire me, frighten me, or give me great hope. Sometimes they spur me to good deeds and positive responses. At other times they lead me down the wrong path. Where they come from and how they operate is surely one of the great mysteries of life.

Learning to deal appropriately with our emotions is not a new problem. Aristotle wrote that "Anyone can become angry—that is easy. But to be angry with the right person, to the right degree, at the right time, for the right purpose, and in the right way—that is not easy."[2] His concern was not with emotions, per se, but with how we deployed them in our lives. Whether wisely and in moderation, or in such a way as to damage our own happiness and that of others. In his book, *Emotional*

Intelligence, Daniel Goleman aptly summarizes Aristotle's goal:

> What is wanted is *appropriate* emotion, feeling
> proportionate to circumstance. When emotions are
> too muted they create dullness and distance; when out
> of control, too extreme and persistent, they become
> pathological, as in immobilizing depression, overwhelming
> anxiety, raging anger, manic agitation.[3]

Learning to manage our emotions, and the moods that they give rise to, can sometimes seem like a full-time job. Many of the choices we make about how we are going to spend our time are intimately related to our desire to "feel better." Triggers for all our various emotional states are before us constantly, so learning how to deal with these triggers—the things that set off negative emotions—is something we all need to make a priority. When the negative emotions begin to take control, they can send out ripples of unhappiness that

Sunset On the River by George Inness, Crystal Bridges Museum, Bentonville

affect our own state of mind as well as that of those who are around.

Which is why the Apostle Paul called on the Philippians to engage with the emotion of rejoicing (Phil. 4:4). He puts it forward more as a command than a suggestion. He is indicating that we are not just at the whims of our emotions, but that we can, in fact, control them. Similarly, the psalmist "speaks" to his soul about the proper response to what is happening in his life, and even when it isn't going well, he calls on his soul to "bless the Lord" (Ps. 103:1 ESV).

We dare not limit ourselves to what our emotions are telling us about reality. Often they are construing it from a limited perspective. Our response is often immediately related to how we are seeing a situation. The early disciples, for example, were beaten and persecuted, and yet they went their way rejoicing (Acts 5:41). Certainly, such a response was not because the persecution really wasn't that painful, but because they had a bigger picture, a larger context in which to frame their experience.

Sometimes we must act "as if." When we act in conformity to an emotion, it further encourages that emotion. When we act counter to an emotion, it sometimes can help us reorient our feelings. As William James has written:

> Every one knows how panic is increased by flight, and how the giving way to the symptoms of grief or anger increases those passions themselves. . . . In rage, it is notorious how we "work ourselves up" to a climax by repeated outbreaks of expression. . . . Whistling to keep up courage is no mere figure of speech. On the other hand, sit all day in a moping posture, sigh, and reply to everything with a dismal voice, and your melancholy lingers.[4]

The growing understanding of the importance of our emotions for living a happy and balanced life has even led to the creation of the EQ test, the emotional quotient. While the IQ is a test of our intellectual capabilities, the EQ is a test for our emotional intelligence, the ability to use our emotions wisely and well. To find real happiness in life means discovering the proper balance between the head and the heart, letting each instruct and influence the other.

When, for example, a coworker takes credit for a project that I have poured my energy into, I have a few split seconds to determine how I am going to deal with the situation. If my emotions simply override my intelligence, I am likely to strike out with aggressive or self-defensive words and accusations. I might even find myself wanting to do violence to the one who is stealing my thunder. But if I allow myself to consider the possible repercussions of such an outburst, I am more likely to find a way to subtly redirect the credit in my direction or realize that it doesn't really matter who gets the glory after all, as long as the project can move forward. That crucial pause can make all the difference between actions I might later regret and a positive outcome. Or when, in a group setting, I have an idea that I think will provide the looked-for solution, sometimes my emotional side will help me to read the mood of the present moment and lead me to wait for a better time to jump into the discussion.

All day, every day, these two kinds of responses need to be allowed to speak into everything we experience. Life offers us a lot of perplexing questions: Should I marry this person? What would really make me most happy? Is there a loving God, or even a God at all? It would be poor advice to simply jump to your first emotional response, as those who have done so can testify. But it is also ineffective and unfulfilling to treat such questions as math problems that can be solved by a logical formula.[5] We need to listen to our heart *and* our brain. To harmonize them is to learn to think with emotional intelligence.

The arts are all about the emotions. Art isn't just primarily about delivering some sort of message or experience, but of casting it in terms of an emotional experience. In doing so, the arts can become a school for the emotions. Daniel Goleman offers a helpful insight here:

> Some of us are naturally more attuned to the emotional mind's special symbolic modes: metaphor and simile, along with poetry, song, and fable, are all cast in the language of the heart. So too are dreams and myths, in which loose associations determine the flow of narrative, abiding by the logic of the emotional mind. Those who have a natural attunement to their own heart's voice— the language of emotion—are sure to be more adept at articulating its messages, whether as a novelist, songwriter, or psychotherapist.[6]

It is possible for the viewer to have an emotional response to almost any kind of art—even art of questionable quality. Probably most of us have experienced sadness or warm feelings at a "by-the-numbers" or "cookie cutter" movie or song. It may be trite and clichéd, but somehow it still manages to burrow its way into our emotions. And we may find ourselves wiping away tears that frankly embarrass us just a little. Such tears can sometimes be a great source of release to us, and they remind us that we are alive and aware and can be moved. Such art can create a moment of catharsis, but it rarely leaves much real change in its wake. But there is art of a different sort, which evokes more complex emotions—that speaks to a place within us where our emotions and our intellect combine or collide or complement each other for a transformative impact—art that is about more than a momentary gush of the expected feeling. The emotions evoked by more challenging forms of art have the tendency to stay with us, to leave a residue of feeling long after the initial emotions of response have faded.

The video artist Bill Viola was visiting a museum when he came across an older painting of the Madonna with a tear trickling down her face. He was so moved by the image that tears sprang to his eyes. He credits it as the experience that helped make him more fully aware of the emotional power of art.[7] Since then, his own work has focused on creating an emotional experience for the viewer. His video installations, normally of people shot on camera at an extremely low rate of speed, are mysterious and very hard to describe, but if a viewer takes the time to sit with them for a few minutes, they will find themselves moved in a way that goes beyond description. Not long ago, at the Denver Art Museum, I stopped momentarily to view one of his slow-motion videos of a man diving into a body of water. At first, I was impatient with the painfully slow progress toward the water, then I became fascinated, and by the time the video was over I had an unexpected and inexplicable lump in my throat.

This emotional response can happen in a few different ways:

1. ***The arts provide an opportunity for us to exercise our positive emotions.*** To feel real tenderness, to experience a wave of compassion course through our hearts, to be exalted and lifted out of the commonplace, to see God through another set of eyes, and to sense God's love. Our lives can sometimes feel so boring, commonplace,

and humdrum, but through art we can have experiences that are new, inspiring, and transformative. If we start to feel dead inside, the arts can evoke our emotions, bring them to the surface, and awaken us to living more fully. Our hearts can be stretched and expanded.

2. *The arts can also give us a cathartic outlet for our negative emotions.* They provide a safe place to experience anger or fear or jealousy and let us work through how we should respond. Reading *Les Misérables*, for example, will give us a full emotional workout. Anger, bitterness, sadness, terror, and desire for revenge are all among those that emerge as we work through its pages. Sometimes a work of art like that provides a teachable moment about the consequences of such moments. At other times, it just brings such feelings out in the open so we can begin to understand and deal with them. They rise to the surface of our usually placid lives and howl for attention like a neglected child. Aristotle famously suggested that by working through these negative emotions in the presence of the art that evokes them, we can lessen their power to negatively affect our day-to-day lives. I must admit that I am not a particular fan of horror movies, but I have several friends who enjoy them immensely. They tell me they like being scared, as it makes them somehow feel more alive and awake. They are shocked into recognizing, among other things, their own mortality. And that is always something we probably should keep in mind.

3. *The arts can also help us learn to differentiate between false or stock responses to life, and those that are rich and true.* Here, the quality of the art definitely comes into play. It is easy for a skillful artist or filmmaker or novelist to make you feel exactly what they want you to feel. But such manipulated feelings never seem to last very long or have much impact. The more complex

artistry will tend to produce more complex, and ultimately more meaningful, feelings. They will be of much greater value in growing in emotional intelligence. So, make sure that your diet of the arts includes not only entertainment, but challenging and thought-provoking and even puzzling works. They will give rise to more emotional nuance in your response and teach you how to be a more complicated person—in the best sense of that word.

It's easy to live on a pretty shallow level and never really get in touch with our emotions.

When I was in junior high, the English department held a poetry contest. I decided I would enter and sat down to pen two poems. One was about a tree that stood sturdy while seasons and people came and went, and the other involved something that now eludes me. Anyway, when the results of the contest were announced, my poem about a tree had placed second and my other poem received an honorable mention. Both were published in a special edition of the school paper.

I felt quite a bit of pride about my work until I arrived at the drawing class I was taking that term. Our art teacher had been instructing us about how we could use our emotions in our drawings, trying to move us away from our semi-photographic approaches toward more originality and honesty in our perception and approach. We shouldn't simply judge our own work by how closely it resembled the "real thing," but find a way to put something of ourselves into it. The afternoon following the publication of our poems, my teacher decided to use them as an example of what he had been trying to teach us.

He held the school paper aloft, and then dropped it to his desk with a thud that resonated throughout the room. He shook his head and said something like, "These poems are dead. And when I read them, I worry that my students are dead too." Well, that woke us up. He read a few of them aloud, and, mercifully, mine was not among them. "These poems are mostly about clichés. Clichéd ideas, clichéd subjects, and clichéd feelings. They don't tell me anything about the person who wrote them." He muttered something about his disappointment at what we'd been learning in our English courses, and after a short diatribe challenged us that we could do better. "I want you to write about an experience that made you feel something deeply inside. I'm not looking for pretty poems or nice rhymes. I want you to write from your gut."

We took out our notebooks and started to work. Frankly, it wasn't easy to pull something out of myself that I really cared about. The raw vulnerability felt risky. Dangerous. The first thing that came to me was the recent loss of a beloved pet. To be honest, it might not have been of much better technical quality than my little ditty about the tree, but it was a believable howl of pain and emotional turmoil. You couldn't read it without sensing something raw and real; without understand how much hurt I was still feeling.

The art teacher gathered our poems, and those of his other classes, and eventually published an alternative collection of poems. Its pages were filled with real emotion. One person wrote about the high-volume arguments her parents would have every evening while she huddled in her bedroom and tried to study. Another gave pretty clear hints of being on the receiving end of abuse, one was about struggling with self-image, and another about suicidal thoughts. Some were about positive experiences, but they too felt honest and authentic. When I read the poems, I had to admit that he was right. Sure, there was a little excessive teenage angst on display, but these poems were alive,

Self-awareness, being cognizant of your emotional life, is one of the most crucial steps on the path to spiritual growth.

and they were a window into real feelings.

What I learned from that art teacher is that the arts can help us discover a deeper set of feelings within us. They can force us to come face-to-face with feelings we'd rather ignore or suppress. They can help awaken real feelings to replace the kind of stock emotions that are the stock in trade of so much popular art, especially popular movies and popular music. We can dance on the surface of real emotion and settle for clichéd responses, or we can find our deeper emotions through plunging deep into better art. Whether you are a creator of art or a consumer of art, real emotion puts you in touch with the deepest things in your soul. Some of them may not be pretty, but being aware of them is the first step in the journey to cleanse your soul of their negative impact. Self-awareness, being cognizant of your emotional life, is one of the most crucial steps on the path to spiritual growth.

Sometimes our lives can feel like a circus. It's a pretty apt metaphor for what it feels like to navigate our daily lives and all the emotions that come to the surface. *Le Cheval de Cirque* is a painting by Marc Chagall, one of the great artists of the twentieth century, and one of my personal favorite painters. This painting, part of a series he created on the theme of the circus, is one of my favorites. It is typical of his colorful, joyous, and playful images, which celebrate life with a sense of childlike wonder. And it causes me to think about the challenges of living a happy, healthy life.

Like the circus, our lives are busy, bustling, and more than a little chaotic at times. Every day it seems like there is so much happening that it's hard to take it all in, along with a good dose of craziness, and all the constant challenges laying claim to our attention.

We are the high-wire artist, desperately trying to maintain our precarious balance.

© 2020 Artists Rights Society (ARS), New York / ADAGP, Paris

Le Cheval de Cirque by Marc Chagall, Private Collection

We are the juggler, struggling to keep all the balls in the air.

We are the acrobat, constantly stretching ourselves beyond our comfort zones.

We are also the clown, covering our difficulties with a greasepaint smile and laughing our way through our stumbles.

It can sometimes feel like we are always putting on a performance. Always aware that others are watching . . . and perhaps judging. We are always "on."

The paradox is that life is—just like the circus—full of joy and play and adventure . . . and at the same time full of risk and danger. And sometimes the elaborate costumes and makeup we don are hiding a lot of pain.

Life is a circus. But if we can lay aside our mask and put away our need to always be performing for others, there is peace that can be found in the middle of all the hubbub. Maybe if we take the time to quiet our inner circus enough to pay attention to the Divine Ringleader, we can find the confidence we need to exercise the role He has assigned to us. Maybe then we can leap and laugh, ride bareback, and not be afraid to take a few risks. Maybe then we can find our place of peace under God's big top.

The arts can be a valuable companion for learning to deal appropriately with our emotions, as they provide several paths for understanding them. For to awaken our emotions is the first step in learning how to deal with them. This is the vicarious power of art. We read a novel or see a film or listen to a song and we find ourselves immersed in another person's life and way of thinking. Through them we have experiences we might never have had ourselves. We come to face things that we might never have faced on our own. We are challenged with temptations we've never known, feel a depth of grief that we might not have previously experienced, or feel our heart race with a fear our normal lives would never present to us. And we must engage with all the accompanying emotions. Sometimes art can teach us how.

In her fascinating book *When Books Went to War*, Molly Guptill Manning reports on how providing books to American soldiers during

World War II was a powerful tool for building morale and helping them understand the cultural values that we were fighting for in the conflict with the powers of the Axis. Early in its pages, she tells the story of a young Marine who had gone through some of the worst fighting in the war and had seen so much death and horror that he had become desensitized to it, which made him feel like he had a "dead heart." He had "gone through hell," and was worried that he had become so numb from his experiences that he would never again be able to feel things as deeply as he had done before. But, while recovering from his wounds in an Army hospital, this young Marine was given a copy of Betty Smith's novel, *A Tree Grows in Brooklyn*. He credits the book with saving him. In a letter to the author he wrote:

> I have read it twice and am halfway through it again . . .
> every time I read it, I feel more deeply than I did before .
> . . I can't explain the emotional reaction that took place,
> I only know that it happened and that this heart of mine
> turned over and became alive again. A surge of confidence
> has swept through me and I feel that maybe a fellow has a
> fighting chance in this world after all.

The novel made the tough young Marine weep, and of that he said, "I'm not ashamed."[8] Nor need he have been.

QUESTIONS AND SPIRITUAL EXERCISES

1. Write a poem or short story about an event in your life that moved you to some sort of powerful emotional response. What does the way you told the story tell you about how much you are in touch with your own emotions?

2. Think about an unhealthy emotion you struggle with. Now, get a Bible concordance and look up the passages that talk about that emotion. What do you learn?

3. Try creating a picture or a piece of music or a poem about a particular mood or emotion. See if you can evoke that same emotion from others when they see or hear what you have done.

4. Consider the classic *Star Trek* television show. Which character best exemplifies your own approach to life? Why?

5. Meditate on the circus painting by Chagall. What elements in the painting reflect truths about your emotional experiences?

CHAPTER SEVEN

We Are Not Alone:

Finding Comfort and Discovering Courage

IN LATE FEBRUARY OF 2020 the first signs of a worldwide pandemic began to make themselves felt in the United States. At first, many people were skeptical, or just thought that "It'll never happen here." Soon, though, the life-changing realities of its effects began to come into focus. Every day the numbers of cases and the number of dead rose in an exponential fashion. Our best scientists scrambled to figure out how to respond to the coronavirus. Before long, people were "sheltering in place" or in some sort of lockdown. Millions lost their jobs as many service industry businesses, among others, were shuttered. Churches ceased to have their normal worship services, and gatherings of any size were forbidden.

In the face of all this, people felt a great deal of fear and uncertainty. The messages from even the most optimistic generally rang false. People worried about their future and struggled with the uncertainty of what might be just around the corner. They found themselves fighting a deadly enemy that was invisible to the naked eye.

So, what did people do in response to this unprecedented event? Some hoarded toilet paper, canned food, and ramen noodles. Others invented bizarre conspiracy theories to explain what had happened. Some hunkered down in their homes feeling a level of fear that they had never known before. But the crisis also brought out the best in many people, who sewed much-needed protective masks for hospital workers, bought groceries for the housebound elderly, and tried to be present (virtually) for those who were lonely and afraid.

And amid all the worry and fear, many people were reminded of the power of the arts to make a difference in our lives. Sure, plenty of folks just used television and movies and music to help distract them from what was going on. But many found that art provided a very real source of comfort during a scary time, and that it served both as a reminder of what is really important and of what it means to be human. The Metropolitan Opera offered free showings of classic opera. Musicians held "live from my living room shows" to boost people's spirits. Museums offered virtual online tours. Libraries made ebooks more easily available. One friend filmed himself giving a Shakespearian recitation about finding courage from *Henry V*. I posted a blog series of meditations based on great works of art. For a lot of us, the connections we made with the arts were among the most significant things for helping get us through this uncertain time. The arts reminded us that we were all in this together, and that the most esssential things in life would continue.

It needn't take a major worldwide crisis, though, for art to touch our hearts and remind us that we are not alone, that there are others going through similar pain and finding a path forward. The arts can give us the comfort we need and the courage we seek for even the smaller and more personal crises in our lives.

If some of the earlier chapters, extolling the wonders and beauty of life, left you thinking—well, yeah, but what about all the pain and suffering and struggle and horror in the world?—then you are right to wave the red flag and ask some questions about the darker side of human existence. This is something great artists haven't been afraid to do.

Life is a messy proposition. It isn't all about ecstatic moments, experiences of beauty and wonder, and the power of love. We also undergo disappointments and betrayals, witness the suffering and death of those we love, experience the immensity of anger and confusion all around us, fall victim to our own psychological failures and those of others, watch cherished relationships crumble, struggle with doubt, hear of evil formed against the innocent and helpless, see dreams crushed, and feel awkward and ignored. The list could go on.

Oscar Wilde once said that "life breaks everybody."[1] Eventually we all come face-to-face with realities that make us sad or fearful or create a desire to withdraw. Some of the great spiritual writers have reminded us that even in the darkest times we can learn and grow. This less appealing path to spiritual maturity is sometimes referred to as the "via negativa." Mechtild of Magdeburg taught that "we are given two wines to drink in this life: the white wine of joy and the red wine of suffering. 'Until we have drunk deeply of both, we have not lived fully.'"[2]

The Bible confirms this truth. It is not just a collection of inspirational and aspirational memes, but a record of the real lives of people whose journey through life was not easy. The men and women whose lives are recorded in the Scriptures dealt with every negative emotion and experience you can imagine. They suffered pain and were wracked with doubt; they were betrayed and disappointed; they were the victims of injustice and sometimes the guilty purveyors of the same. The

Bible isn't interested in painting a rosy picture of human existence. And the life of faith is not a matter of finding out-of-context "promises" of happiness and prosperity. Such passages of inspiring victory are balanced by passages of defeat and lament.

Throughout the Psalms, for example, we read passages that glorify God as the trustworthy One, as well as passages that lament the hurt, heartbreak, and brokenness of life, and those calling out its unfairness. One whole book of the Bible, Lamentations is an extended inquiry into why things have gone so wrong. Like the Bible, the arts can offer an affirmation of what is good in life, but they can also be a mirror of suffering and struggle. We tend to want to spend our time with art that affirms us, but we would do well to acquaint ourselves with some of the art of struggle. To tell the truth fully is to speak of both affirmation and struggle.

To really make a lasting difference in our lives, art needs to be honest about what life is really like. Too much of our "fast food" Christian art, music, and literature suffers from excessive and false cheeriness or from taking a position of triumphalism. In the attempt to be positive and inspiring, it can seem to imply that having faith makes life easier and guarantees more happiness and success. Or that there is a simple solution to all our problems: Just trust Jesus. Find a promise in God's Word. Stand up against the devil. Speak positively. And though there may be some help to be found in all these, when you are in pain it can feel as though these are all one great big scheme to avoid the pain of real life. Honestly, hearing these concepts tossed out as the simple answer to one's suffering often just makes the suffering that much worse.

We are going to experience a lot of pain here on earth before the curtain comes down on our lives. We are going to lose loved ones, be at odds with people we care about, be rejected or belittled. We are going to experience sickness and the pains of growing old. We are going to have moments when our faith doesn't seem to be helping and we are left feeling confused or with doubts niggling at the back of our mind.

We have a great hope, but it is rooted in the reality that we are fallen people living in a fallen world. At times we are victims of unkindness or injustice or malice, and at other times we are the perpetrators of the same. Our hope comes not because we can avoid struggling with any of these things, but because hope can be found amid all our pain and hurt and failures and doubts.

One of the things that makes art such an indispensable companion on our journey of life is that artists have recorded their own struggles with these things through their works of art. They tell us their own stories and the stories of others. They reflect on their own pain and alienation and questioning. They make us privy to their own emotional responses. And in the process, we are reminded that we are not alone with ours.

The Great Wave Off Kanagawa by Katushika Hokusai, Metropolitan Museum of Art, New York

When an artist awakens himself, he can wake others. When an artist looks inside herself, she can help others understand themselves a little bit better.

When my father died, I needed someone to talk to. I found that many people were quick to offer well-meaning sympathy. A couple wanted to offer some sort of theological insight, along the lines of the not-very-helpful "well, everything happens for a reason." But there was one category of people whom I found it very helpful to talk with— those who had recently suffered a similar loss in their lives. They didn't have a bunch of pre-packaged answers for me. In fact, they mostly just listened, then shared about their own feelings and what they had struggled with after losing someone who was important to them. Along with that select group of listeners, the other important thing that came alongside me was the arts—songs, poems, stories, and pictures in which I could identify a fellow struggler; someone who truly understood.

When we are hurting or confused or discouraged or filled with doubts, sometimes the most helpful thing is to realize that we are not alone in our suffering—that others have walked the road before us . . . and that they have come through, even if just a little the worse for wear. The creative person can use their own pain and struggles and doubts in a redemptive manner, using these to bring understanding and hope and healing to others.

So much of popular music is about our experiences of loss and lone- liness, and the songs chronicle the death of a beloved parent or lover, of finding yourself alone at the bar or standing in the rain, of missing a train or losing a job, or struggling against harsh economic realities. And these realities are made even more real because they are usually unfolded in the context of a story. Country music especially excels at storytelling, and it doesn't shy away from some of the saddest stories. It bravely faces up to the hurt and injustices of life, as well as the pain we bring upon ourselves by our foolish choices.

Many of the greatest country artists were born into grinding poverty. Loretta Lynn was the daughter of a coal miner, who worked hard to scrape together a subsistence living for his family, and Johnny Cash grew up picking cotton alongside the other members of his family. The music of these artists eventually became their ticket out of poverty. Some, like Hank Williams, struggled against alcoholism and substance abuse. He lost that battle all too young, but not before leaving behind some of the saddest and most moving songs ever written. His song "I'm So Lonesome I Could Cry" weds the weeping sound of a steel guitar with lyrics that express the idea that nature itself (the whippoorwill and the robin) join him in this hymn to loss and loneliness. There is a good reason why some have called him "the Hillbilly Shakespeare." Williams knew how to express the darkest of emotions with a halting voice of honesty and the gentlest touch of grace.

Much of country music reflects the twin poles of our existence: "Saturday night" (a life of sin and the despair and sadness it creates) and "Sunday morning" (the comfort and hope found in faith). It isn't an either/or for most country artists. Both experiences are very real to them. So, many of them sang two types of songs, both delivered with passion: regular country blues and gospel songs. Taken together they offer a message about the effects of living in a fallen world, and the hope that we might find even in the midst of it. The same Hank Williams, who could cause tears to sprout in the corners of your eye, could also write such hope-filled gospel songs as "I Saw the Light," which celebrates a deliverance from a life of sin. Williams was not alone in seeing both sides of reality. At its best, country music holds together a tension that we all know to be true—that we are broken people in a broken world, and that we might still find hope and meaning in the middle of it all. These are songs of redemption. If redemption is not found here, then in a world beyond, as in "I'll Fly

Away," and "In the Sweet By and By."

Johnny Cash perhaps illustrates this tension as well as any other country musician. He did battle with various addictions throughout his life, and he raised a middle finger at authority and hypocrisy. He also had a tenacious faith in God throughout his career, sometimes ebbing, sometimes coming to the fore, but always there. He could sing to prisoners who identified with the violence and darkness in his stories and songs, and he could belt out a gospel song with complete conviction at a Billy Graham crusade. There was no conflict in him. Just a reminder that we oftentimes will find ourselves in a pit of our own digging before we emerge to the light of God's grace.

The rock group U2 reveals this same kind of tension in their music, though for them faith and doubt often inhabit the very same song, as in the powerful, "I Still Haven't Found What I'm Looking For." This song is a reminder that though Jesus has "carried the cross of my shame," that doesn't mean that all our questions will be put to rest or our experiences will always be joyful. Life isn't simple, and faith doesn't end our struggles or provide an easy answer to every thorny question. In fact, in my own experience, faith actually makes life more challenging—though infinitely more satisfying.

> A living faith is a faith that is at war with the darkness we find within ourselves.

The members of U2 have been outspoken about their faith, and they commonly use biblical tropes and references in their songs. The better you know the Bible, the more of it you'll find in their music. But they are also very open about their failings and the temptations of being rock stars. Their lead singer, Bono, admits to not being a very good advertisement for God. He has a particular love for the book of Psalms because it gives voice to praise for God and is honest about the struggles of living faith out in this world. As he once said in an interview: "I'm holding out for Grace. I'm holding out that Jesus took my sins onto the Cross."[3] A living faith, U2 reminds us, is a faith that is at war with the darkness we find within ourselves. Such a faith recognizes that there are not simple answers to many of the problems we face; that God doesn't usually step in and magically make everything comfortable. This is the theme of their popular song, "I Still Haven't Found What I'm Looking For."

C. S. Lewis had a similarly realistic perspective about life:

> If you think of this world as a place intended simply for our happiness, you find it quite intolerable: think of it as a place of training and correction and it's not so bad.
>
> Imagine a set of people all living in the same building. Half of them think it is a hotel, the other half think it is a prison... The people who try to hold an optimistic view of this world would become pessimists; the people who hold a pretty stern view of it become optimistic.[4]

Our hope is not based upon wishful thinking or "group-think" or some method of positive thinking. Our hope is based upon the fact that God has a bigger agenda for our lives than merely our present happiness. He walks with us through a broken world, calls us to be agents of change within it, and offers to transform us through all the challenges we face. We can learn a lot from the pain we experience. Perhaps the hope that arises from struggle is the greatest form of hope. As Wendell Berry expresses so beautifully, writing about the sound of water as it trips along over the rocks in a riverbed, "The impeded stream is the one that sings."[5]

Even when we are realistic with ourselves about our expectations for what life will be like, we still may need a reminder that we don't walk through our lives alone: that God is with us during our darkest hours.

We all need comfort from time to time, and the arts can be very helpful for finding it. Art can move us from comfort to courage, and from courage to hope.

Recently I awoke with a start from a nightmare. Shuddering, I glanced at the clock, trying to get my mind off the horrors that had just paraded across the interior screen of my mind. As is often the case with such nocturnal experiences, I didn't even remember the details of the bad dream, but it had left a bit of fear in its wake. So, to shake off its influence, I eased myself out of bed, used the bathroom, and had a drink of cold water, hoping that these activities would dispel the bad taste left by the dream. My plan kind of worked. I stopped replaying the scenes from the nightmare and shook off the emotional aftereffect. But then I found myself awake enough that I began to replay some of the stresses of the previous day and worry about the responsibilities of the next one.

> **Art can move us from comfort to courage, and from courage to hope.**

Tossing and turning for a bit, I knew I needed something to settle me, so I asked my bedside smart device to play an album that has never ceased to make me feel a little more peaceful: John Michael Talbot's *Come to the Quiet*, a gentle acoustic performance of several Psalms and other passages of Scripture. As I lay there in the dark and let these familiar healing words of the Bible wash over my soul, I was able to settle into a peace-inducing trust that God was present in my struggles and would help me through them. A couple of songs in, I drifted off into a peaceful slumber.

This and other albums by Talbot contain settings of various

Scriptural texts that helped lodge them deeply in my memory. When I need them, I can recall these passages of the Bible with greater ease because the musical accompaniment aids in learning them by heart. To have the insights of Scripture readily at hand in our mind is a great help for facing whatever life might throw at us. And it is music, better than any other art form, that cements the words into our brain, and brings us the comfort we need through the way it moves our heart.

This is certainly one of the reasons that music is an important part of a worship service. The music not only engages our emotions, but by speaking the words aloud they seem to become more real to us—a form of confession. As we sing the great hymns of the faith or modern worship songs, they become part of our inner life, truths made more real to us as we express them aloud. They become truths we can stand upon. Comfort we can receive. Hope we can hold onto.

The English Puritans generally focused solely on metrical versions of the Psalms. Their tunes tended to be a bit stiff, and their approach to the lyrics was more cerebral and doctrinal. For them, music was not meant to arouse emotions, and if it did, they frankly didn't approve. But a group of eighteenth-century hymn writers changed all that. They sought to make the music of the church more enjoyable, relatable, and artistically satisfying through the original hymns they penned. They were part of a movement to make the faith more emotionally satisfying and relevant for everyday life.

The young Isaac Watts was dissatisfied with the music he heard in church, and he wanted to improve the quality of congregational singing, so he took on the challenge of creating his own hymns. Over seven hundred in number, they included such classics as "When I Survey the Wondrous Cross," "Jesus Shall Reign," "O God Our Help in Ages Past," and "Joy to the World."

John and Charles Wesley each had intensely powerful experiences of God moving on their hearts that changed the way they understood their relationship with God, and so they focused their teaching and their hymnody on a religion of the heart, encouraging hearty, passionate singing. Their hymns included "O for a Thousand Tongues to Sing," "Come Thou Long Expected Jesus," "Hark the Herald Angels Sing," "Christ the Lord Is Risen Today," and "Love Divine, All Loves Excelling."

One of the greatest hymn writers was certainly the most unlikely. John Newton had been a slave trader and a self-confessed moral degenerate before he experienced a powerful conversion to Christ. Because he wanted to share the joy he had found in his faith, he partnered with the poet William Cowper to create a collection of hymns especially for his congregation, but they were so appealing that they soon spread far and wide. One of them, "Amazing Grace" is probably the most oft-sung hymn all around the world. It is a hymn of personal testimony, an expression of how grace transformed the life of one very lost soul, and how it still has the power to do that today.

The singing of hymns allows people to express their faith with a robust sound that reflects the hope to be found in the truth of the Gospel. The best of the hymns crystallize the great truths of the faith and demonstrate how those truths can impact our lives in the midst of our struggles. Many of the most popular hymns are about finding a deep trust in God even in the middle of the storms of life. "It Is Well with My Soul," for example, was written by Horatio Spafford following the drowning of his four daughters in a shipwreck. It is a somber song but builds to a swelling confession of confidence; an inspiring affirmation of naked trust in the face of tragedy. Or one might think of the popular "Rock of Ages," which clings to the promise that God is a rock in whom we can "hide" when life threatens to overwhelm us.

There is something about lifting our voice in song or hearing a talented singer offer one of these great hymns of the faith that provides so much hope and comfort. At their best, many modern-day worship songs or contemporary Christian music songs are carrying on this tradition. They give us words we can use to affirm our confidence that we have a place of spiritual safety even in the worst of storms.

Sometimes our struggles are not merely about how we feel, but about what we can believe. We might, at times, find ourselves asking serious questions of our faith. Is it really true? Can I really believe in God and His love? In Emily Dickinson's poetry, her emotional and intellectual struggles became the primary theme for so many of her poems. She puzzled aloud over life's difficult questions and most perplexing mysteries. She distrusted the overly simplistic answers that seemed to satisfy many of her friends, and she set out to explore the most vexing responses she found within herself. It began, for Dickinson, with interrogating herself about her own motives.

Many of her best poems are the record of her wrestling with God. She had an ongoing lovers quarrel with her Maker about the things that perplexed her most. At times her poetry seems rooted in a firm conviction of faith, and at other times it is full of questions and doubts about the usual answers people were offering. She once wrote, "We both believe and disbelieve a hundred times an Hour, which keeps Believing nimble."[6] Her own nimble beliefs were as much about questions as answers. Dickinson was never very comfortable with organized religion, but she worshipped God in the beauty and wonder and awe she found in her own garden. In one poem she wrote of how her faith was inspired outside of the institutional church:

> Some keep the Sabbath going to Church—
> I keep it, staying at Home—
> With a Bobolink for a Chorister—
> And an Orchard, for a Dome—
>
> Some keep the Sabbath in Surplice—
> I just wear my Wings—
> And instead of tolling the Bell, for Church,
> Our little Sexton—sings.
>
> God preaches, a noted Clergyman—
> And the sermon is never long,
> So instead of getting to Heaven, at last—
> I'm going, all along.[7]

By the time she had written this poem, Dickinson had largely become a recluse, and rarely left the confines of her home. But she still found evidence of God in her back garden amid the singing of a winged choir of birds. She is, in a sense, the patron saint of questioners, and one who reminds me that I can find glimpses of the Divine outside of normal religious boundaries.

Graham Greene was one of the greatest 20th century novelists. His classic novels such as *The Power and the Glory*, *Brighton Rock*, *The Heart of the Matter*, *The End of the Affair*, and *Monsignor Quixote* all feature characters who are struggling between faith and doubt and determining the right course of action in the midst of very complex ethical situations. In Greene's novels, faith always has a cost to extract from those who cling to it, but there is also a moral heroism that undergirds the choices his characters make. In Greene's novels, God uses even the most imperfect people to accomplish His will.

Greene himself was an imperfect fellow, one who made a lot of poor choices in his life but still held onto faith, even if sometimes by only a thread. He doubted God, he doubted others, he doubted himself, and he even doubted his doubts. As he wrote, "I don't believe in my disbelief."[8]

He clung tenaciously to a faith of which he could never satisfactorily convince himself, just as so many of the flawed characters in his stories. Nevertheless, in these stories, God shows up again and again in unexpected and surprising ways, a reminder of the Scriptural statement: "My ways are not your ways" (Isa. 55:8).

Sometimes when I read Greene's work I can identify with the thoughts and feelings of his characters. I too am a doubter at times, but one who continues to grasp ahold of faith even when the questions seem overwhelming. And I am reminded that a world without God is much more unlikely than a world where God is present, but sometimes seems to be in hiding.

Artists earn a hearing by their honesty and their willingness to uncover even the uncomfortable truths about life and about themselves. They are at their best when they tell the truth. Yes, sometimes art is about affirming what we believe, but just as often it is about our struggles to keep believing. Faith is that sometimes it can be a struggle—with doubt, with our failures to overcome our besetting sins, with questions about our own worthiness, and with uncertainty about God's love for us. We all have moments of great confidence and we all have moments when everything is a question. By giving us insight into their own mysterious dance with doubt, and their own engagement with life's pain, the great artists remind us that we are not alone with our own struggles, questions, and pains. In this, they are valued fellow travelers on the road of life.

WikiCommons

The Raising of the Cross by Rembrandt, Alte Pinakothek, Munich

Sometimes the suffering we experience in our lives is a result of our own poor choices, but more often it is simply the result of being a fallen person living in a fallen world. Our sins, both personal and societal, conspire to make this a less-than-perfect world. We are all guilty, the apostle Paul reminds us (Rom. 3:23). The arts can serve as a mirror to help us see ourselves as we really are, as well as provoke a proper attitude of repentance for our complicity in the darkness around us and within us. They can provide the words and images we might need to bring us to a state of recognition of our fallenness and inspire a heartfelt humility toward God. Which is why Rembrandt painted himself into a scene where Christ is being hoisted up onto the cross. He recognized that, in a spiritual sense, he was among those who nailed Jesus to the cross. His sins were to blame. And so are yours and mine.

Sometimes art literally gives voice to a response of repentance. Alfred Schnittke was born in 1934 to German-Jewish parents living in the Soviet Union and made a name for himself with a thoroughly modern and rather dissonant style of composition. He converted to Catholicism in 1982, which marked a significant move toward a more traditional sound. Starting in 1985, he experienced a series of life-threatening strokes, which seemed to have the effect of making him consider more profoundly his own mortality.

The result was an immensely powerful work called *Psalms of Repentance*, a collection of twelve choral pieces that was given its premier about the time that Gorbachev's *Perestroika* program was opening the door for reconsideration of the place of religion in Russian culture. These chant-like pieces are musically spare, very intimate, and provide a window into Schnittke's own spiritual convictions. The tone throughout is funereal but strangely beautiful, making effective use of each of the divisions of his choir. The lyrics give voice to what it means to lose connection with God—the bitterness and judgment and sorrow we feel—but also to cry out for God's forgiveness and deliverance.

These "psalms" offer a window into a God who cares for us, who sympathizes with our brokenness and sorrow. The fruit of repentance is extolled in the latter psalms, and then the twelfth psalm dispenses with words altogether, replaced with wordless humming from which arises an atmosphere of transcendent mystery. To listen and meditate on these words and music is to be reminded of our need for confession and for the absolution of our sins.

One of the most beloved of Rembrandt's paintings is his *The Return of the Prodigal Son*, which is based on the parable Jesus told in Luke 15:11–32. In this painting, we see an illustration of the extent of God's forgiveness and acceptance. Rembrandt has used light in this painting to draw our focus to the returning prodigal, who has wasted away his life and his inheritance with bad choices, and now kneels before his father seeking pardon. His clothes tell the story of what he has been through. They are worn and ragged, and his battered shoes are coming apart.

WikiCommons

The Return of the Prodigal Son by Rembrandt, Hermitage Museum, St. Petersburg

As he buries his face in the bosom of his father, he is held there by a tender embrace. Take note of the way the father's hands rest ever so gently on the prodigal's shoulders as he leans forward to encircle his beloved son. Though the other siblings look on disap-

provingly, the face of the father is full of love. In that face, Rembrandt reveals the tenderness of God the Father, whom this earthly father is intended to represent. The prodigal has not only been forgiven, but he has been restored to his place in the family.

Rembrandt has given a human face to all our abstract ideas about God, a face that speaks of the expansiveness of that love. As recorded in Luke, we learn that the father doesn't wait for his son to come groveling before him, but rather he spies his son "a long way off," lifts up the hem of his robe, and runs to meet him halfway. The son confesses his sin to his father, but the father is more interested in celebrating the return than in acknowledging the guilt. The great painter has given us a powerful illustration of how readily God accepts us, even in our failure.

In his book, *The Return of the Prodigal Son*, Henri Nouwen writes movingly of his own experience with this painting, and how it helped him through a time of loneliness and spiritual crisis. In the father's embrace he came to understand more clearly the embrace of God's love. For him, that embrace represented his true home.

> The tender embrace of father and son expressed everything
> I desired at that moment. I was, indeed, the son exhausted
> from long travels; I wanted to be embraced; I was looking
> for a home where I could feel safe. . . .
> The painting has become a mysterious window
> through which I can step into the Kingdom of God.[9]

Nouwen's experience is one that many have found in the arts— finding a window into deeper understanding and deeper communion with God.

We need to find inner courage as we travel the journey of our lives. We are often so beset by fear, which can sometimes be the most daunting hurdle standing between us and the life we would like to embrace. Fear is not only debilitating; it is also one of the most common human emotions. Sometimes fear can be a natural and reasonable response to a threatening situation. There are times when it would be foolish and ignorant not to be afraid. But when it becomes fixated on things we can do little about, or when it overwhelms us and keeps us in a state of unrest, fear can be a very negative emotional response. It can detour us from moving forward in life. It can keep us from growing and maturing, from venturing out from the familiar and doing something new. It can keep us from taking the actions we need to take, freezing us in our tracks.

Honestly, there is always something to fear. We are surrounded by scary realities, or even just scary perceptions, all the time. There are always things threatening our safety and security. So, how can we keep moving forward in spite of our fears? We need courage.

I want to suggest that courage is, in part, an act of the imagination. Courage demands that we put aside our fears and imagine a better world, or even a "better me." If we can entertain positive changes and transformations as a possibility, we can find a different perspective on our struggles. We can see them differently. When we contemplate what is in front of us or what might lie in the future, one of our greatest sources of strength can be found in imagining that things can be made better, and that we may need to be the one to bring that change about.

> **Courage demands that we put aside our fears and imagine a better world.**

This is another way that the arts can be of help to us. They can provide a vantage point from which to step outside our comfort zone and our own limited perspective into a bigger and brighter future. Without imagination, we can only rely on our own feelings, our own finite resources of strength, and our own coping skills. With imagination we can picture and embrace new solutions. We can visualize a path forward, and bypass the emotions of the moment, stretching toward a better future. We need a vision. Proverbs 29:18 reminds us that we perish for the lack of one.

So, what kinds of courage do we need? And how does the imaginative power of art help us find that courage?

The arts can give us ***the courage to stand for others.*** The Bible speaks often about our duty to stand against injustice and defend the oppressed and marginalized. This was the consistent message of the prophets of the Old Testament. We'll devote an entire chapter in this book to the prophetic power of the arts to help us stand against injustice.

The arts can give us ***the courage to change.*** In the same museum in Florence that houses Michelangelo's iconic statue, *David*, there is a grouping of roughhewn sculptures flanking either side of the walkway that leads toward *David*. Michelangelo named this series, *The Prisoners*. Whether or not they were purposely left in an unfinished state is a question we cannot answer, but they provide an instructive contrast with the finished perfection of *David*. These figures are seemingly tearing themselves out of the stone that has imprisoned them, and their effort is immense.

These statues are perhaps a recognition that our lives are more likely to be a work in progress than a finished masterpiece. As Michelangelo's prisoners remind us, change doesn't come without some pain. It doesn't just magically happen within us. There is a price that comes with transformation. It isn't easy to change course, to step outside of what is comfortable, and to

The Prisoners: Awakening Slave by Michelangelo, Galleria dell' Accademia, Florence.

stand up against evil inclinations we find within ourselves. It isn't easy to tear ourselves out of our own shells. These sculptures remind us that if we want to become the perfected David, first we must be torn out of the stone that imprisons us. We need to allow the great Master Artist to chisel away the imperfections to reveal what is beautiful inside. This means finding the courage to change and accepting its cost.

The arts can also give us *the courage to persevere and overcome.* Sometimes art can stoke the heroism within us and challenge us to overcome our most challenging circumstances by giving us examples of courage and heroism in action. In the film, *The Shawshank Redemption*, we are presented with the story of a man falsely accused of a murder and locked away in prison, who refuses to give up hope. In *Of Gods and Men*, based upon a true story, a small group of monks experience persecution and eventually martyrdom from a repressive Muslim regime. Despite the clear danger of staying where they are, the monks remain faithful to their ministry to the impoverished Muslim community near their monastery. In the end, with quiet dignity, they give their lives for the sake of others. But first, they must walk a path that requires a God-given courage. The best art reminds us that life is hard, and that it will sometimes require more of us than we think we have within us. Art can tell us stories about those who have endured the unimaginable—which helps us imagine how we might also endure.

Art can tell us stories about those who have endured the unimaginable—which helps us imagine how we might also endure.

Finally, the arts can give us *the courage to hope.* The arts can help us believe that there is a future that will be better than the present, help us refuse to be limited by the way we might feel at this moment, and imagine and envision a brighter tomorrow. Such hope is not about ignoring reality but believing in a bigger and better reality. Beauty gives us hope, like a message sent from another world.

René Magritte's *The Empire of Light II* is a playful painting about such a perspective, reminding us that though we dwell in the midst of darkness, there is a light above us. We often need a new perspective so that we are not locked into only seeing the darkness that surrounds us.

© 2020 C. Herscovici / Artists Rights Society (ARS), New York

The Empire of Light II by René Magritte, Metropolitan Museum of Art, New York

No matter what our current circumstances, there is a light coming from a source we cannot see. Sometimes, in order to see clearly, we don't just need to look around—we need to look up. In the words of Frederick Buechner, "Here is the world. Beautiful and terrible things will happen. Don't be afraid."[10] The reason we can find the comfort and courage and hope to be unafraid is that we are not alone. God is with us.

As He hung on the cross, the Gospels record Jesus' seven last words. Among them are His anguished cry, "My God, my God, why have you forsaken me?" and His very final words, "Father, into your hands I commit my spirit." Our entire Christian experience is reflected in the tension between these two statements. Though it may sometimes seem like we are alone and forsaken in our pain and struggles, our best response is always to once again, with intentionality, place ourselves in the hands of the One whom we can always trust. In those hands, peace can be found whatever storms might rage around us or whatever fears might seek to hem us in.

QUESTIONS AND SPIRITUAL EXERCISES

1. How can the art of a Christian balance an affirmation with honesty about human struggles? What songs, poems, paintings, or pieces of literature do you think do this most effectively?

2. Find a hymnbook and slowly read through some of your favorite hymns. What do they tell you about God and your relationship to Him? What images within them do you find particularly helpful and inspiring? Now, sing them in praise to God.

3. In what ways can you identify with Michelangelo's *The Prisoners*?

4. What pieces of art, music, or literature have you found most comforting? How do they accomplish that?

5. What pieces of art, music, or literature give you hope? What kind of hope does it give you?

CHAPTER EIGHT

A World Bigger Than Me:

Making Us More Empathetic

NOT LONG AGO I WAS IN A HURRY to get somewhere to do something that seemed important at the time, and I was reciting all the things in my head that were currently making me anxious and frustrated. I was thinking about job stresses, relationship issues, some minor health concerns, and a certain book whose deadline was approaching. I was moving along the sidewalk, head down, walking fast, and not making any eye contact, when I nearly bowled over a man who had a little cup and a forlorn expression. He shook it to suggest that I add to the change that he had accumulated, and he asked if I could help. I didn't miss a beat. I just shrugged him off and kept walking.

And it bothered me the rest of the day. Because I am learning to try to be more empathetic, and I am making some good steps in that direction, but I still have a way to go. I've heard so many stories about homeless folks using the money they beg to buy drugs and booze, and I've read articles about how a handout sometimes does more harm than good in the long run to the one who receives it. Plus, I'm not excited about the way the streets are littered with garbage by those whose home is the street, but they can't be bothered to pick up after themselves. I could go on with all the reasons not to help.

But.

What has changed my mind and made me more likely to at least flash a smile and say a few words (even when that doesn't feel comfortable) has been my opportunities to serve some homeless people through local programs and get to know them not as unfortunate victims, but as people. Their underlying worries, stresses, fears, and hopes aren't that different from mine. Miss a couple paychecks and I could be one of them. I've grown to appreciate the struggles they face daily and yet marvel at the generally positive outlook so many of them have, or their sense of humor. It is a hard life, but they are often just doing the best they know.

> **Sentimentality doesn't keep anyone clothed and fed.**

When I get to know others, it becomes much harder to place them in a category and then dismiss them out of hand or look down upon them from my privileged perch. Instead, I want to be the kind of person for whom the phrase "be kind and loving to everyone" isn't just an aspirational meme. It can often be no more than a sentimental slogan that helps no one unless it is undergirded by a strong sense of empathy. Sentimentality doesn't keep anyone clothed and fed. It doesn't release anyone from the grip of hopelessness.

But real empathy is trying to imagine what it might be like to be in the desperate situation someone else is in or envisioning what kind of pain and hopelessness they might be facing. Empathy takes my focus off myself and reminds me that my choices shouldn't be only about what is good for me or in my best interest. And the arts are one of the potent tools I have found for gaining that kind of understanding, for my putting concerns into action.

Maybe all my own important stuff isn't really that important. Maybe I should stop to buy my homeless neighbor a cup of coffee or a healthy meal. Or, at the very least, I should offer a warm smile and send a sincere prayer heavenward on his behalf, that he finds safety and a more secure future. The arts can awaken me to the needs of the wider world and help me become more compassionate and empathetic through opening my eyes to the lives of others.

———————

When you look at a painting like Paula Modersohn-Becker's *The Old Peasant Woman*, you see more than just compositional style and use of color. Doesn't it also raise questions in your mind? Who is this woman? What is she thinking? What is she feeling? You can't help but feel some sort of emotional response to a painting like this. Doesn't it make you wonder about the backstory of this woman's life? I can't help but be moved by it. When an artist is doing their job well, they usually draw an emotional response from those who are looking at their work.

The Old Peasant Woman by Paula Moderssohn-Becker, Kunsthalle Hamburg

WikiCommons

And often that response is one of empathy toward the characters being depicted in a painting, a film, or a novel.

When we view a work of art like this one, the longer we look, the more we wonder about this woman and what has given her a look of such weariness and sadness. When the art form is one where you spend more time with the characters involved—as in a novel—you often come to *care* very deeply. You might even shed a tear on their behalf. You find yourself involved in their struggles, their heartbreaks, and their failures, as well as their triumphs and transformations. And you'll feel that you have lived alongside them for a time, and even been privileged with a glimpse into their inner lives.

Responses such as these are why the arts can be such an effective tool for strengthening our empathy.

In experiencing great art, we go places we've never been, see things we've never seen, face brand new temptations and conflicts and moral dilemmas that we've never grappled with in our own life. When, for example, we read a great novel, such as those of Dostoevsky, Tolstoy, Victor Hugo, George Eliot, or the work of any number of great contemporary novelists, we are given the opportunity to expand our fund of life experiences and face moral conundrums that we might not otherwise entertain. We get more than pleasure out of such reading, though we certainly get that.

We can actually get an education about human life; about the kinds of challenges that life might one day throw our way. So, if we allow ourselves that level of involvement, the book might have something to teach us about how we should respond if we are ever in a similar situation. Through reading great literature, we can begin to see a bigger, more expansive perspective on what might come our way in the course of life. In his underappreciated book *An Experiment in*

Criticism, C. S. Lewis argues for the great value of reading in making us broader and better people:

> Those of us who have been true readers all our life seldom fully realise the enormous extension of our being which we owe to authors. We realise it best when we talk with an unliterary friend. He may be full of goodness and good sense but he inhabits a tiny world. In it we should be suffocated. The man who is contented to be only himself, and therefore less a self, is in prison. My own eyes are not enough for me. I will see through those of others.[1]

What he is saying here, it seems to me, is that our ability to think and feel what others are thinking and feeling is exercised and strengthened by our exposure to great literature, and I think, by extension, to other forms of art that tell stories about individuals and their lives. Later in the essay, Lewis memorably remarks, "In reading great literature I become a thousand men and yet remain myself . . . I see with a myriad eyes, but it is still I who see."[2]

When we partake of great art, we are given an opportunity to stretch ourselves beyond the comfortable and familiar boundaries of our own life experience as we are temporarily placed inside the world of another person. We come to understand from that vantage point that there is always a story behind every person's attitudes and actions, which, if we knew it, might make us more patient and forgiving. Through narrative art, we are given a window into what would otherwise be unfamiliar. We're taken inside, and it changes us from the

When we partake of great art, we are given an opportunity to stretch ourselves beyond the comfortable and familiar boundaries of our own life experience.

inside out. And as our empathy and understanding grows, so will our emotional investment in others.

Our word "empathy" comes from the Greek word *empathia*, which means to *feel into*, to understand the subjective experience of another person. It means to, at least temporarily, see with someone else's eyes rather than merely seeing through our own. This is not our natural way of seeing. It is usually hard for us to be concerned about anything that isn't somehow to our own advantage. That's why empathy is a learned response, something we must develop, a way in which our heart needs to be stretched and expanded. While some might be more naturally empathetic, anyone can grow in this area. The more emotionally healthy we are, the easier it is for us to see the needs of others.

Those who are more self-aware and open concerning their own emotions have a greater capacity to read or intuit the emotions of others. Which is what must happen if we are to be empathetic—we must learn to read others, and we must understand that our own life is actually connected to theirs. What affects others, affects you. When we understand this, we begin to see the connection between empathy and caring. Paul encourages this kind of fellow-feeling in his letter to the Romans, "Rejoice with this those who rejoice; mourn with those who mourn" (Rom. 12:15). This is the kind of attitude that marks the spiritually mature believer. We also see this emphasis in 1 Peter 3:8: "Finally, all of you, be like-minded, be sympathetic, love one another, be compassionate and humble." Empathy is the key to strong relationships and robust emotional health.

There is an important difference between *empathy* and *sympathy*, two words we often mistakenly use interchangeably. When you feel sympathy for someone, it means you are experiencing an emotion of sadness for their fate. That's useful, but it isn't the same as empathy. Empathy goes further. To feel empathy is to "feel into" another's situation. To be empathetic is to imaginatively enter into another person's world and let that encounter change the

> **Without empathy, we inhabit a very small world of our own making.**

way you think and feel and experience your own life. Whereas sympathy can sometimes strike an almost condescending posture, empathy is about recognizing that you could easily find yourself in the same position if the circumstances were just a little different. To be empathetic means you are experiencing someone else's pain vicariously, and wanting, by extension, to bring that pain to an end.

Without empathy, we inhabit a very small world of our own making. We are locked into our own individual perspective. But with empathy, we find our perspective broadened and are inspired into making an impact on someone else's world. We not only have an intellectual grasp of their needs and struggles, but we *feel* those needs and struggles at the deepest level. Just as our physical muscles are strengthened with use, so our "moral muscles" of compassion grow more agile as they are exercised.

To get inside the head of another person requires an act of imagination. Imagination can not only let you peer into the exterior circumstances of someone else's life, but also put you, in a very real way, inside their consciousness. Usually, however, it begins with allowing you to get a glimpse into their world and its struggles. This has been the project of many great creative artists.

One of the most empathetic artists of modern times was Käthe

Kollwitz, a German printmaker who came to prominence in a time of economic crisis and hyper-inflation in the aftermath of World War I. Times were hard for most of society, but especially for those already on the lower rungs of society. Kollwitz's prints accurately and unsparingly captured the harrowing effects of hardship and social injustice that arose out of this situation. Women were often the ones most affected, so she concentrated much of her work on illuminating the results of inhumane and unjust policies on them and their children. Kollwitz was not consciously creating political propaganda as much as she was intent on honestly portraying the horrible conditions and hopelessness of the lives of those affected.

In some prints she also illustrated the effects of war upon the populace, stripping these military endeavors of their empty glory and showing their actual effect on real people. She avoided melodrama and manipulative exaggeration in her work, instead somberly recounting the real pain and suffering that lower-class women were experiencing. Viewing her work then, and now, one is struck by the emotional and psychological truth of her portrayal of human misery. There is a profound sense of empathy etched in every line of her work, and she renders the facial gestures of human emotion with great facility and unabashed authenticity.

In her *The Mothers* of

WikiCommons

Woman Thinking by Käthe Kollwitz, San Paulo Museum of Art

1919, she powerfully evoked the extreme cost of the war and the effects its aftermath had on women and children. In it we glimpse her own deep maternal concern for the innocent victims of the war machine. Other works, like *The Weavers*, addressed the catastrophic economic effects of the industrial revolution on the weavers, whose livelihood was being replaced by machines and factories. When, in desperation, they tried to revolt, they were put down without mercy. She captured the pitiless horror of it all.

The Weavers was part of a series of prints that represented a first in visual art—the sympathetic depiction of the plight of the workers who were on the losing end of social change. These images were a sensation when they were first exhibited, though they raised the ire of the Emperor, who called them "gutter art." Similarly, the Nazis later labeled her art as degenerate, saying it was not morally uplifting. Telling the truth is often not appreciated by those in power.

But despite the criticisms of the authorities, her art was widely embraced by the common folk because she was telling the truth about their conditions. Her art also effectively moved the hearts (and empathy) of some in the upper classes, who were inspired by it to call for social change.

Georges Rouault was an important modern painter, as well as a very committed Christian. As a young man he had apprenticed as a stained-glass artist, which is reflected in the black outlines and luminous colors of his mature style. His religious paintings, especially his images of the suffering Jesus, are very powerful. But equally powerful are his paintings of clowns and prostitutes, and those at the fringes of respectable society. The critics who called his work ugly and repulsive failed to understand what he was up to. Rouault wanted to capture both the sacred and the fallen with his brush. He once wrote that "All my work is religious for those who know how to look at it."[3]

We see the depth of empathy he felt for the outcasts of society in his moving painting, *The Injured Clown*. We feel the sadness of the cluster of clowns as two of them come to the aid of the injured one. We are reminded that we live in a broken world filled with broken people. We sense the sympathy of the artist, and our own sympathies rise in response. Rouault said of this painting, "In my view, it is quite possibly as religious as compositions with a biblical theme."[4]

In this and other paintings of clowns, Rouault depicts those who smile and frolic for the entertainment of others, yet hide sadness and a feeling of exclusion behind their painted faces. Similarly, when he created a series of pictures of prostitutes, there was no glamorizing of that dehumanizing profession. He illustrated the ugliness and hopelessness of their condition, slaves to the lusts of men. Rouault wanted to evoke empathy from the viewer and understanding for the fallen state of humanity. He wanted to help us find tenderness and pity in our own hearts.

Among his major works was a series of engravings, *Miserere et Guerre*, which explored the horrors of war, death, and man's inhumanity to man. These engravings are a testament to the depth of human suffering, and some of the images are dark and disturbing. But the series culminates in a series of engravings of the passion of Christ. For, said Rouault, all human suffering is taken up into His redemptive anguish on our behalf. He believed that the only answer to human suffering was to begin with meditating on the suffering of Jesus.

The modern British novelist Julian Barnes once wrote that "it was through books that I first realised there were other worlds beyond my own; first imagined what it might be like to be another person."[5] Many of us know exactly what he meant by that. Great literature takes us outside our world and into an alternative one. Novels can remap our own reality. By reading a well-written novel that immerses us inside its world, our imagination can be compelled into a different way of seeing the world we are already familiar with. Even when an author such as Dickens exaggerates or heightens the social conditions to make them seem as dire as possible for dramatic effect, he is revealing the extent to which things can go wrong in a culture and illustrating the grindingly horrific impact of poverty and injustice on particular individuals.

Through novels like *David Copperfield*, *Great Expectations*, and *Hard Times*, we are given a fresh perspective of the world, one that causes our current perception to shift and enlarge if we will allow that to happen. A recent revisit of Victor Hugo's *Les Misérables* had a similar effect on me. I found both anger boiling up at instances of inhumanity in the novel, as well as a powerful wave of compassion rising up inside me. Every time I read the book or see a filmed adaptation, I exit the experience feeling a little more human than I was before I entered it.

One of the great factors in igniting a new concern for the social well-being of others in the late eighteenth and early nineteenth centuries was the rise of novels as a popular literary form—novels that vividly captured the struggle of the lives of those in the neglected lower classes. Some historians have suggested that this "reading revolution" in the late eighteenth and ninteenth centuries was closely connected to the growth of numerous humanitarian movements. Through reading newspapers, and especially through reading novels, a wider world was opened to readers, and issues of social injustice came into a sharper focus. And especially because this recognition was wed to the power of a story to move readers at a visceral and emotional level, the result was a cry for amelioration of these inhumane conditions, a greater concern for the impoverished, and an impetus for major social transformations.

Three important ninteenth century novelists were at the forefront of creating fiction that inspired change. Harriett Beecher Stowe's bestselling *Uncle Tom's Cabin*, whatever its literary shortcomings, was extremely effective at exposing the evils of slavery. It helped to transform the thinking of a generation of readers who were moved by its storytelling. So important was this book to the abolitionist cause that when Abraham Lincoln met her in 1862, he reportedly said, "So, you're the little woman who wrote the book that started this great war!" Stowe had the courage to tell the truth about the abysmal conditions of slaves; a truth that many people outside the South had never seen, and many others, both North and South, really didn't want to see. She let readers see how slavery affected the lives of actual human beings. And her novel moved her readers to a new way of looking at this form of inhumanity. It made a difference.

Charles Dickens wrote many novels that also proved to be important to the cause of reform. Several of them, directly or indirectly, exposed the inhumane working conditions in English factories during the nineteenth century and especially unmasked the abuses of child labor. When he wrote about the impoverished in his books, Dickens portrayed the depth of their despair and revealed living conditions that were not fit for human beings. Over the course of his novels,

Dickens created unforgettable characters from every social class and displayed the dignity that could be found in each of them. The emotional power of his popular books stirred the consciences of countless readers and helped forge a movement to demand more legal protections for workers, and especially for children in the workforce.

Elizabeth Gaskell created the same sort of awareness in novels such as *Mary Barton*, but her main characters were usually working-class women, a part of society that was often neglected in the public consciousness. By taking her readers into their lives and experiences, her novels opened people's eyes and minds and hearts. Her books gave a new dignity to women whose situation had largely been ignored and neglected.

Of course, this tradition lives on today in the pages of the best of our contemporary novelists. Writers like Chimamanda Ngozi Adichie, Sandra Cisneros, Amy Tan, and Alan Paton are among those whose books have helped modern readers vicariously experience the lives of those who struggle against various forms of oppression.

> **In well-written novels we experience the depth and complexity of other lives, and our own understanding is deepened in the process.**

Scientific studies have confirmed the positive effect of reading fiction (particularly literary fiction, which focuses on fully realized characters) on increasing both empathy and its related attribute, emotional intelligence. A study published in the journal *Science* found that "after reading literary fiction, as opposed to popular fiction or serious nonfiction, people performed better on tests measuring empathy, social perception and emotional intelligence—skills that come in especially handy when you are trying to read someone's body language or gauge what they might be thinking."[6]

The finding suggests that in well-written novels we experience the depth and complexity of other lives, and our own understanding is deepened in the process. One of my friends, who is probably the most empathetic and understanding person I know, is also someone who reads constantly, and most of what she reads is literary fiction and memoir. From these books she has learned enviable skills for relating with others, and she is quick to credit her reading for much of what she has learned. Books have opened the lives of others up to her in a more powerful way.

Because of their immersive qualities, films can also be an effective tool for enlarging our empathies. The great film critic, Roger Ebert, once said that "movies are like a machine that generates empathy."[7] They "enlarge us, they civilize us, they make us more decent people."[8]

One of the things I love about the best films is this very quality—their effectiveness for letting me spend some time in the shoes of another person, to see how they live, the injustices they encounter, the temptations they face, and their very different life situations. When you choose to view films about people from other cultures and races, it has the effect of broadening your world and taking you outside of your own comfort zone. You can imaginatively experience what it might be like to struggle with the issues other people must cope with, sometimes on a daily basis. When I watch such films, I am, at least for a couple of hours, no longer stuck just being me. And when I emerge out of the darkness of the cinema, I emerge a little more tolerant, a little more understanding, and a little more empathetic. I am enlarged, and hopefully a little better citizen of the world. For the world I know after viewing such films is a bigger world, and a world more inclusive.

For that reason, I have made an effort to view films from all over the world. Once you learn to cope with subtitles, which really isn't difficult, a whole world opens before you. In recent years I have watched films from Italy, Spain, Russia, Japan, China, India, Poland, Czechoslovakia, Hungary, Brazil, Iran, Israel, and countless other places. I've found it fascinating to gain a deeper appreciation for how other cultures live, and what kinds of things they struggle with. Some might be surprised to learn that Iran, for example, has a wonderful tradition of thought-provoking and creative filmmaking.

Experiencing Iranian cinema and vicariously entering the lives of ordinary Iranian people makes it impossible for me to sustain a simplistic view of what the Iranians are like. Of course, that country has struggled under oppressive leadership and been at odds with my own nation, but that doesn't mean that individual Iranians are all simply part of that system. No, they are unique people who struggle with many issues that are like those that confront me. The films of Iranian director Asghar Farhadi (who has received two Academy Awards for best foreign language film) explore issues of social class, marital discord, resistance to cultural norms,

> **We find greater empathy in films that open up worlds that might be unfamiliar to us.**

and even religious tolerance with an unflinching realism. When I watch one of his pictures (among the best are *A Separation* and *The Salesman*), I learn a lot about the lives of Iranian people, but I also learn something about our universal human nature. About the things we all have in common. His films are a window into the world in which Farhadi lives and works, but also a window into my own.

Within some of the best American films you can find this same kind of concern for exploring the lives of people who are locked out of many of the best opportunities of our society. For them, life is a daily struggle, and movies can make that struggle come to life. Movies should not only entertain us; sometimes they should challenge us. When it comes to choosing how you are going to spend a couple hours at the theater, it might be advisable to put aside your desire for mindless entertainment and sometimes allow yourself to be challenged and made uncomfortable by what you see and hear. The discomfort you feel when watching such movies might well be evidence that empathy is growing inside you.

We find greater empathy in films that open up worlds that might be unfamiliar to us and place us deep inside the life experiences of people very different from us. What does it feel like to be a member of a minority who is regularly treated like a third-class human being? What does it feel like to be unfairly jailed by a prejudiced and racist legal system? What does it feel like to be a single mom who is just barely eking out an existence in horrific living conditions? What does it feel like to a young man whose father treats him with contempt and violence, or a woman who is only valued for her sexuality? What does it feel like to be the victim of persecution, ridicule, bigotry, rape, violence, or hate?

Through watching films that raise these issues, we have the opportunity to expand our empathy. Just a handful of the recent films that have dealt with such issues could include *Just Mercy, Fences, The Florida Project, Lion, The Green Book, If Beale Street Could Talk*, and *The Hate U Give*. Each of these films tells a morally complex story. The line between right and wrong is sometimes, as in life, blurrier than we wish it was. Such films ask us to struggle with the complexity involved and not rush to simple judgment. They expose the all-too-frequent ugliness of human interactions, and the abysmal way we sometimes treat those who are different from us. Such films are all peopled with real human beings. No one in such films is purely good or evil. We might tend to like things to be nice and tidy, but honestly, a smiling optimism about human nature doesn't really make for good theology.

There is particular power to be found in films about cultural confrontations, like the classic *To Kill a Mockingbird*, which illustrates the clash between black and white in the deep South and argues for fairness, justice, and a recognition of common humanity. Or *Monster's Ball*, where the segregationist code and a cycle of generational prejudice and hatred is finally overcome by human understanding and a recognition of shared pain. What makes us suffer, this film reminds us, is part of what constitutes our shared humanity. Or *The Visitor*, about the friendship between a college professor and an immigrant couple who end up living in his New York apartment and help him see his life a little differently.

Clint Eastwood's *Gran Torino* is another such movie, where Eastwood plays a retired auto worker who must come to terms with his own prejudice against Asian Americans when he encounters and comes to better understand his Hmong neighbors. As he begins to recognize their humanity and the difficulties of their lives, decades of misunderstanding and racism finally start to crumble. Spike Lee has been a master at creating films that challenge us to take a sober look at how hard it is for blacks and whites to really understand each other, especially in films such as *Do the Right Thing*, *Malcolm X*, and *BlacKkKlansman*.

Historical reenactments of the lives of past crusaders for justice or those who had an impact at key moments can also give us much to ponder as we ask ourselves how much has really changed between then and now. There are many powerful films in this genre such as *Selma* (Martin Luther King), *Gandhi* (Mahatmas Gandhi), *Harriett*

(Harriett Tubman), and *Hidden Figures* (about the African American women who were crucial to the space program).

Yes, there's a place for watching movies just for the fun of it. I eagerly await (though am often disappointed in) the latest installments in the *Star Wars* series and the James Bond movies. Sitting in the dark with a tub of popcorn and an escapist movie is sometimes just what I need. But just like I wouldn't try to exist on a diet of Mountain Dew and Twinkies, so I won't limit my filmgoing to movies that are sugary and easy to watch. Films tend to have one of two approaches: they can either reflect a fantasy dream world of unreality, or they can provide a deeper revelation of what it feels like to be alive. Make sure you make room for this second kind of theatrical experience.

Let films not only entertain you, let them educate you. Let them make you more empathetic.

A picture, it is said, is worth a thousand words. And this is nowhere more true than in the art form of documentary photography, where photographers use their gifts to shed light on current social issues. This can be a highly effective way of opening people's eyes to injustice and creating more empathy in their hearts. These photographers made it their business to disclose some of the horrors that might be otherwise hidden from sight. Lewis Hine took pictures that exposed the effects of child labor in a time when there were few regulations in place to protect the young workers. His heart-rending photos of children performing dangerous industrial tasks were published in numerous magazines across the United States and led to a massive public outcry for change. The photos were so devastating that they

Public domain

Photo by Lewis Hine

convinced people of the need for much stricter laws.

Similarly, Dorothea Lange's photographs taken during the migrations caused by the Dust Bowl shed light on the depth of poverty among the "okies." Many of her photos have become iconic, showing the desperation of mothers and their young children. Another example of documentary photography is the famous photo by Nick Ut of a naked young girl and other terrified children fleeing from a napalm attack, running down the middle of a road during the Vietnam War. This photo proved instrumental in mobilizing opposition to that war, as it provoked shock, horror, guilt, and anger from many of those who viewed it. It perhaps encapsulates the high cost of war on innocent civilians better than any other single image. The work of these and other documentary photographers achieved what they set out to do—they made viewers feel deeply. And deep feelings often lead to change.

Whether through a novel, a painting, a film, a song, or a photograph, art has the power to transport us into the lives of others and create a sense of empathy for what they are facing in their lives. Preaching or hectoring others about the need to "love everybody" rarely seems to accomplish its intended goal. Empathy isn't so much about changing our mind as it is about changing our heart. Stories, in whatever form they are told, have the power to touch us and nudge us in a more empathetic direction.

When I listen to the heartbreaking story songs of Bruce Springsteen, I am not being offered a set of directives about how I should think about others. Instead, I am dropped down in the middle of the life of one of his characters and privileged to witness their struggles and small victories. Whether it be the desperate would-be romantics in "Jungleland," or the weary young blue-collar worker who feels his life has reached a dead end in "The River," Springsteen knows how to make us feel without ever telling us how we should feel.

Similarly, the films of the Belgian filmmakers Jeanne-Pierre and Luc Dardenne give us quiet and dignified glimpses into the lives of people whose social and economic situations have pressed them into making difficult moral decisions, or whose troubled pasts have created seemingly insuperable barriers to finding happiness. The Dardenne brothers, in unforgettable films like *L'Enfante, The Unknown Girl,* and *Two Days, One Night* do not offer any tidy answers or dispense judgment on their characters. They just let us live for a couple hours in the presence of people whose circumstances are complex and whose choices have consequences. Their movies don't conclude with tidy happy endings, but instead leave the viewer to draw their own conclusions about what they have just experienced. If the plight of these characters doesn't move you, then maybe nothing will. They are most empathetic of filmmakers.

What happens when we become more empathetic? I think it creates several important transformations within us.

Empathy creates a deeper sense of compassion for others. It takes social issues outside the realm of political argumentation and causes us to feel the effects of policies. It also helps us find more kindness and patience within ourselves for those we encounter every day.

Empathy makes us a little less judgmental. When we are empathetic, we come to understand that behind every act that we might disapprove of, there may well be a story or a set of circumstances that at least possibly might explain it. This doesn't mean we can never make a judgment of disapproval, but it means we should be a bit slower to judge others.

Empathy helps us offer the dignity that every person deserves. Everyone merits being treated with respect and honor, and when we are more empathetic, it becomes easier to do just that.

Empathy releases us from the prison of our self-absorption, reminding us that life isn't all about us. Empathy is the very opposite of narcissism. Empathy doesn't allow us to make all our decisions about what is best for us, and it helps us live out the gospel call toward putting the needs of others first.

Empathy for others can also impact the way we see ourselves. The more we see the mixture of good and bad in others, the more we must recognize that same mixture within ourselves. If we can learn some patience for others, we might grow to become more patient with ourselves. Empathy can guide us toward the possibility of change when we stop beating ourselves up and begin seeing ourselves not only for what we are, but for what we are becoming. As we experience great

DISCOVERING GOD THROUGH THE ARTS

> **When we see through eyes of love, we are seeing through the eyes of God.**

art, our hearts and minds are stocked up with new experiences that we might never have for ourselves, but that art can provide vicariously. In the process, our minds are stretched beyond our present perspectives, our hearts widened to accept new feelings, and our compassion for others—and for ourselves—grows deeper.

Growing in empathy gives us a better understanding of how God, the ultimate Empath, feels about us—His mercy, love, acceptance, and compassion. When we see through eyes of love, we are seeing through the eyes of God—a bigger picture, and a bigger story that takes place outside our own little world.

Empathy is the best of motivators for prayer. It moves us to petition God on behalf of others, which is a good thing since our prayers so often become mostly focused on our own wants and needs. An empathetic frame of mind provides us with plenty of passion that we can channel into our intercession for others. It teaches us to watch for needs that others haven't even expressed and take them to God in prayer. It helps us pray not just with our mind, but with our hearts, adding passion and urgency to our petitions.

There is an old Native American saying that you cannot judge someone until you've walked a mile in their moccasins. Perhaps what our broken and divided world needs more than anything else right now is a tribe of empathetic people, people who try to see life from beyond their own comfortable spheres and are filled with the kind of compassion that can start to change the world. If you want to join this tribe, great literature and great films might be a good way to start your initiation.

QUESTIONS AND SPIRITUAL EXERCISES

1. What is the best definition you can offer of the trait of empathy? Why do you think some people seem to be more naturally empathetic than others?

2. Treat yourself to a couple films that reflect the lives of people in another culture. See the appendix for more suggestions, though they are just the tip of the iceberg.

3. Read one of the novels mentioned in this chapter, looking for how it helps you see the world a little differently.

4. Spend time praying that God will create a more empathetic heart within you.

5. Put your empathy into action. Volunteer at a soup kitchen or homeless shelter, stop and have a real conversation with a homeless person, visit a shut-in or a stranger at a local nursing home, or bake some cookies for that person you find so hard to get along with.

CHAPTER NINE

Prophetic Voices:

Awakening a Passion for Justice

WHEN I BECAME MORE SERIOUS ABOUT MY FAITH during my high school years, I developed a fascination for the topic of Bible prophecy. I ravenously devoured the books of people like Hal Lindsey, Salem Kirban, John Walvoord, and a host of others. I remember most of the prophecy gurus agreeing that the Second Coming would take place within the next handful of years, and surely before the dawn of the new millennium. It was just around the corner, many asserted, so I memorized the relevant Bible verses and charts that confirmed a vision of the "end times," and pored over Revelation, Daniel, and the prophetic books of the Old Testament looking for insight. It became a bit of an obsession for me, and I liked having "insider information" about how prophecy was being fulfilled all around me.

Flash forward to the present. My eschatology (theological beliefs about the last things) has changed a lot since then. I am no longer concerned with trying to pin the tail on the Antichrist or place the latest events of the evening news into a prophetic timeline. And I have some serious questions about the way many prophecy "experts" interpret the Bible. What changed my mind? Well, there are a number of primarily theological concerns that led me to a different way of thinking, but I'm not interested in arguing about these in the context of this book.

What is relevant for the present chapter is the change that occurred in the way I read the Old Testament prophets. I used to search for verses that might tell me something about the future, never spending much time thinking about what the primary message of these men and women might be. As I read more carefully, I came to realize that they were usually more interested in what was happening in their current context than in their visions of future times.

Sure, it is indisputable that some of their words were about the future they foresaw, a time when God would show Himself fully in all His power and all His grace. But much of what the prophets spoke about—and often thundered about—were the problems of idolatry and injustice, which were so real and so urgent in their own day. I'd been so busy looking for information about the future that I'd missed the way their words spoke to their contemporary moment, as well as to present concerns today. They weren't interested in creating data for us to place in a chart or timeline or making us feel confident of our spiritual dedication. They were calling us to wake up.

When we talk about growing in spiritual maturity, we are usually referring to the disciplines by which our personal growth might be nourished—prayer, Scripture study, meditation, fasting, and other practices. These are the practices that help us mature in our personal relationship with God. But there is a tradition going back to the Old Testament prophets that challenges the value of such spiritual activities if they are divorced from actions that promote justice. Pursuing personal spiritual maturity, the prophets indicated, is not enough. God calls His people to combine a commitment to loving Him with a commitment to caring about the needs of others.

The prophet Isaiah, for example, while acknowledging the dedication of God's people to fasting, challenged the value of fasting if the Israelites' lives did not prioritize compassion, justice, and demonstrating concern for the poor. One imagines him observing all the dedication to personal faith that he saw in the people of Israel, and then deploying thundering words of rebuke about what they were neglecting while they worked to purify their hearts. God was calling them to back up their spiritual practices with a commitment to the needs of those on the margins of society, and to delivering justice for all the people of Israel. For Isaiah, true faith was demonstrated by how God's people cared for others.

> **God calls His people to combine a commitment to loving Him with a commitment to caring about the needs of others.**

> "Yet on the day of your fasting, you do as you please
>> and exploit all your workers. . . .
> You cannot fast as you do today
>> and expect your voice to be heard on high. . . .
> Is not this the kind of fasting I have chosen:
> to loose the chains of injustice
>> and untie the cords of the yoke,

> to set the oppressed free
>   and break every yoke?
> Is it not to share your food with the hungry
>   and to provide the poor wanderer with shelter—
> when you see the naked, to clothe them,
>   and not to turn away from your own flesh and blood?"
> (Isa. 58:3–4, 6–7)

Here Isaiah focuses on one of the most demanding of spiritual exercises—that of denying yourself food for a period of time—and says that even such an act of spiritual sacrifice is meaningless and unacceptable in God's eyes if it is not paired with an active concern for others that leads to deeds that improve the circumstances of the poor and needy. As James writes in his New Testament letter, "Religion that God our Father accepts as pure and faultless is this: to look after orphans and widows in their distress and to keep oneself from being polluted by the world" (James 1:27).

For most of us, it is much easier to pray for a needy person than it is to reach out to them, engage with them in a dignified way, and do what we can to meet their practical needs. None of us gets off the hook because we are busy, uncomfortable, or don't know where to start. An important part of our spiritual growth should be about serving those who have less than we do. Lest we forget to prioritize this part of being a follower of Jesus, the Bible contains lots of reminders. The tradition of the biblical prophets challenges you and me to rethink our priorities and make some changes, just as the Israelites of old were called to do. Let's not get tied up in the arguments about whether social justice is part of the gospel message. Whether it is or it isn't, it is without question a significant theme throughout the entire

Bible. So, let's take it seriously. In our own time we also have the work of creative "prophets" of all sorts—musicians, novelists, filmmakers, artists, and poets, who have carried on the task of awakening us to unmet needs and calling us to do something about them.

In the previous chapter we discussed how the arts can help us develop more empathy and compassion, igniting our hearts to respond with a heartfelt concern about the lives of others. But just feeling sorrow and sympathy and compassion is not enough. We are called to seek justice alongside righteousness.

Compassion addresses the symptoms that arise in people's lives by meeting immediate needs, such as food, housing, education, and medical care. But we need more than just compassion. We need to work for justice as well. Justice calls us to do more than alleviate immediate suffering. It calls us to address the systemic injustices in our society. The pursuit of justice should seek to transform (or if necessary, overturn) the institutions and structures that are at the root of poverty, disease, racism, inequality, and injustice. If we don't fix the problems at their source, we are just putting a temporary Band-Aid over the problem.

As someone has said, compassion is when we see someone drowning in a river and respond by pulling them out. Justice is when we go upstream and find ways to keep people from falling into the river in the first place.

The prophets of the Old Testament frequently used imagination and vivid word pictures to call into question the inequality, injustice, and unrighteousness of their culture. They were people who had an uncommon access to the mind and heart of God, with a passion for pure religion and authentic social justice. They were not primarily predictors of a predetermined future, but barometers of a present that was on a path toward God's judgment. These prophets saw things differently than most of the people around them. They were outsiders even to their own culture, and stood apart from the status quo.

The prophets offered a different perspective: revealing how God felt about the current state of affairs, while putting the passion and pathos of God on display in their words and actions. The prophet was a poet, a preacher, a social critic, and a moralist—all at the same time.

What is important for our purposes here is also to note the high degree of artistry they brought to their proclamations. They were not satisfied with straightforward preachments or hectoring lectures, but wrapped their messages in poetry, creative expression, storytelling, and dramatic enactments. They were, in the fullest sense of the word, artists.

Isaiah by Michelangelo, Sistine Chapel (detail), Rome

Like artists today, the prophets were unauthorized and uncredentialed voices. They worked outside the system, and usually without the approval of the government or the religious authorities. The only authority they claimed was the authority of God. They saw silence as a way of maintaining an unjust status quo, so they were compelled to speak up and speak out against injustice and to imagine a better future.

Their messages were especially targeted at those in their society who were infatuated with human wisdom, military might, and the security of wealth. They condemned the oppression of the poor, the neglect of the marginalized, the greed of the wealthy, the unjust taxation by the leaders of the nation, and the religious justification of all such evils.

So, the prophets spoke out against the perversion of justice, and here is just the smallest sampling of the kind of things they said:

> "'What do you mean by crushing my people
>   and grinding the faces of the poor?'
>   declares the Lord, the LORD Almighty" (Isa. 3:15).

> "And what does the LORD require of you?
>   To act justly and to love mercy
>   and and to walk humbly with your God" (Micah 6:8).

> "Away with the noise of your songs!
>   I will not listen to the music of your harps.
> But let justice roll on like a river,
>   righteousness like a never-failing stream" (Amos 5:23–24).

> "They do not seek justice.
> They do not promote the case of the fatherless;
>   they do not defend the just cause of the poor" (Jer. 5:28).

Abraham Heschel translates these verses for our time, "Men may not drown the cries of the oppressed with the noise of hymns, nor buy off the Lord with increased offerings."[1]

The words of the prophets are just as relevant to us today. As Walter

Brueggemann points out, the "triad of *exploitative labor, unjust taxation, and exhibition of surplus wealth* was judged by these poets [the prophets] as both antineighborly and in defiance of the will of the covenantal God."[2] That same triad still haunts our contemporary culture.

The prophets spoke of the Divine sorrow over the moral and spiritual deficit on God's people when it came to such issues. God, they insisted, is not indifferent or apathetic but is *emotionally invested* in the well-being of His people, especially the ones who are victims of an unjust system. As Abraham Heschel, an expert of the prophets, reminds us, "All prophecy is one great exclamation; God is not indifferent to evil! He is always concerned, He is personally affected by what man does to man."[3] All the prophetic predictions of disaster and judgment we read in the prophets are paired with exhortations to repentance. They call for a turning, a forsaking of a former way of living. For them, the future is not written in stone, but subject to change based upon our response.

The method the prophets used for delivering their urgent message was not preaching as much as poetry. They used poetic rhythms and forms, powerful word pictures, stories that revealed deeper truths, and visionary images. These methods of communication create a communication that was more imperative and more unforgettable to their listeners and readers. Some of the prophets were almost like ancient performance artists, who backed up their thundering words with symbolic acts that unveiled a fresh perspective. By God's command, Hosea married a woman whom he knew would be unfaithful as a picture of God's long-suffering patience. Jeremiah went to see a potter and observed how a lump of clay could be fashioned into something beautiful, an image of how God desired to shape His people. Isaiah walked barefoot for three years as a sign and warning. And Jeremiah performed all kinds of seemingly irrational acts to illustrate his message.

Many artists have carried on the traditions of the prophets, of speaking boldly and creatively against the wrongdoing and injustice they see around them, as well as against those who think, "Thank you very much, I can get along just fine without God." Like the prophets of old, these artists are not concerned with being comforting and inspirational as much as challenging and even a bit shocking when necessary. We need to hear them. If we only partake of art that makes us feel good and refuses to look at the hard or challenging truths, we cut ourselves off from a source for seeing what needs to be done. Sometimes the arts need to ruffle our feathers if true compassion is to take root.

> **We need prophetic artistry to help us balance our pursuit of spiritual discipline with a passion for social justice.**

The arts can exercise prophetic power as they speak against the sins of our culture and call us back to a neglected truth, and they also can give a voice to the voiceless and the marginalized. Sometimes a work of art, because it bypasses mere intellectual argumentation and reaches the heart and the emotions, can persuade at the deepest level, convincing those who encounter it of truths they might not be able to argue for or against. Art is a different kind of communication, and it is one especially well-suited for calling for change. We need these voices and the messages they can deliver to us. We need prophetic artistry to help us balance our pursuit of spiritual discipline with a passion for social justice.

When we ponder Dante's *Divine Comedy*, we probably think of it as a powerful image-driven meditation on the spiritual journey. It is that, but it is more than that. Before he penned his great poem, Dante had written an earlier book, *On the Monarchy*, which argued forcefully for the separation of church and state. He saw the abuses that occurred when the two were not allowed to operate in their separate spheres, and he brought this same concern to his *Divine Comedy.*

When he wrote of his fictional travels to hell, purgatory, and heaven, Dante peopled its verses not only with famous saints and sinners of the past, but with actual individuals living in his own time. Dante's hell contains not only kings and rulers, but also bishops and popes, and many of them are portrayed in a very unflattering way. His grand poem is not only about the heights and depths of spiritual experience, but also about the corruption and hypocrisy that was rampant in current Florentine politics and religion. He went so far as to place the pope at the time, the power-hungry Boniface VII, in one of the circles of hell. Dante was using his timeless artistry to also comment on the problems and injustices of his own time.

William Blake was another poet who raised his voice against the injustice of his day, using his verse to challenge cultural norms. Among the poems in *Songs of Innocence and Experience* are verses attacking economic injustice, religious hypocrisy, and the use of children in dangerous industrial labor. Though the industrial revolution was only in its infancy when he penned his work, Blake foresaw the dire consequences this new technology would have on the poor, especially when it was in the hands of greedy industrialists. He saw the new factories where people labored for subsistence wages in terrible working conditions as "dark Satanic mills."[4]

Blake called for a return to a simpler way of life and a childlike innocence as an alternative to the heartless injustice he saw all around him. His poems revealed what needed to change for that to happen.

The beloved novelist Jane Austen is often considered to be little more than an insightful commentator on love and relationships, but there was something more than that going on in her books. In novels such as *Pride and Prejudice*, she effectively satirized the inequalities of the class system of her day and argued for a love not based on social climbing and getting ahead financially, but on recognizing admirable character in a potential spouse rather than succumbing to the emptiness of mere charm.

A recent study by Oxford scholar Helena Kelly, *Jane Austen: The Secret Radical*, reflects on how Austen took up such topics as slavery, poverty, and the limited roles of women with a gentle but incisive critique. As Kelly notes, her novels are:

> Not an undifferentiated procession of witty, ironical stories about romance and drawing rooms, but books in which an authoress reflects back to her readers their world as it really is—complicated, messy, filled with error and injustice. This is a world in which parents and guardians can be stupid and selfish; in which the Church ignores the needs of the faithful; in which landowners and magistrates—the people with local power—are eager to enrich themselves even when that means driving the poorest into criminality. Jane's novels, in truth, are as revolutionary, at their heart, as anything that Wollstonecraft or Tom Paine wrote.[5]

This is an often-overlooked aspect of her wonderful novels, and she serves as an example of how social issues can be addressed artfully rather than with a hammering and bombastic rhetoric. I love to think of prim and proper Jane Austen as a gentle revolutionary.

Nearer our own time, Walker Percy was one of the most entertaining critics of our wayward American society. His graceful style, perfect comic timing, and unwavering eye for human behavior make him compulsively readable. Wedded to this was a sincere Christian faith, and a frustration for the trappings of Christian culture. Percy was a novelist who saw modern civilization as being in the grip of despair, a despair so deep that few recognized it for what it was.

Trained as a doctor, Percy sought to write what he called "diagnostic novels"[6] to uncover what has gone amiss in the modern world. "Something is indeed wrong," he wrote, "and one of the tasks of the novelists is, if not to isolate the bacillus under the microscope, at least to give the sickness a name, to render the unspeakable speakable."[7] He did this through a series of satirical and comedic works that were deeply serious at heart. As a committed Catholic, Percy wanted to point toward Christianity as the only way out of the modern malaise, but realized that there are immense challenges in doing so:

> The old words, God, grace, sin, redemption . . . now tend
> to be either exhausted, worn slick as poker chips and
> signifying as little, or else are heard as the almost random
> noise of radio and TV preachers. The very word 'Christian'
> is not good news to most readers."[8]

And so, Percy set himself the challenge of finding new ways to talk about faith, with brutal honesty about human failings and a great good humor. He is one of my favorite modern writers because he is so able to wed critique with an ultimate hope for humanity. His flawed main characters are each on a spiritual search of one sort or another, and through the pages of his novels, each of them stumbles ever closer to the Kingdom of God.

Music has proven, in our modern times, to be one of the most enduring and effective ways of challenging the status quo, calling our cultural values into question and pointing out our various forms of injustice and hypocrisy. Music also has a unique power of creating a communal identity among those who hear and embrace a message of change. Let's take an all-too-brief musical journey through African American music, and trace how it has been an important conduit for addressing the needs of a people who have often found themselves under the heel of a dominant white culture. As the novelist Ralph Ellison has lamented: "the art—the blues, the spirituals, the jazz, the dance—was what we had in place of freedom."[9]

Slavery was the context by which most of the Africans were introduced into American culture, and it was a dehumanizing, cruel, and utterly unjust system. The myth of the contented slave has been perpetrated by some to disguise or diminish the horrifying reality. On the auction block, no family ties were recognized. Families were broken up, husbands and wives separated, and their children sold away from their parents. For most slaves, slavery meant working fifteen to twenty hours a day and being beaten if one showed signs of fatigue. It is appalling that Christianity was often used to defend slavery and slaveholders, justifying it through a desire to "civilize" and "Christianize" the slaves, and employing scriptural texts to make a "biblical" case for the practice.

While many slaves came to accept the faith of their oppressors, it did not dull their desire for freedom and liberation. In fact, the slave community appropriated the story of the exodus of the Israelites as a parallel to their own situation. They created a genre of songs that have come to be known as "spirituals," which affirmed their value as human beings, asserted their dignity and humanity, and spoke of hope and freedom. These songs provided strength and courage as they defined the black experience in their own terms, not in the terms of the oppressors. W. E. B. Du Bois wrote about the spirituals, which he called Sorrow Songs: "Through all the sorrow of the Sorrow Songs there breathes a hope—a faith in the ultimate justice of things."[10]

The spirituals embraced the suffering of Jesus during His earthly sojourn and identified their own pain with His. Interestingly, these songs rarely addressed the white people who had enslaved them with hate or scorn. Perhaps they had given up expecting anything but evil from their captors. Since whites had demonstrated themselves to be so lacking in understanding and compassion, they seemed to imply that it wasn't even worth addressing their cruelty and hypocrisy. They were not able to deal with the white slaveholders on moral, human grounds. So, the songs were their own way of communicating with each other about what they were experiencing and what they hoped for.

> **The spirituals embraced the suffering of Jesus during His earthly sojourn and identified their own pain with His.**

As their titles indicate, these were largely songs about liberation: "Go Down Moses," "O, Freedom," and "Mary Don't You Weep." Like the Israelites of old, the slaves dreamed of a future promised land where they would be free, and they sang of a God who was involved in history, including their own history, on the side of the ones who had been wronged. Many of the songs were focused on the relief they hoped to find in the afterlife ("Swing Low, Sweet Chariot," "I Want to Go to Heaven When I Die," and "Get On Board That Gospel Train"), but these were not songs of passive acceptance of their lot, but instead a way of keeping a more hopeful vision of the future in front of their eyes. The hope of Heaven was an anticipation of a new order of peace and justice, and their deep longings for freedom were encoded into songs with meanings meant for their own community. The immediate hope was for a promised land in the free North. The long-term hope was for freedom and dignity beyond death.

Harriett Tubman even used the songs to spread coded messages about escape. Some have speculated that "Follow the Drinking Gourd" for example, was used as a guide for slaves escaping North, its verses providing a sort of musical map of signs to look for on each step of the perilous journey.

Like the spirituals, the blues were birthed from the experience of slavery and oppression, which is why James Cone refers to this genre as a "secular spiritual."[11] The blues depict the difficult realities of the black experience: hard luck, broken families, and a general dissatisfaction with a cold and uncaring world. Even after the political liberation of the slaves, their circumstances often remained very difficult. But unlike the communal statements of the spirituals, the blues are an individual expression. They are a music of catharsis—affirming the struggles of life while refusing to surrender to despair; a way to help one transcend their troubles by understanding the universality of pain.

As jazz developed, it too became a way to address injustice, and some musicians did this very directly. John Coltrane played eight benefit concerts in support of Martin Luther King and the civil rights movement. He wrote several songs dedicated to the cause, but "Alabama" is especially gripping. The notes and phrasing of the music are based upon the words that Dr. King preached at the memorial service for the little girls who died in the Birmingham church bombing. Just as King's speech escalates in intensity, so "Alabama" begins with a plaintive tone and subdued mood before sliding into a crackling surge of energy, reflecting outrage and a strengthened determination to achieve justice.

Billie Holiday's haunting recording of "Strange Fruit" threatens to overcome the listener with its overwhelming emotion. Inspired by the 1930 lynching of two young black men, it shines a light on the horror of racism. It became Holliday's signature song, and an anthem of the early civil rights movement. If you don't know the words to this classic song, take a moment to look them up. Holliday will not let us avert our eyes from a grave and horrifying injustice.

In 1957, Arkansas governor Orval Faubus used the National Guard to prevent black students from entering a newly desegregated public high school. Charles Mingus displayed his outrage by composing a piece entitled "Fables of Faubus," which offers a harsh critique of the Jim Crow attitudes of the South using the tools of sarcasm and ridicule.

Early soul music followed in the tradition of speaking up against social inequality. Talented artists like Sam Cooke, Curtis Mayfield, and Marvin Gaye even caught the attention of white audiences with their music and helped reshape a generation's perceptions of African Americans. The mainstream acceptance of this music helped elevate the status of black Americans. Marvin Gaye's *What's Going On* remains a classic pop/soul record and was particularly effective in highlighting deteriorating social conditions and the damaging public policies of the 1960s and 70s.

Hip-hop and rap music have carried similar messages into our own times. Originally a purely celebrative dance music, it became a vehicle for the expression of righteous indignation. Grandmaster Flash's "The Message," released in 1982, sketches a harrowing picture of the struggles of life in the South Bronx where one in three young people were unemployed, where jobs were scarce, and where poverty abounded. The city was heavily populated by junkies, hookers, pimps, bag ladies, hoodlums, and predatory drug dealers. Grandmaster Flash spelled out his grievances about oppressive living conditions and an environment where young people were brought up without any real hope for escape from the cycle of oppressive poverty.

In his excellent book, *Hip-Hop Redemption*, Ralph Basui Watkins explains the significance of this music: "Hip-hop is a child of the city. Young prophets cry out as they live in a world that those who could escape have escaped. African American youth and young adults face what appear to be hopeless odds, and they fight back through the prophetic arm of hip-hop."[12]

For the next generation of hip-hop and rap artists, a more aggressive sound and message came to the fore. Spike Lee asked Public Enemy to create "an anthem to scream out against the hypocrisies and wrongdoings [of] the system" for his film, *Do the Right Thing*. Their answer was a song called "Fight the Power," which contained a message of repudiation for the non-violent approach of the civil rights movement.[13] Their message was that they simply weren't going to take it anymore.

The West Coast band N.W.A. brought their experiences with gang culture, police brutality, and drugs to rap music. Their album, *Straight Outta Compton*, opens with the promise of dispensing "street knowledge" to the listener. They are storytellers, and the story they are telling isn't a pleasant one. But it was influential because many African American listeners found it true to their experience. Their songs were rage-fueled and profanity-laced, a war cry against the system. While Public Enemy were driven by a black empowerment philosophy, N.W.A. just seemed to be saying that if you were going to treat them like animals, well then, they were going to act like animals.

What developed in rap music is a reminder that art of protest can easily lose its artfulness and become something quite different. The "gangsta rap" message was closely tied to the gang culture, which had done nothing to lift young African Americans out of their plight. In short order, their themes of violence, antisemitism, threats against Korean grocers, misogyny, a celebration of ostentatious materialism, and a mainstreaming of gang culture all conspired to create a fierce backlash. Everything exploded with the Watts riots of 1992 and the Rodney King verdict.

The nineties brought two effective artistic voices to the fore that focused on a God-centered critique of both the dominant culture and the hip-hop culture. Talib Kweli's *Eardrum* suggested that those who celebrate violence, misogyny, and drugs are part of the problem. His song "Hostile Gospel Part 1" is both a lament and a prayer for deliverance. And Lauryn Hill's immensely popular *The Miseducation of Lauryn Hill* challenges some of the thinking of hip-hop culture. Her song "Zion," for example, tells her story of deciding not to abort her baby, even though she knew becoming a mother would be hard on her musical career. Such artists are models for critiquing the dominant culture while not closing their eyes to the problems inherent in their own.

Hip-hop continues to be a place where social justice issues take precedence, for example, in the music of Kendrick Lamar, J. Cole, and Meek Mill. These artists are carrying on a tradition that started with the slave spirituals and is bringing a message of justice and liberation into the twenty-first century.

———

Bob Dylan is arguably the greatest singer/songwriter of modern times, and issues of justice and social equality have always been part of the message of his music. As a young man, Dylan moved to New York City to become part of a burgeoning movement of folk music and social activism. Part of the attraction for moving east from Minnesota was the presence of Woody Guthrie, who was in a hospital in upstate New York. Initially Dylan seemed intent on mimicking his iconic hero, though he soon developed his own unique vocal and writing style. Compared to the socially active folksingers who had preceded him, Dylan's work was more poetic, more lyrical, and more psychologically complex.

He tackled issues such as civil rights, war, censorship, and economic injustice, as well as hypocrisy in governmental and religious institutions—all with great freshness of approach and unparalleled creativity. His approach was generally not the sloganeering that characterized many in the folk world but showed an awareness of the complexity of the issues. For Dylan, throughout his career, the answers to the problems he was writing about were never simple. Possibly as a result of his Jewish heritage, Dylan always had a deep suspicion about the perfectibility of human beings or institutions.

Especially in his early work, I think we can discern at least four major approaches he took to writing and singing about social justice, which showcase some different approaches an artist might take to exploring these issues. First, he wrote songs that might be called *musical journalism*, which revealed existing injustice through storytelling and cultural reportage. Songs such as "The Ballad of Hollis Brown," "The Lonesome Death of Hattie Carroll," and "The Death of Emmitt Till" were meant to shock listeners. These songs tear off the blinders of ignorance (whether innocent or chosen) and force the listener to see how things really are. In "The Lonesome Death of Hattie Carroll," for example, Dylan exposes the inequities in the justice system through telling the true story of a rich young white man who only gets a slap on the wrist for killing an older black woman in a fit of rage. Such songs are predicated on the assumption that hearing about evil can lead to taking a stand against it.

Second, Dylan wrote direct **protest songs,** angry indictments of the evils that society had come to accept as a norm. "Master of War," for example, is a blistering attack on the military-industrial complex, those who are building fortunes at the expense of young men dying in battles fought for reasons they don't understand. In the final verse he exhibits a sort of righteous indignation in the hope that he will one day see these masters of war lowered into their own graves. This song, one critic suggests, "is a vehicle for all those dangerous, unpacifistic emotions that antiwar movements rarely allow themselves to express—that feeling of hating violence so much that all you want to do is match it with a violence of your own."[14]

As we learned in the late sixties, this kind of pent-up anger does not end up being an entirely successful way to combat society's problems. Dylan's "A Hard Rain's A-Gonna Fall" offered a new approach to protest singing: less direct, and more creative and allusive. This song is about a world that is destroying itself. At the time it was written, many suggested it was a warning about nuclear annihilation, though in recent times some have proposed that it also holds a relevant warning about the dangers of climate change. It is a perfect example of how some of the best social justice art can be open to multiple interpretations and continuing relevance.

Third, Dylan penned many **songs of sarcastic indignation,** using humor and sarcasm as a weapon against society's evils. Songs such as "The Paranoid John Birch Society Blues" and "Only a Pawn in Their Game" held out ridicule for beliefs and institutions that support racism, exclusivist nationalism, and a mindset of conformity. Dylan exposes the irrationality at the heart of such dangerous beliefs by using humor rather than heated rhetoric. Especially powerful is his song "With God on Their Side," which is a challenge to those who conflate national agendas with religious commitments. As Dylan recounts how God has been used to justify all kinds of evils, he asks the listener to step back and reconsider the dangers of this kind of thinking.

Fourth, and most enduring (there is probably a lesson in that), are the *songs of hope for a better future.* Songs such as "Blowing in the Wind," "When the Ship Comes In," and "The Times They Are A-Changing" asked the listener to imagine a better and more just society. These songs didn't so much prescribe a lot of specific answers to the problems before us, as to raise awareness of the issues and remind us that there is always hope for change. The status quo always needs to be questioned, and higher values need to be sought. If you are not part of the solution, Dylan seems to be saying, then you are still part of the problem.

After three early albums of what he would later call "finger pointing songs," and after being hailed as the voice of his generation, Dylan's songwriting continued to evolve. The more direct protest music was replaced by more poetic, personal, intuitive, and lyrically ambiguous songs. He would later write in his autobiography, "Protest songs are difficult to write without making them come off as preachy and one-dimensional. You have to show people a side of themselves that they don't know is there."[15]

That became the strategy of many of his later songs that deal with issues of social justice. Songs such as "Black Diamond Bay," "George Jackson," "Blind Willie McTell," and "License to Kill" used a more creative approach to unmasking the absurdity, unpredictability, and irrationality of modern life. Dylan delivered his messages with more nuance, more individualism, more imagination, and more ambiguity than had

> **For Bob Dylan, the quest for justice begins by seeking to repair what has gone wrong inside the heart of every human being—starting with yourself.**

previously been the case, but with no less of a powerful call for justice. Those who are producing art from a Christian worldview could do well to pay attention to the effectiveness of a less in-your-face approach.

Dylan's songs sought to understand the underlying causes of injustice in our society, and he saw the darkness in human hearts as the key to his understanding. The problem was more than just politics. For him, the quest for justice begins by seeking to repair what has gone wrong inside the heart of every human being—starting with yourself. This evolving sense of living in a world gone wrong (the title of one of his albums) may explain Dylan's embrace of Christianity with its foundational belief in original sin. In later albums he frequently combined cultural criticism with a biblical perspective.

In novels we read of injustice, and in music we hear a voice of dissent, but in the visual arts we can *see* it for ourselves.

Goya's searing painting, *The Third of May, 1808* addressed our human tendency to perpetrate horror upon each other in times of war. It was not the first time that Goya had addressed the topic of war and the injustices it spawned. From 1810 through 1820, he created a series of eighty-two etchings that illustrated the horrors of war. These etchings were harsh, haunting, macabre, and horrific, probably the most vivid depiction of what really happens to soldiers and non-combatants in the heat of war, an unveiling of the inhumanity of which we are all capable. Mutilation, torture, and rape are all manifest. On

WikiCommons

The Third of May, 1808 by Francisco Goya, The Prado, Madrid

a few of the etchings, perhaps to confirm that he wasn't just using his imagination, Goya scribbled, "I saw it."

The Third of May, 1808 was commissioned to depict the heroism of those who stood up against invading French soldiers. Goya illustrates an actual historical scene, with Spanish patriots who had fought against the French and were now being rounded up and executed. It is not an image that glorifies the heroic dignity of war, but rather a testament to its cruelty and cost. Faceless soldiers take aim at a figure in white, who is not a famous hero, but an ordinary man in a Christlike pose. He is surrounded by those who have already been victims and the cold-blooded executioners are almost machine-like in their efficiency. All face their fate with fear. This is the truth that Goya felt must be told about war, and many years later another Spaniard, Pablo Picasso, also used his palette for a similar protest.

On April 26, 1937, during the Spanish Civil War, the small town of Guernica was bombed by fascist forces, utterly destroyed by German fighter planes acting under an agreement between Spain's fascist dictator, Francisco Franco, and Adolf Hitler. Guernica was not a strategic target but served as an excuse for the Nazi regime to test the efficiency of Herman Goering's Luftwaffe. The enemy was, under the Nazi "total war" doctrine, not just the opposing army, but anyone and everyone who supported them. The Nazis were eager to assess the effectiveness of their concept of *blitzkrieg* ("lightning war") and see how the shock of such a sudden attack could demoralize an enemy.

Large squadrons of bombers came in three waves and dropped hundreds of bombs, which demolished all the public buildings in the town and 71% of the private homes. They also bombed nearby farms. The bombers were followed by fighter planes who swooped low and machine-gunned the civilians who were trying to escape. It was a merciless slaughter. Finally, a few hours later they dropped hundreds of incendiary bombs, which whipped up a firestorm that burned anything that was left. The devastation was almost unimaginable, but a famous artist decided to help people imagine it.

Pablo Picasso, a Spaniard, was living in Paris when he got the news about this unspeakable act. Within a week he began making sketches for a monumental painting that would respond to this horror. The resulting painting was *Guernica*.

Picasso's fractured cubist style captured the horror of that day more effectively than any photograph possibly could. The massive canvas was nearly eight meters wide and more than twice his height, so he had to use a precarious ladder to reach its upper regions. The resulting masterpiece is a terrifying and shocking nightmare of a picture, a mass of broken bodies and screams of pain, the aftermath of

© 2020 Estate of Pablo Picasso / Artists Rights Society (ARS), New York

Guernica by Pablo Picasso, Museo Reina Sofia, Madrid

unspeakable violence. Picasso offered his painting as a loud shout of "no" against the inhumanity of this event, but also against all wars. It quickly became, and remains, a powerful symbol of the immorality of the fascist regimes, as well as a symbol of the anti-war movement. Picasso's brush said more than his voice alone ever could, a testament to the power of art to unmask the evil humans perpetrate on one another. It became a powerful weapon in the war against war.

Occasionally, one of the occupying Nazi officials would drop by Picasso's studio to do a random search or engage in some general harassment. When one of those Nazi officials saw a sketch for this painting, he asked with a tone of disgust, "Did you do this?"

"No," Picasso coldly replied, "you did."

———————

In the last chapter we discussed the ability of films to move us to empathy. Films, like other works of art, can also be used to move us to action. They can be prophetic, raising their voice against injustice and affirming the courage to stand against it. Fictional films can be as powerful as documentaries in their ability to reveal injustices. But those films that bring true stories to life are especially effective at revealing the deep evils in our world.

I could offer countless examples, but will instead suggest the viewing of three recent films that do this very powerfully: *A Hidden Life* (the story of a man who paid a heavy price for his refusal to be a part of the Nazi war machine), *Just Mercy* (about a man scheduled for execution despite the weakness of the case built against him),

> True prophetic art invites a conversation, full of nuance and complexity.

and *Dark Waters* (a legal thriller about the fight to shut down a manufacturing plant that is knowingly poisoning the water of unsuspecting citizens). Each of these, in its own unique way, asks important questions and should cause us to think about our responses to the various faces of evil in our world.

Prophetic art is always in danger of descending to the level of becoming merely useful propaganda—superficial and full of sloganeering. That kind of art, which is in abundant supply on every side of every issue, usually fails to achieve what it is setting out to do. While propaganda shoves a message in one's face, true prophetic art invites a conversation, full of nuance and complexity.

Prophetic art ultimately seeks for a sort of "conversion" to take place within the heart of the one who hears or sees it. It attempts to awaken the conscience to compassion for the plight of another or challenge people to work to repair an unjust society. Sometimes the purpose of the prophetic artist will be to shock or shame the viewer, awakening them out of a moral slumber and causing them to re-think their commitments. Unlike more triumphalist art, the idea isn't to reinforce what the viewer already believes, but to challenge them to a different way of seeing. Prophetic art is focused on illuminating what its recipient isn't really paying adequate attention to. Such art has a moral urgency. It is meant to make you uncomfortable; it gets up in your grill.

Prophetic art calls those who attend to it to heroism, to find the courage to stand up for others. It can be a way of calling out unrighteousness and inspiring large and small acts of heroism. Our world today needs heroes like this more than it needs superheroes. We need ordinary people who will stand in the way of evil and challenge it. Who will draw lines and question the cultural status quo. Who will refuse to let greed and hatred and lust for power get the final word. Such art can arouse the conscience of those who are morally asleep, and calls us not only to pray and to care, but to act.

This is the kind of heroism we see in Tolkien's *The Lord of the Rings*. In this recounting of an epic mythic quest, the fate of Middle Earth hangs upon very ordinary humble heroes, such as Frodo Baggins and Sam Gamgee. And also, upon very ordinary virtues such as loyalty, integrity, perseverance, and self-sacrifice.

This is the kind of heroism we see in *To Kill a Mockingbird*. Who can forget the scene where Atticus Finch leaves the courtroom and all of the African American spectators in the gallery stand in respect for an ordinary man who would not accept the status quo, and who fought against racism by defending an innocent man in the face of the enormous social pressure that was arrayed against him?

Each of us needs that kind of courage to stand against the evils of our own time, and against the evils that are in our own heart. The arts can help expose what has gone wrong with the world and provide a vantage point for us to step outside our comfort zone and into a bigger and better future. Without imagination, we can only rely on our own feelings and our own experiences and our own finite resources of strength. With imagination, we can picture and embrace new solutions. We can visualize a path forward. We can bypass the limits of our own comfort and stretch toward a better future. We can make art, and partake of art, that is committed to making a difference.

QUESTIONS AND SPIRITUAL EXERCISES

1. What are some instances of social injustice in our world today, and how might these be addressed through the arts?

2. How is the message of the Old Testament prophets relevant for our own time? Which issues they address are still problems in our contemporary world?

3. What does a biblical approach to social injustice involve? How prevalent are these issues in the Bible?

4. Sample some of the music discussed in this chapter. What approaches are these artists taking to social issues? How effective and persuasive do you find them to be?

5. What are some ways that you can become a hero in your world?

CHAPTER TEN

Quiet Places:

Assisting Us in Prayer and Contemplation

I GUESS YOU COULD SAY THAT I HAVE BEEN PRAYING all my life. From a very young age I was taught the simple "Now I lay me down to sleep" prayer, and my grandmother even bought me a little cross-stitched wall-hanging of that prayer, which showed children playing with a puppy, ice skating, and kneeling down at their bedside. I would dutifully follow their example, folding my hands and whispering a list of people whom I asked God to bless when I got to the end of the prayer: mommy, daddy, my sister, my grandparents, and anyone else whom I happened to think of that particular evening. I don't recall ever being bothered by the words, "If I should die before I wake, I pray the Lord my soul to take." Life seemed secure enough that any likelihood of passing away in my sleep seemed distant, and even if I did, the prayer had my eternal destination covered.

I suppose prayer seems a bit more complicated to me these days. In addition to the question of why I need to tell a God who already knows everything that is happening, there are the questions about why some of my most earnest prayers seem to go unanswered and my trivial, off-the-cuff ones sometimes get a seemingly miraculous response. It's all a little puzzling. As I have grown in my faith, though, such questions trouble me much less than they used to. I've begun to see that asking for things I need and want isn't really the major purpose of my prayer life anyway. Instead, I've come to understand prayer more as a sort of dialogue with my Maker, a way of keeping the channels of communication open.

But it's always easy to find excuses not to take the time to pray. I have more to do these days than play with my puppy and ice skates. I have lots of responsibilities to meet, people with whom relationships are tricky, and long to-do lists nagging at the edge of my consciousness. The decisions I have to make are infinitely more complex than when I was a kid, and frankly that often leaves me not really knowing exactly how I should be praying. It's difficult at times to push past all this inner hubbub and quiet myself down enough for prayer to be meaningful time spent with God instead of a duty to check off my list. Focusing and centering myself can be the first challenge for prayer, and this is where the arts have often proven so helpful.

> **The work of artists and musicians and poets can put me in a state of mind that is more receptive, focused, and inspired.**

The work of artists and musicians and poets can put me in a state of mind that is more receptive, focused, and inspired. They can help me find inner stillness. They can usher me into a sense of greater awareness of God. And they can give me words to pray when words seem to fail me. Which is why I'll sometimes listen to a short piece by a favorite composer, a hymn, or a worship chorus before entering a time of prayer, or why I'll read a favorite poem by T. S. Eliot, George Herbert, Mary Oliver, or Gerard Manley Hopkins as a way to kick-start my conversations with God. Engaging with the arts regularly fuels my prayers.

What is prayer? What is its purpose? I've found no better answer to that question than the one provided by George Herbert in his poem, "Prayer (1)," which offers one of the most unforgettable descriptions I have ever come across. The language isn't exactly contemporary, but read it carefully and you'll see what I mean:

> Prayer the Church's banquet, Angels' age,
>> God's breath in man returning to his birth,
>> The soul in paraphrase, heart in pilgrimage,
> The Christian plummet sounding heav'n and earth;
>
> Engine against th' Almighty, sinners' tower,
>> Reversed thunder, Christ-side-piercing spear,
>> The six-days world transposing in an hour,
> A kind of tune, which all things hear and fear;
>
> Softness, and peace, and joy, and love, and bliss,
>> Exalted Manna, gladness of the best,
>> Heaven in ordinary, man well drest,
> The milky way, the bird of Paradise,
>
>> Church-bells beyond the stars heard, the soul's blood,
>> The land of spices; something understood.[1]

With this riotous rush of imagery, Herbert offers us a multifaceted look at what prayer is and what it does. Through the twenty-seven images offered in this short poem, he reminds us of prayer's mystery and its power to transform a life. Considering each of them could easily occupy an entire book all its own. Rather than try to unpack them here, I'd like to suggest that you find some quiet minutes to slowly read and savor each phrase, meditating on what it can tell you about what happens when you lift your heart and voice to God in prayer. I particularly like the line about prayer being a "heart in pilgrimage." Perhaps that, more than anything else, is what prayer feels like to me. It is a process of discovery; learning more about God, and, as a consequence, learning more about myself every time I talk with Him.

Hopefully we can dismiss the idea that the primary purpose of prayer is getting our needs and desires met, as though God were a cosmic valet just waiting to serve up whatever we might request. There has been enough foolishness and nonsense along that line from television preachers and "health and wealth" teachers to bring confusion to many earnest seekers. But we should not let such false teachings keep us from talking with God about the things that are heavy on our hearts. When we are in a relationship with someone, our hopes and dreams and desires and disappointments and desperation are natural topics of conversation. So, it will sometimes be in our conversations with God. When we are facing a health crisis, difficulties in a relationship, trouble at work, a deep sense of loss, or whatever it might be, we ask God to step in and change things, or at the very least help us through the pain. For some, these moments of crisis are really the only time they think to pray; prayer becomes a desperate last grasp at something that might help them in a time of need. Since God is a loving Father, He hears all such prayers. Even the kind of self-centered ones. Which is why Jesus encouraged us to bring our needs to Him.

Sometimes such prayers receive an immediate answer, and when that happens, we call it a miracle. But the very use of the word "miracle" connotes an event that is outside our normal experience. It wouldn't be a miracle if we could count on it every day. Miracles are an exception to the normal order of things.

Sometimes that answer is "wait," and in the waiting we learn that God, in His wisdom, didn't give us what we asked for because the timing was not right. Sometimes answers, when they come, unfold slowly, like a flower in the springtime. They aren't on our preferred schedule.

And sometimes the answer is "no," because we ask for things that might prove harmful to us; because we don't really understand what it is that we need, and what we are asking for is not, in the big picture, even good for us. As James writes, "When you ask, you do not receive, because you ask with wrong motives, that you may spend what you get on your pleasures" (James 4:3). I am thankful for many of the unanswered prayers in my life, because I eventually came to see that there was something better God had in mind. I think it was Martin Luther who wrote that we pray for silver, but sometimes God gives us gold instead. Country artist Garth Brooks has a moving song called "Unanswered Prayers" about coming to realize that he is much better off because God didn't give him what he thought he wanted. Whatever kind of answer we might receive, God is never ignoring our pleas. We might not always get the answer we want or the way we want, but He always answers.

People sometimes speak about "the mystery of unanswered prayer," but the real mystery is why we somehow think our lives should always be filled with pleasure and we should be exempt from pain. If we look at the big picture of Scripture, rather than focusing on scattered verses here and there, we find that many of the great biblical saints, people who had the most intimate experiences with God, were also people whose lives were punctuated with pain and suffering and doubt. And yet, we are invited to pray. We don't have to first puzzle out exactly when we should or shouldn't pray about something that concerns us. We just need to remember that He will only give us good things, but that sometimes His definition of good is not the same as ours.

Prayer isn't primarily about claiming promises or pleading for answers. It is about nurturing a relationship. Can you imagine a meaningful friendship with someone with whom you seldom spent any time, with whom you were rarely vulnerable about your needs, wants, hopes, and desires, and for whom you only made time when it was convenient for you? It wouldn't be much of a relationship.

Praying Hands by Albrecht Dürer, Albertina, Vienna

To have intimacy with another requires both time and vulnerability, and if we want an intimate connection with God it seems to pretty much require the same. Prayer is the beating heart of the spiritual life. It is impossible to imagine authentic spiritual growth without the practice of prayer. Prayer is what transforms religion into a relationship. When we give ourselves to prayer, our faith no longer consists of lofty thoughts and philosophies and doctrines *about* God, but it becomes the basis for a friendship *with* God. The model for prayer that Jesus Himself gave us is based upon a familial closeness; upon the fact that we can address God as "Our Father." This is no mere formal address, but the very foundation upon which prayer rests.

In our prayers we can expose our true selves to God. Any prayer meant to curry favor with Him, demand things from Him, or somehow underline our piety isn't really true prayer. Prayer begins with vulnerability, and vulnerability is a difficult thing for most of us. But we can always consider ourselves safe in being vulnerable with Him. We can share everything that is on our hearts: fears, worries, guilt, aspirations, dreams, desires, and needs. And God bestows upon us the dignity of listening to everything we say—no matter how foolish, self-centered, and self-indulgent it might be. He hears and He cares.

The arts can prepare us for prayer by stilling the heart and mind. One of the biggest obstacles to prayer is the ceaseless inner chatter of our minds and the corresponding ups and downs of our emotions. Martin Laird memorably refers to it as "the cocktail party going on in our heads."[2] There is often a cacophony of clashing inner voices that won't let us focus and settle ourselves to pray. We find ourselves following every fleeting distraction. This state is what the Buddhist monks call "the monkey mind," as they picture their thoughts swinging wildly from branch to branch with no clear direction. With all this going on in our brains, it is no wonder that it is hard to settle down to pray with real concentration.

Silence is such an important part of prayer, but we are surrounded by things that tug at our attention like a dog whose teeth have fastened upon the hem of our trousers. When we pray, it is like when we compose a poem. First, we must compose ourselves. We must give up our fear of the silence and be patient enough to wait for the words to come. And if they don't come quickly, that isn't a problem. Just sitting quietly with God might be one of the highest forms of prayer. As Robert Hudson has suggested, "One important thing that poetry and prayer have in common is that they are not so much forms of expression as forms of expectation, of waiting to see what God, who fills the silence, will do next. They are ways of listening."[3]

The arts can help us throttle down all our random thoughts and babbling musings, and really focus on one thing. Certain works of visual art have proven to be very helpful to me finding such a focus. For example, Claude Monet's lovely winterscape *The Magpie* is a painting that exudes the very essence of peace and quietude. He has captured a moment of absolute stillness in the wintry French country-side. A solitary magpie sits atop the ramshackle gate, surrounded by a stone wall that is, like the trees, covered in a blanket of snow.

Looking at the blue-grey shadows that stretch upon the almost undisturbed ground, I can feel the chill of this winter morning. As I

The Magpie by Claude Monet, Musee d'Orsay, Paris

Wiki Commons

look, I half expect to see my breath, cloudlike, as I pull my coat snug around my body. I can almost hear the soft thud of a clump of snow dropping from the branches above. I stand transfixed. If I pass over such a sight too quickly, I have missed the gift that it is. I have missed an opportunity to find that inner stillness I desire. There are many paintings that have this kind of power to still our inner turmoil and give us a reminder to stop and pray.

There are two very different kinds of paintings that I have found helpful: images of nature and the abstract images of modern art. The images of nature have a calming effect like that of taking a walk in the woods or along the seaside. Sometimes I will sit for an extended period, poring over a book containing the luminous images of the Hudson River School painters. Or I will ponder the glorious black and white nature photography of Ansel Adams, many of whose photographs seem to shout of the glory of God. I find myself wanting to respond, and that response is a prayer.

I've found that certain works of modern art can also be very effective as a tool for putting myself in a contemplative space. An abstract or non-objective painting does not allow us to easily identify the subject matter of the painting and then move on. Instead, because it lacks a recognizable subject, we are freed to look slowly and patiently, letting our eyes travel over the entire expanse of the canvas. I have found that the work of Mark Rothko engages me in this way, as in the staggering paintings in the Rothko Chapel in Houston, as do the vibrant explosions of color in the work of Wassily Kandinsky, who believed that colors had the power to communicate spiritual and emotional states, or very minimalist paintings like "The Stations of the Cross" series by Barnett Newman, which ask me to focus on a solitary line against a single colored background.

One of my favorite contemporary painters is the Japanese American artist Makoto Fujimura, an outspoken Christian whose work has received widespread acclaim throughout the art world. His paintings are not generally images of any particular object in our world, but rather are a world in themselves. They demand slow and patient looking. They cannot be grasped in a glance but require the viewer to take time with them. A painter who grinds his own pigments out of precious minerals, his work accentuates the physicality of the colors and materials that are found in nature. His is a grounded abstraction.

Fujimura often applies the pigments in semi-transparent layers, which, in effect, trap light within and between them, and allow it to shine through with an effect that cannot be fully experienced without seeing one of these paintings in all their physical glory. There is a resulting depth and ambiguity to what you are seeing, and a surface that seems alive. As he writes of the process, "Coarser mineral pigments, being literally sand, create ripples of color when allowed to cascade down. I stand the painting against the wall, and using broader strokes with abundant water, let the pigments cover the painting. When displayed in a gallery, the pigments reflect the light and shimmer like stars."[4]

So, what does this have to do with prayer and contemplation? Fujimura uses the biblical story of Mary pouring perfume upon Jesus' travel-weary feet to explain. "The act of painting with precious minerals is like Mary anointing the feet of Jesus . . . I desire to transform the metaphorical language of abstraction and make the reality of Mary's act of adoration come alive today. In this sense, my work is not 'abstract;' it is a representational depiction of God's space."[5]

Fujimura's paintings ask us to stand reverently before a mystery and let it be a revelation to us. For those who cannot see how an abstraction can point toward God, Fujimura answers in an essay entitled "How to 'See' My Painting":

> Art can train us to "see" with our eyes, or even "listen"
> through our eyes, and that experience can help to tap into
> the "eyes of your heart." Your faith journey depends on
> being able to see things through these eyes, to see through
> the "dangers of the world" to the "mystery of the Gospel"
> that St. Paul speaks of.
>
> So, after seeing my work, my desire is that you open
> the eyes of your heart, and see the world and the people
> around you a little differently. Instead of being filled with
> anxiety about the world, we can truly see the prismatic
> possibilities of the world around us.[6]

Opening the eyes of our heart is an excellent preparation for heart-to-heart communication with God.

John Drury has suggested that art "entails a contemplative waiting upon them [the paintings] which puts us alongside those who painted and viewed them so devoutly by putting us in the realm of prayer, with its passive expectancy, its active openness."[7] This openness can be a gateway to prayer.

So, what do we do when we can't seem to find the words to express what we want to say to God? Perhaps we can draw an example from modern courtship. When it comes to a budding romance, there are few things as effective for letting someone know your thoughts and feelings than in sharing with them a poem or a song that causes you to think of them. Sometimes the right poem or song can perfectly express those deep feelings for which you can't find the words. And the one who receives the gift of a song or a poem knows that you chose them specifically for them, as an expression of your passion. Even though they know the words are not actually your own, they are treasured just as though they had come from your own mouth or pen.

Similarly, we should not be afraid to use the words of others as guides in our praying. Praying written prayers can be a wonderful addition to your prayer experience. One of the things they accomplish is relieving us of the necessity of finding the right words and let us just focus on the sentiment we want to raise before God. Both written and extemporaneous prayers can be part of our practice. I think that God treasures our fumbling attempts to express what is in our hearts, no matter how halting and unpoetic they may be. To Him, these are as beautiful as the prayers of the most poetically gifted saint.

Though God loves our imperfect prayers, sometimes we can all use a little help in finding the right words to express ourselves from the prayers of others. Praying written prayers is a practice I have followed in my own spiritual journey, and it has enriched my life as I have slowly savored the great prayers of the past and expanded my own vocabulary of prayer. I even published a little collection of some of my favorite prayers from across the centuries that have been particularly helpful to me.[8] Included in it are prayers that we love due to their beauty of expression, or their soul-searching honesty, or for the window they give us into God's love and our own weakness.

When we pray the prayers of others, we can embrace the way they have captured things that we feel but didn't know how to put into words. We are reminded of how universal our spiritual longings and spiritual struggles really are. Joining them in prayer, we are joining that great chorus of petitioners down through the centuries who sought

God with fierce passion. And there is something special about the fact that many of these prayers have been repeated countless times by other people of faith who found focus, solace, and a deeper experience with God through these shared words. We have no hesitation about singing hymns of praise that were penned by others, so why should we be shy about using the prayers of others to lift our hearts toward God? One that I have prayed many times is this prayer from Thomas Merton, who was not only an insightful writer on the spiritual life, but also a published poet. I can so easily identify with the honesty of his prayer:

> My Lord God, I have no idea where I am going. I do not see
> the road ahead of me. I cannot know for certain where it will
> end. Nor do I really know myself, and the fact that I think
> I am following your will does not mean that I am actually
> doing so. But I believe that the desire to please you does in
> fact please you. And I hope I have that desire in all that I am
> doing. I hope that I will never do anything apart from that
> desire. And I know that if I do this you will lead me by the
> right road, though I may know nothing about it. Therefore I
> will trust you always though I may seem to be lost and in the
> shadow of death. I will not fear, for you are ever with me,
> and you will never leave me to face my perils alone.[9]

I could not have said it better myself, which is the whole point of using the written prayers of others. Merton provides the words for what is in my heart, and so I offer them to God as my own.

In addition to such written prayers, I have found that poetry can be a powerful tool for expressing my heart toward God, especially the prayer poems of writers like George Herbert, Gerard Manley

Hopkins, Thomas Traherne, and John Donne.

George Herbert's poem "The Call," for example, is a poetic invitation for God to invade every area of our lives, and his constant use of the personal pronoun "my" allows us to make this a prayer of our own. It is a poem of gratitude and celebration for the One who calls us:

> Come, my Way, my Truth, my Life:
> Such a Way, as gives us breath:
> Such a Truth, as ends all strife:
> Such a Life, as killeth death.
>
> Come, my Light, my Feast, my Strength:
> Such a Light, as shows a Feast:
> Such a Feast, as mends at length:
> Such a Strength, as makes his guest.
>
> Come, my Joy, my Love, my Heart:
> Such a Joy as none can move:
> Such a Love, as none can part:
> Such a Heart, as joys in love.[10]

If the previous prayer poem by George Herbert is a summons for God's active presence in each of our lives, the following prayer poem by John Donne can be a model for honest confession and a cry for healing:

> Batter my heart, three-personed God; for, You
> As yet but knock, breathe, shine, and seek to mend;
> That I may rise and stand, o'erthrow me, and bend
> Your force, to break, blow, burn, and make me new.
> I, like an usurped town to, another due,
> Labour to admit you, but oh, to no end,
> Reason your viceroy in me, me should defend,
> But is captived, and proves weak or untrue.
> Yet dearly I love You, and would be loved fain,

But am bethrothed unto your enemy:
Divorce me, untie, or break that knot again,
Take me to you, imprison me, for I
Except you enthrall me, never shall be free,
Nor ever chaste, except you ravish me.[11]

Donne understands that he is a slave to sin, with a mind and heart easily captivated by evil purposes. He is bold enough to plead for the violent disruption of grace into his life, for he knows that only God can rescue him and make him free from sin's imprisonment. The poem, "Holy Sonnet XIV," is the kind of honest cry for help that should sometimes be a part of all our prayers.

I have found that novels and short stories can be valuable for helping me step outside myself and get a clearer picture of my own sinfulness. They can be like a mirror in which I see unflattering aspects of myself in the characters I am reading about. For example, the short stories of Flannery O'Connor are especially good for helping me see my own hypocrisies and giving me a glimpse of the magnitude of sin even among the "Good People." There are, she tells us through the vehicle of her sometimes shocking stories, no truly good people. We are all in need of grace.

In all the messiness of life in a broken world, I regularly make the wrong decisions or turn in the wrong direction. My selfishness and carelessness sometimes hurt others. I say the wrong thing, sometimes even when I *know* it is the wrong thing. I follow pleasures of the moment and neglect the eternal priorities I should be following. *The Book of Common Prayer* gives me words for my situation: "Most merciful God, we confess that we have sinned against Thee in thought, word, and deed; by what we have done, and by what we have left undone."[12] This perfectly encapsulates the reality in which we live— all of us broken and breaking others, all of us hurting and hurting others, all of us ashamed and intent on shaming others.

It is best not to pretty up this reality with fancy evasions or psychological explanations. Instead, it is much better to recognize it and call it what it is: sin. It isn't surprising that we should feel embarrassment and recognize our shortcomings when we approach God in prayer. He knows our actions and, more frighteningly, knows our thoughts. When we come to Him in prayer, we come with all our imperfections, or we do not come at all.

All the baggage we carry can become the thing that seems to separate us from God, or we can acknowledge our sin and accept forgiveness. "If we confess our sins," the apostle John writes, "he is faithful and just and will forgive us our sins and purify us from all unrighteousness" (1 John 1:9). Receiving that forgiveness is the result of our vulnerability, our willingness to own up and say that we are sorry. Just as in every other relationship in our life, it is often the unspoken and hidden things that are the most damaging. Solving any relationship problem usually begins with talking it out. In confession I can talk it out with God. Since I live in constant need of forgiveness, my acknowledgment of that fact is what keeps the channel of communication clear and unhindered.

One poem that has become an inexhaustible source of inspiration for me is T. S. Eliot's *Four Quartets*. Eliot uses exalted poetic language to say things that almost cannot be said, as he weds his imagery to a mystical wisdom that is specifically Christian, drawing on such writers as John of the Cross, Julian of Norwich, and the anonymous author of *The Cloud of Unknowing*. He tackles such themes as time, memory, human suffering, and the nature of a living faith. As he attempts to encompass these weighty topics, he also reflects upon the limits of language for expressing them: "Words strain / Crack and sometimes break, under the burden / Under the tension, slip, slide, perish / Decay with imprecision, will not stay in place."[13] (I have felt the reality of this description on every page of this book as I have tried to put words around the topic of beauty and art and faith).

But in spite of the difficulty, Eliot wrestles memorably to find the words to explore the only hope for humanity—the God who is found both in the Word and in the silence. Numerous are the times I have tucked this small volume under my arm and found a quiet place outdoors to read it slowly and let it provide me with fodder for my prayers.

If you want to appreciate a poem, you must slow down and read it carefully, ruminating over each line; exploring the ambiguities, uncovering the metaphors, and taking notice of how each line and word is related to each other. Prayer is similar in many ways. We should not rush to finish, and we should not be afraid of the silences between the sentences. With both poetry and prayer, we should not rush to speak what we already know, but to be open to the impartation of new meanings and new understandings in our relationship with God.

We might use the classic methodology of *lectio divina* that believers have used for centuries when they read Scripture. This way of reading emphasized slowing down to consider the text word by word, phrase by phrase, thereby taking in the fulness of what is being offered and then turning it back to God in prayer. Each insight, sometimes several for each verse, would become something to be used for praying, whether it might suggest praise, confession, intercession, or whatever.

John LeClercq wrote of this method of meditating on Scripture:

To meditate is to attach oneself closely to the sentence

being recited and weigh all its words in order to sound
the depths of their full meaning. It means assimilating the
content of a text by means of a kind of meditation which
releases its full flavor. . . . The Holy Scripture is the well
of Jacob from which the waters are drawn which will be
poured out later in prayer.[14]

Similarly, we can approach a poem as a text that might inspire us
to understand more deeply, and then to respond in prayer. Of course,
not every poem is usable in this way, but if you are willing to be a little
adventurous you might find unexpected spiritual riches in even the
most unlikely of places.

Prayer is a love poem to a loving God. We offer love and appreciation,
not primarily for what God has done for us, but for who He is. Such
praise is often triggered by reminders of God's glory, such as what I
experienced recently on a drive home from work. The sun was setting,
and the sky was lit up as though there was a fire ablaze somewhere in
the heavens. I was filled with a sense of deepest awe, and words of praise
rose unbidden from deep inside. As I drove, I could not find the words
for what I was feeling, so I sang the hymn "Be Thou My Vision." As one
wise saint once suggested, the person who sings prays twice.

If I was paying better attention to the gifts God has so lavishly
strewn around me, I would probably have an experience like that
every day. There is so much to appreciate, and so much to be thankful
for. An important element of prayer can be found in the expression of
such a realization, and a mindset of receptivity to the glories we see all
around us. As the great English spiritual writer William Law wrote:

> Receive, therefore, every day as a resurrection from death,
> as a new enjoyment of life, meet every rising sun with such
> sentiments of God's goodness as if you had seen it and
> all things new created upon your account, and under the
> sense of so great a blessing let your joyful heart praise and
> magnify so good and glorious a Creator.[15]

Praise music is all about putting such sentiments to a musical accompaniment. Many of the greatest hymns and worship songs can give us words when words fail us.

So can the great choral arrangements of Scripture passages by classical musicians. Handel's *Messiah*, for example, is a great storehouse of biblical riches, using key Old Testament and New Testament passages to inspire the listener with the story of redemption. Bach's *St. Matthew Passion* is a powerful setting of the latter chapters of the Gospel of Matthew. Haydn sets the opening chapters of Genesis to music in *The Creation*. Stravinsky created a choral masterpiece from the Psalms in *Symphony of Psalms*. Then there are the settings of the Mass or Requiems by the likes of Mozart, Beethoven, Shubert, Brahms, Faure, and countless others.

One of my favorite contemporary composers is Arvo Pärt, a committed Orthodox Christian who is well-read in theology and spirituality. One of his favorite books is also one of mine, *The Imitation of Christ*. Most of Pärt's music is built around religious ideas and sacred texts, yet it is even beloved by many non-believers for its quiet, calming effect. His works offer what can only be described as an intense quietude. Whether choral or instrumental, his music is sonically dense and complex, but somehow sounds simple and pared down. Some have referred to Pärt's music as "holy minimalism." While he resists that description, it accurately captures the mood that his music creates; an almost otherworldly sense of peace and calm for those who listen. As I listen to one of his compositions, they often transport me to a higher awareness of God's presence, and they quiet my inner turmoil. In a way I can't explain, they draw me closer to God. He has written music that sounds eternal, which puts my heart in a place of receptivity and prayer. His music sets aside the sweeping romanticism so common to many religious compositions and offers instead a music that is marked by tranquility and contemplation.

When our prayers are not in the context of our personal time with God, they are usually occurring in a congregational setting in a place set aside for worship. Here our music gives wings to our prayers. What would our worship services be like without music? The instrumental and choral and congregational singing give voice to our feelings and commitments, they inspire, they console, they provide a glimpse of the glory of God, they connect us with other worshippers, they testify of God's greatness, and they lift our hearts.

Henry Ward Beecher offered an unforgettable picture of the effect of an organ on a group of worshippers:

> I am accustomed to think of a congregation with an organ
> as of a fleet of boats in the harbor, or on the waters. The
> organ is the flood, and the people are the boats; and they
> are buoyed up and carried along upon its current as boats
> are borne upon the depths of the sea. So, aside from mere
> musical reasons, there is this power that comes upon
> people, that encircles them, that fills them—this great,
> mighty ocean-tone; and that helps them to sing.[16]

What he says about the organ could be extended to the piano or to the modern worship band. The music carries us forward in unison; while the music plays, we are one. Music calls forth a host of metaphors that occur again and again in common speech and speaks to fundamental realities about our lives. Consider, for example, how often we talk about a situation being "harmonious" or "discordant," or about the tempo of life, or the need to improvise, about something being finely tuned, about reaching a crescendo or a fevered pitch, how a truth resonates, how we might need to jazz things up, and about modulating the tone of a discussion. Music gives us so many of our best metaphors about communication, and prayer is, at its root, all about communicating with God.

Hymns have always had an important place in the church, beyond just their uses for congregational singing. In the early church they were used to confirm and promote orthodox theology against its heretical opponents. In the medieval church, they focused on the mystery of the presence of God in the sacraments. In the Reformation, they proclaimed a rediscovered understanding of faith, grace, and justification. In the African American spiritual tradition they offered a vision of freedom from bondage in this world and the next. In the guise of worship songs, they have focused on the worshipper's personal connection with God. And in the modern social reawakening, they call us to action against injustice and inequality. Throughout the history of the church, hymns have been an indispensable companion for the journey.

The greatest of all hymns can be found right there in the center of our Bibles in the book of Psalms. The musical poetry of the Psalms has been a part of worship from the days of the Hebrews to our modern Christian congregations. From the very beginnings of the monastic movement, for example, the singing and chanting of the Psalms was a regular part of their daily devotion. Perhaps, in our own way, we can join in by indulging our ears with a recording of Gregorian chants. I have a dear friend who finds herself easily stressed and made physically sick by too many loud noises. In our day and age, such a racket isn't easy to avoid, so when she finds herself especially anxious or tense, she puts in her earbuds and, in her own words, "listens to my monks." She never fails to find the chants calming and healing. The fifth-century spiritual theologian John Cassian had some helpful words to offer about singing the Psalms:

> He will take into himself all the thoughts of the Psalms and will begin to sing them in such a way that he will utter them with the deepest emotion of heart not as if they were the compositions of the Psalmist, but rather as if they were his own utterances and his very own prayer; and will certainly take them as aimed at himself, and will recognize that their words were not only fulfilled formerly by or in the person of the prophet, but that they are fulfilled and carried out daily in his own case.[17]

As Cassian suggests, we can make the Psalms our own. We can let their words help us to praise God, confess our sin, appeal for help, or glory in God's created world. They are a treasure that continues to reveal themselves. Modern singer songwriters have mined the Psalms for expressions of praise and worship. A number of the best contemporary worship songs are paraphrases of various psalms. So is U2's song "40." John Michael Talbot has set many of them to music over the course of numerous albums. Even a songwriter like Sinead O'Connor, whose own wandering spiritual journey can be perplexing at times, released an album entitled *Theology* during one phase of her career that contained heartfelt and gorgeous songs based mostly on the Psalms. It is an album I return to with regularity.

Both C. S. Lewis and Dietrich Bonhoeffer have written memorably about the idea that the Psalms are a prayer book for the Christian.[18] When we can speak or sing the Psalms, we will discover the transformative power of praise within them. They are poetry that is on fire with a longing for God.

Prayer doesn't end when we finish speaking. Prayer is also about listening. Prayer is not like putting a message in a bottle and tossing it into the sea of eternity, where we hope it will reach its destination, but we never know for sure. Instead, prayer should be like a phone call, with much back and forth. It takes two people to have a conversation, and prayer is, at heart, a conversation. Of course, we are not listening for an audible voice. Instead, we listen for a voice that arises from within, from the quiet depths of our hearts. It isn't about "hearing voices," but about becoming attuned to God's quiet inner nudges. Which is why an interior silence is so important for prayers of listening. God speaks, as He did to Elijah on the mountain, not in the storms and fires of our ecstatic emotional experiences, as in a quiet "still small voice" (1 Kings 19:9–13 KJV).

My most profound experiences of prayer, the ones that have truly changed me, are usually the ones that are birthed in an inner silence. In Psalm 62:5, the psalmist speaks to himself, and these words are relevant for you and me, "My soul, wait in silence for God only" (NASB). And in Psalm 46:10, we find the familiar command: "Be still, and know that I am God." There is something life-transforming about resting in a quiet consciousness of God's presence, which can best be encountered in silence.

It marked a turning point in my own prayer life when I discovered a small book entitled *The Practice of the Presence of God*, which opened my eyes to a simple but powerful form of prayer, the usually wordless prayer of presence. This form of prayer consists of simply placing yourself in the presence of God and enjoying the fellowship of close intimacy with Him.

God is always with us. But are we aware of His presence? Such an awareness can grow in us as we seek to be conscious of God during all the activities of our day, and when we set aside time for silent listening or for just resting in that presence. Our prayers don't always have to involve words. In everything we do, we can find the solace that He is with us.

So, whether I am sitting at my desk at work, playing a round of golf, listening to a piece of music, gazing at a painting, reading a book, sitting in the waiting room at my physician's office, taking a walk, or doing dishes (just like Lawrence), I can call to mind that I am in the very presence of God, and I can lift my heart toward Him in wordless prayers of love and appreciation. Practicing His presence has the power to transform every activity of my life, and it causes me to long even more for those moments when I can find an opportunity to sit in quiet contemplation and rest in His presence.

Sometimes a painting or drawing can put me in mind of praying and inspire me to stop what I am doing and talk with God. An example might be the popular Albrecht Dürer woodcut called "Praying Hands," with its weathered, well-veined, world-worn hands folded in prayer.

One of my favorite visual calls to prayer is Jean-François Millet's "The Angelus." While many of his contemporaries were busy painting urban scenes of life in the cities, Millet chose to focus his talents on depicting the lives of the peasants and farmers in the rural countryside.

In this painting, he calls our attention to the moment when a farmer and his wife have put aside their tools and lower their heads in prayer. It is a quiet and sacred moment of stillness. The sky is bright with the announcement of the nearness of the day's end. The farmer has removed his hat out of respect for God and clutches it close to his body. His wife sets aside the basket of potatoes she has been gathering, and reverently folds her hands as she bows her head. This moment is probably in response to the bells ringing out from the church whose steeple rises in the distance, their

The Angelus by Jean-Francois Millet, Musee d'Orsay, Paris

sound a summons to prayer. Millet has created an image of gratitude, of thankfulness for the small blessings of life, and it serves as a reminder that prayer should be a central activity of each of our lives; that we are invited to refocus our eyes—away from life's struggles and hardships, and onto the God who is present with us in every detail of every day. Maybe we just need a reminder to stop and acknowledge His grace. Sometimes art, music, or literature will provide just such a reminder.

QUESTIONS AND SPIRITUAL EXERCISES

1. Write a poem that you can use as a prayer. This is likely just for your own use, so don't be worried about its aesthetic quality as much as its authenticity.

2. Find a collection of prayers written by others and look for prayers that say the things you'd like to communicate to God. You might even want to start a notebook and gather some favorites you can use often.

3. Choose a piece of art from the pages of this book (or another favorite), and let it be an inspiration for a time of prayer. What thoughts arise that you want to place before God as you look at the art?

4. Get a hymnbook and try praying some of the hymns. Which ones are especially meaningful to you?

5. Create your own "sacred space" for praying. What art or books might you place in that space?

6. Memorize a short poem or a couple stanzas of a longer one. Or write it out on a 3x5 card or slip of paper. Carry it with you for a week or two, and refer to it often, until it becomes part of your "mental furniture."

CHAPTER ELEVEN

Soul Food:

Resources for Your Spiritual Journey

EVERY YEAR I TAKE A PERSONAL SPIRITUAL RETREAT—a few days away to reexamine the direction of my life and an opportunity to ask some new questions about where I need to refocus. Often I'll drive out to the Oregon coast, where there will be an opportunity to walk along the beach, watch the waves march in and retreat, and stare out upon the vastness of the ocean, looking out to where it seems to become one with the sky. Other times I'll head up into the mountains, where I can smell the sweetness of the pine forests, ramble along pathways lined with giant trees, and hear the streams gurgle along their way over the rocks and then come roaring down in waterfalls. Less frequently I will head to a large city, where I can get a downtown hotel room from which to go exploring, walking along the streets and listening to the hiss of tires, the low roar of automobiles, and the babble of unknown strangers as I meander the streets and lose myself in the anonymity of the urban setting. Each setting has something to teach me, and each offers me different opportunities for praying and meditating on my life and how God is working in it. Variety is good.

For my times of retreat, I will sometimes take a little food along with me, maybe something that fits the environment. Or maybe I will look for a restaurant that has just the right kind of food for that setting. At the coast, I'll sample some seafood. In the mountains I might grill a hot dog over the fire or indulge in some s'mores. In the city I might investigate some interesting new cuisine I haven't tried or visit a small restaurant that just looks interesting. Variety is good.

Variety is a good thing in our spiritual journey as well, especially when it comes to feeding ourselves with art, music, literature, or film. It can become easy to fall back on what is familiar to us, always listening to the same music, re-watching the same films, and falling back on the delights of familiar authors. Some of this "comfort food" might be wonderful and affirming. It feels good and familiar; it might just hit the spot. Then there is the creative "fast food" that we can snack on when we don't want to bother with a full meal. Both comfort food and fast food can be tasty, but you don't want to make either one your only nutritional source or your only source of gastronomic pleasure. Such food is often utilitarian. It provides immediate satisfaction and the cessation of hunger, but it really doesn't satisfy at the deepest level. And as much as you might enjoy any particular cuisine, you'll eventually grow tired of it if you eat it too often. The law of diminishing return can affect our diet.

Why should we be willing to settle for a steady diet consisting of the convenience of fast food or the safe dependability of comfort food when there is so much more we can experience? Why would we settle, then, for an aesthetic diet of easily digestible movies, television, popular music, and bestsellers when we have available to us the work of the master chefs of the imagination, artists and musicians and writers and filmmakers who have cooked for us a spiritual, intellectual, and emotional feast—a feast that offers savory and unforgettable new flavors to enjoy, to feed our soul, and with which to enhance our lives?

You can think of this last chapter as a menu for a lifetime of feasting. Hey, it's even got more options than that huge menu at the Cheesecake Factory, and all of them are awaiting your inspection and enjoyment—to read, listen, watch, look, and explore. You probably won't like everything on these lists (though I have enjoyed all of them at one time or another). For you, some of my suggestions might be like Indian food has been for me. At first, I didn't care much for it, and it took me a little while to learn to appreciate it. But I'm glad I hung in there, for now I have discovered it has flavors I've never experienced elsewhere.

You might need to be patient. You might need to stretch yourself. And a lot of these artistic dishes are a bit on the spicy side. You'll find suggestions on some of the lists for books and films and recordings that are most definitely not family-friendly but deal with hard issues that adults really can't afford to ignore, even if they aren't comfortable to talk about. These lists are meant to expose you to great works of art, and many of them aren't by fellow believers. I've cast my net wide.

Sometimes the work of non-believers, seekers, and strugglers has inspired me more than the safer creations of fellow believers. They have taught me to be honest about my feelings, ask better questions, and more deeply understand the complexities of human experience. Every Christian is also a human being, and as such we mostly share the same questions and struggles as our fellow residents of this planet. I find it disappointing that sometimes Christian art, in a mistaken attempt to be safe and uplifting and inspiring, doesn't actually come across like it was created by a real living, breathing, struggling person. If you are paying any attention at all, you know that life isn't always safe and uplifting and inspiring. In fact, there is much in the Bible itself that frankly isn't very safe or uplifting or inspiring. A lot of it is hard and confusing and maybe even occasionally puzzling or off-putting. It is a book that tells the stories of real people who are often really messed up. Why would we want to create art that doesn't have this same connection to real life? God meets people in all the messiness of their lives. After all, isn't that the meaning of grace?

That doesn't mean that discernment isn't important. Not all art is good for you. Some of it is nihilistic, pornographic, and just plain hopeless. Such work is probably best ignored, especially if it touches on things that you struggle with in your own life or might cause you to stumble. Even then, such art can be a window into the hearts and minds of the people you and I rub shoulders with day in and day out. If we want to have more meaningful spiritual conversations with them, it can help to know where they are coming from, and art can be the most helpful window into their souls. What moves them, and why?

The arts can help make you a better person, but only when they are wedded to a life of integrity and spiritual discipline.

Still, caution can be wisdom. Just don't be so cautious that you insulate yourself from the darker realities of human existence. If you do, your words to others about the good news may come across as merely empty inspirational aspirations that are detached from real life.

One final caveat before the lists. And this is important. It may be obvious, but it probably needs to be said: Despite all the things I have shared in this book about using the arts to deepen your spiritual experience, developing a love for the arts will not necessarily make you a better Christian. In fact, there is always the danger that it might just make you an insufferable aesthetic snob. The arts are not a badge of superiority. Partaking of them doesn't automatically make you a better person. Don't forget that some of the men who worked as guards and administrators in the Nazi concentration camps went home at night and listened with serene pleasure to their recordings of Mozart and Beethoven. The arts can help make you a better person, but only when they are wedded to a life of integrity and spiritual discipline. Partaking of great art should not, of course, be a substitute for engaging with the spiritual disciplines. But the arts are something we can use alongside them. Your prayer, Bible reading, church attendance, and other spiritual practices can be enhanced by the arts, but certainly can't replace them.

The following suggestions are very personal in nature. I've put them in short categorized lists just for fun. These are poems, novels, films, paintings, and pieces of music that have inspired me and others. The list is unapologetically personal, but I hope you might find joy and insight in exploring some of them. While some affirm the glories of faith, others are more focused on seeking for spiritual truth, or the struggle to be a good human being. We probably need all these perspectives if we are going to let the arts transform our lives.

If you have suggestions for great stuff that I haven't listed in all of these categories (and maybe haven't discovered yet), I'd love to hear your suggestions. I'm planning a spot on my website (www.terry-glaspey.com) to post these for all of us to enjoy.

Poetry has been a much-valued companion on my spiritual journey, and often an impetus toward prayer. The best of the poets have caused me to think more deeply about my life and my experience with God, as well as teaching me to pay closer attention to the world around me. Here are a couple of lists of poets whom I especially treasure as fellow travelers on the spiritual path, though it pains me to consider how many wonderful voices I haven't been able to include in the service of brevity. These provide, at least, a good place to get started on your personal exploration of the world of poetry.

Ten of My Favorite Christian Poets

1. Gerard Manley Hopkins
2. T. S. Eliot
3. George Herbert
4. John Donne
5. Thomas Merton
6. Malcolm Guite
7. Wendell Berry
8. Steve Turner
9. Luci Shaw
10. Thomas Traherne

Ten Favorite Poets Who Are Spiritual Seekers, and May, Or May Not, Be Believers

1. Mary Oliver
2. Antonio Machado
3. Czesław Miłosz
4. William Wordsworth
5. Rainer Maria Rilke
6. Denise Levertov
7. Emily Dickinson
8. Seamus Heaney
9. William Carlos Williams
10. Rumi

If you haven't read much poetry and want to sample some great poets, the best way to begin might be through browsing through an anthology of poems. Here are a handful of my favorites:

Sister Wendy Beckett, ed., *Speaking to the Heart* (New York: Carroll and Graf Publishers, 2006)

Mark S. Burrows, ed., *The Paraclete Poetry Anthology* (Brewster, MA: Paraclete Press, 2016)

William Harmon, ed., *The Top 500 Poems* (New York: Columbia University Press, 1992)

Roger Housden, ed., *Risking Everything* (New York: Harmony Books, 2003)

Czesław Miłocz, ed., *A Book of Luminous Things* (New York: Harcourt Brace and Company, 1996)

Ben Witherington III and Christopher Mead Armitage, eds., *The Poetry of Piety* (Grand Rapids, MI: Baker Books, 2002)

And here are a handful of books that take a deeper look at the art of poetry:

Malcolm Guite, *Faith, Hope, and Poetry* (London: Routledge, 2008)

Edward Hirsch, *How to Read a Poem* (New York: Harcourt Books, 1999)

Robert Hudson, *The Art of the Almost Said* (Friendswood, TX: Bold Vision Books, 2019)

Marilyn McEntyre, *When Poets Pray* (Grand Rapids, MI: William B. Eerdmans, 2019)

Someone once said that writing about music is like dancing about architecture. It's hard to really understand how music moves our heart and emotions so powerfully, but we have all felt it do so. Music can connect us with memories, quicken our pulse, create a mood, settle our thoughts, or set our feet to dancing. But music is one of the places where it is easy to get into an aesthetic rut. We all know people who will only listen to classical music, only listen to jazz, only listen to contemporary Christian music, only listen to country, or only listen to the top contemporary singers and songwriters. To limit ourselves in this way is to miss the grand variety that is available to us, a buffet of riches of all sorts. I have learned to appreciate just about every kind of music out there, and you can too.

Here are a few admittedly inadequate lists for beginning your exploration. Those with expertise in any of the genres can testify to the inadequacy of my suggestions. I can hear them saying, "Yes, but what about _____?" You can fill in the blank. I doubt that any of these imagined critics would not agree with the greatness of the pieces included in these sparse recommendations, though I admit to being not as up-to-date on great new musical artists as I'd like to be.

Twelve Great Works of Classical Music by Christians

1. Johann Sebastian Bach, *St. Matthew Passion* (also explore *Magnificat*, *The Mass in B Minor*, and his cantatas)
2. George Frideric Handel, *The Messiah*
3. Franz Joseph Haydn, *The Creation*
4. Wolfgang Amadeus Mozart, *The Requiem*
5. Henryk Górecki, *The Symphony of Sorrowful Songs (#3)*
6. Olivier Messiaen, *Quartet for the End of Time*
7. Anton Bruckner, Psalm settings
8. Felix Mendelssohn, *The Reformation Symphony (#5)*
9. Arvo Pärt, *Tabula Rasa* (and numerous similar works)
10. Tomás Luis de Victoria, Sacred Choral Music
11. Francis Poulenc, *Dialogues of the Carmelites* (an opera)
12. Gregorian Chants (there are many good collections available)

Fifteen Great Works of Classical Music That Never Fail to Lift My Spirits

1. Johann Sebastian Bach, *The Brandenburg Concertos*
2. Samuel Barber, *Adagio for Strings*
3. Ludwig van Beethoven, *Pastoral Symphony (#6)*
4. Frédéric Chopin, Piano music
5. Aaron Copland, *Appalachian Spring*
6. Antonín Dvořárak, *The New World Symphony (#9)*
7. Gerald Finzi, *Clarinet Concerto*
8. George Gershwin, *Rhapsody in Blue*
9. Wolfgang Amadeus Mozart, *Eine Kleine Nachtmusik*
10. Franz Schubert, *The Trout Quintet*

11. Jean Sibelius, *Finlandia*
12. Bedřich Smetana, *The Moldau*
13. Johann Strauss II, Waltzes
14. Antonio Vivaldi, *The Four Seasons*
15. Ralph Vaughan Williams, *The Lark Ascending*

Eleven Indisputably Great Works of Jazz

1. Louis Armstrong, *Hot Fives*
2. Art Blakey and the Jazz Messengers, *Moanin'*
3. Dave Brubeck, *Time Out*
4. John Coltrane, *A Love Supreme*
5. Miles Davis, *Kind of Blue*
6. Duke Ellington, *Live at Newport 1956*
7. Billie Holiday & Lester Young, *A Musical Romance*
8. Charles Mingus, *Mingus Ah Um*
9. Sonny Rollins, *Way Out West*
10. Thelonious Monk, *Brilliant Corners*
11. Weather Report, *Heavy Weather*

Twenty-Four Great Modern Christian Musicians

1. Bob Bennett, esp. *Matters of the Heart*
2. T-Bone Burnett, esp. *Truth Decay, The Criminal Under My Own Hat*
3. The Call, esp. *Let the Day Begin, Reconciled*
4. Kate Campbell, esp. *Visions of Plenty, Rosaryville*
5. Michael Card, esp. *The Ancient Faith, The Life*
6. Johnny Cash, esp. *Johnny Cash at San Quentin, The Gospel Road*
7. James Cleveland, *Greatest Hits*
8. Bruce Cockburn, esp. *Dancing in the Dragon's Jaws, Humans, Bone on Bone*
9. Daniel Amos, esp. *The Alarma Chronicles, MotorCycle, Mr. Buechner's Dream*
10. Bob Dylan, esp. *Blood on the Tracks, Slow Train Coming, Infidels*
11. Aretha Franklin, esp. *One Lord, One Faith, One Baptism*
12. Keith Green, esp. *For Him Who Has Ears, No Compromise*

13. Mark Heard, esp. *Victims of the Age, Dry Bones Dance, Second Hand*
14. Garth Hewitt, esp. *Love Song for the Earth, Scars, Stealing Jesus Back*
15. Mahalia Jackson, esp. *Gospels, Spirituals, and Hymns, Everytime I Feel the Spirit*
16. Rich Mullins, esp. *The World as Best As I Remember It, Volume 2, A Liturgy, a Legacy, and a Ragamuffin Band*
17. Larry Norman, esp. *Only Visiting This Planet, So Long Ago the Garden, In Another Land*
18. Over the Rhine, esp. *Good Dog, Bad Dog, Drunkard's Prayer*
19. Pierce Pettis, esp. *While the Serpent Lies Sleeping, Making Light of It, Everything Matters*
20. Randy Stonehill, esp. *Welcome to Paradise, Equator, Return to Paradise*
21. John Michael Talbot, esp. *Come to the Quiet, The Painter, Troubadour of the Great King*
22. U2, esp. *War, The Joshua Tree, All That You Can't Leave Behind*
23. David Wilcox, esp. *Big Horizon, Turning Point*
24. Hank Williams, esp. *Greatest Hits*

Fifteen Spiritual Seekers in Modern Music

1. Arcade Fire, esp. *Neon Bible*
2. Bright Eyes, esp. *I'm Wide Awake, It's Morning, Lifted*
3. The Byrds, *Sweetheart of the Rodeo*
4. Nick Cave, *Abattior Blues/The Lyre of Orpheus, Skelton Tree*
5. Leonard Cohen, esp. *Recent Songs, The Future, You Want it Darker*
6. John Coltrane, esp. *A Love Supreme*
7. The Indigo Girls, esp. *Indigo Girls, Nomads, Indians, Saints*
8. Loreena McKennitt, esp. *The Mask and the Mirror, The Book of Secrets*
9. Van Morrison, esp. *Into the Music, Avalon Sunset, Hymns to the Silence*
10. Carrie Newcomer, esp. *The Gathering of Spirits, Betty's Diner*
11. Sinead O'Connor, esp. *Theology*
12. Richard Shindell, esp. *Somewhere Near Paterson, Reunion Hill*

13. Bruce Springsteen, esp. *Born to Run, The River, The Rising*
14. Cat Stevens, esp. *Tea for the Tillerman, The Teaser and the Firecat*
15. Lucinda Williams, esp. *Sweet Old World, Car Wheels on a Gravel Road, Blessed*

Here are a few books on music that I have found especially helpful and insightful:

Robert Greenberg, *How to Listen to Great Music* (New York: Plume Books, 2011)[1]

Jay R. Howard and John M. Streck, *Apostles of Rock* (Lexington, KY: University of Kentucky Press, 1999)

Patrick Kavanaugh, *The Music of Angels* (Chicago: Loyola Press, 1999)

Jan Swafford, *Language of the Spirit* (New York: Basic Books, 2017)

Steve Turner, *Hungry for Heaven* (Downers Grove, IL: InterVarsity Press, 1995)

Gene Edward Veith and Thomas L. Wilmeth, *Honky-Tonk Gospel*, (Grand Rapids, MI: Baker Books, 2001)

There is no experience with art that quite compares with getting lost in a good novel, given the opportunity to live with characters and ideas for a more extended period of time than with any other art form. I have learned much from them about the joys and struggles of life and have been both entertained and inspired and convicted as I wandered through their pages. Here are some very selective lists of favorites:

Twenty-Five Great Novelists Who Affirm Faith

1. Georges Bernanos, esp. *The Diary of a Country Priest, Under Satan's Sun*
2. Wendell Berry, esp. *Jayber Crow, A Place in Time*
3. Frederick Buechner, esp. *Godric, The Book of Bebb*
4. Willa Cather, esp. *Death Comes to the Archbishop, Shadows on the Rock*

5. G. K. Chesterton, esp. *The Man Who Was Thursday, The Father Brown Stories*
6. Fyodor Dostoyevsky, esp. *The Brothers Karamazov, Crime and Punishment, The Idiot*
7. Sūusaku Endō, *Silence, Scandal, The Golden Country*
8. Gail Godwin, *Father Melancholy's Daughter, Evensong*
9. Ron Hansen, *Mariette in Ecstasy, Exiles*
10. Susan Howatch, esp. *Glittering Images, Glamorous Powers*
11. C. S. Lewis, esp. *The Chronicles of Narnia, The Great Divorce, Till We Have Faces*
12. George MacDonald, esp. *At the Back of the North Wind, The Princess and Curdie, Fairy Tales*
13. François Mauriac, esp. *Therese Desqueyroux, Vipers Tangle*
14. Flannery O'Connor, esp. *Short Stories*
15. Walker Percy, esp. *The Second Coming, Love in the Ruins, The Moviegoer*
16. Marilynne Robinson, esp. *Gilead, Lila*
17. Dorothy L. Sayers, *The Man Born to Be King*
18. Alexander Solzhenitsyn, *One Day in the Life of Ivan Denisovich, Cancer Ward, The First Circle*
19. J. R. R. Tolkien, *The Lord of the Rings, The Hobbit*
20. Leo Tolstoy, esp. *The Death of Ivan Ilych, Anna Karenina, Short Stories*
21. Anthony Trollope, *The Warden, Barchester Towers*
22. Sigrid Undset, *Kristin Lavransdatter*
23. Walter Wangerin, esp. *The Book of the Dun Cow, The Book of God*
24. Evelyn Waugh, esp. *Brideshead Revisited, A Handful of Dust*
25. Charles Williams, esp. *Descent Into Hell, Place of the Lion*

Fifteen Great Novelists Who Write About Spiritual Seekers
1. Douglas Coupland, esp. *Life After God*
2. David James Duncan, *The River Why, The Brothers K*
3. George Eliot, *Middlemarch*
4. Graham Greene, esp. *The Power and the Glory, Brighton Rock, The Heart of the Matter, Monsignor Quixote*
5. Hermann Hesse, esp. *Narcissus and Goldmund, Siddhartha*

6. Zora Neale Hurston, *Their Eyes Were Watching God*
7. John Irving, *A Prayer for Owen Meany*
8. Barbara Kingsolver, *The Poisonwood Bible*
9. Yann Martel, *Life of Pi*
10. Robert M. Pirsig, *Zen and the Art of Motorcycle Maintenance*
11. Chaim Potok, esp. *The Chosen, My Name is Asher Lev*
12. J. D. Salinger, *Franny and Zooey*
13. Isaac Bashevis Singer, esp. *Gimpel the Fool, The Penitent*
14. John Updike, esp. *Pigeon Feathers, Roger's Version, In the Beauty of the Lilies*
15. Anne Tyler, *Saint Maybe*

Twenty Great Novelists Who Write About What It Means to Be Human

1. Chimamanda Ngozi Adichie, *Purple Hibiscus*
2. Jane Austen, esp. *Pride and Prejudice, Sense and Sensibility*
3. Saul Bellow, esp. *Humboldt's Gift, Herzog*
4. Charles Dickens, esp. *Great Expectations, Hard Times, David Copperfield*
5. Anthony Doerr, *All the Light We Cannot See*
6. Ralph Ellison, *Invisible Man*
7. Jonathan Safran Foer, *Everything is Illuminated*
8. William Golding, *Lord of the Flies, The Spire*
9. Jon Hassler, esp. *Staggerford, A Green Journey, Dear James*
10. Robert Hellenga, *The Fall of a Sparrow*
11. Mark Helprin, esp. *A Soldier of the Great War, A Winter's Tale, Paris in the Present Tense*
12. Dara Horn, esp. *The World to Come, All Other Nights*
13. Victor Hugo, *Les Misérables*
14. Harper Lee, *To Kill a Mockingbird*
15. Gabriel García Márquez, *One Hundred Years of Solitude*
16. Haruki Murakami, *Hard Boiled Wonderland and the End of the World, IQ84*
17. Ann Patchett, *Bel Canto*
18. Arundhati Roy, *The God of Small Things*
19. Zadie Smith, *White Teeth*
20. Amor Towles, *A Gentleman in Moscow*

There are a lot of good books on the relationship between literature and faith, but here are six of my favorites:

Jerram Barrs, *Echoes of Eden* (Wheaton, IL: Crossway, 2013)

W. Dale Brown, *Of Fiction and Faith* (Grand Rapids, MI: Eerdmans, 1997)

David L. Larsen, *The Company of the Creative* (Grand Rapids, MI: Kregel, 1999)

C. S. Lewis, *An Experiment in Criticism* (Cambridge: Cambridge University Press, 1961)

Joseph Pearce, *Literary Converts* (San Francisco: Ignatius Press, 1999)

William H. Willimon, *Reading with Deeper Eyes* (Nashville: Upper Room Books, 1998)

Films are the ultimate collaborative art form. They combine sight and sound with the work of writers, directors, and actors to create a cinematic story. Films are also probably the most influential artistic form in our contemporary world. There aren't many novels or recordings that sell a million copies, but it isn't uncommon for a film to have millions of viewers. Unfortunately, the quality does not always match the popularity of the movies, so I'm suggesting some that are definitely worth your time. What I mentioned at the opening of this chapter is especially true for these lists—not everything in them will be appropriate for all ages. But all of them will inspire you, challenge you, or at least make you think a little differently.

Twenty-Five Films That Affirm Faith

1. *Andrei Rublev* (1969)
2. *The Apostle* (1997)
3. *Babette's Feast* (1987)
4. *A Beautiful Day in the Neighborhood* (2019)
5. *Brother Sun, Sister Moon* (1972)
6. *Chariots of Fire* (1981)
7. *Diary of a Country Priest* (1951)

8. *The Flowers of St. Francis* (1950)
9. *Going My Way* (1944)
10. *A Hidden Life* (2019)
11. *The Hiding Place* (1975)
12. *Into Great Silence* (2007)
13. *The Lion, the Witch and the Wardrobe* (2006)
14. *Luther* (2003)
15. *The Mission* (1986)
16. *Monsignor Quixote* (1987)
17. *Of Gods and Men* (2011)
18. *Ordet* (1955)
19. *The Passion of Joan of Arc* (1928)
20. *Romero* (1989)
21. *The Scarlet and the Black* (1983)
22. *Shadowlands* (1993)
23. *Silence* (2017)
24. *The Tree of Life* (2011)
25. *The Two Popes* (2019)

Twenty Films to Extend Your Empathy
1. *About Schmidt* (2002)
2. *Dead Man Walking* (1995)
3. *Do the Right Thing* (1989)
4. *The Florida Project* (2017)
5. *The Grapes of Wrath* (1940)
6. *Green Book* (2018)
7. *The Hate U Give* (2018)
8. *The Insult* (2017)
9. *Land of Plenty* (2004)
10. *Make Way for Tomorrow* (1937)
11. *Monster's Ball* (2001)
12. *Selma* (2014)
13. *Seven Up!* and its sequels (1964–2019)
14. *Shoplifters* (2019)
15. *Sparrows* (1927)
16. *The Unknown Girl* (2016)
17. *To Kill a Mockingbird* (1962)

18. *Tokyo Story* (1953)
19. *Two Days, One Night* (2014)
20. *Umberto D.* (1952)

Eight Films on Biblical Stories

1. *Ben-Hur* (1959)
2. *The Gospel According to St. Matthew* (1964)
3. *Jesus of Nazareth* (1977)
4. *Last Days in the Desert* (2016)
5. *The Passion of the Christ* (2004)
6. *Paul, Apostle of Christ* (2018)
7. *Risen* (2016)
8. *The Ten Commandments* (1956)

Twenty-Five Films About Spiritual Seekers and Strugglers

1. *Breaking the Waves* (1996)
2. *The Burmese Harp* (1956)
3. *Calvary* (2014)
4. *Corpus Christi* (2019)
5. *Crimes and Misdemeanors* (1989)
6. *Europe '51* (1952)
7. *The Fall* (2008)
8. *Find Me* (2019)
9. *First Reformed* (2018)
10. *Hannah and Her Sisters* (1986)
11. *Henry Poole is Here* (2007)
12. *Ida* (2014)
13. *Ikiru* (1952)
14. *Léon Morin, Priest* (1961)
15. *Loving Vincent* (2017)
16. *My Night at Maud's* (1969)
17. *On the Waterfront* (1954)
18. *Philomena* (2014)
19. *The Sacrifice* (1986)
20. *The Seventh Seal* (1957)
21. *Stalker* (1979)
22. *Tender Mercies* (1983)

23. *The Thin Red Line* (1998)
24. *Wild Strawberries* (1957)
25. *Wings of Desire* (1987)

Twenty Films About the Struggles of Being Human

1. *12 Angry Men* (1957)
2. *Before Sunrise* (1995) and its sequels
3. *Bicycle Thieves* (1949)
4. *Citizen Kane* (1940)
5. *Dead Poets Society* (1989)
6. *Decalogue* (1987)
7. *The Godfather* (1972) and *The Godfather Part II* (1974)
8. *Life is Beautiful* (1998)
9. *Magnolia* (1999)
10. *The Matrix* (1999)
11. *The Night of the Hunter* (1955)
12. *Rashomon* (1950)
13. *The Royal Tenenbaums* (2001)
14. *Saving Private Ryan* (1998)
15. *Schindler's List* (1993)
16. *A Separation* (2011)
17. *The Shawshank Redemption* (1994)
18. *Sullivan's Travels* (1942)
19. *Sunrise* (1927)
20. *The Third Man* (1949)

If you want to learn more about the history of film, I would suggest:

Mark Cousins, *The Story of Film* (London: Pavillion, 2011)[2]
Gerald Mast, *A Short History of the Movies* (New York: Macmillan, 1992)
David Thomson, *The Big Screen* (New York: Farrar, Straus, and Giroux, 2012)

On the relationship between faith and film, here are a few of my favorites:

> Roy Anker, *Of Pilgrims and Fire: When God Shows Up at the Movies* (Grand Rapids, MI: Eerdmans, 2010)
>
> Gareth Higgins, *How Movies Helped Save My Soul* (Lake Mary, FL: Relevant Books, 2003)
>
> Robert K. Johnston, *Reel Spirituality* (Grand Rapids, MI: Baker Books, 2000)
>
> Jeffrey Overstreet, *Through a Screen Darkly* (Ventura, CA: Gospel Light Books, 2007)

Painting is one of the harder art forms to share. To see great works of art in person means visiting a museum or attending a special exhibition, and the great paintings are scattered all over the world in various locations. Most of us don't have the money to travel around the United States, much less fly overseas in quest of great art. I've had some opportunities to take a couple of art vacations, and let me tell you it is worth the effort and expense to build a vacation around seeing unforgettable masterpieces. There is no substitution for the real thing. In the meantime, however, you'll probably have to settle for exploring art on the internet or through books of art prints. These days, a simple Google search will unearth riches, and many of the best museums have virtual tours available. Here are some artists you'll want to check out, and a list of museums that you can add to your bucket list and hopefully visit someday:

Twenty-Five Artists Whose Work Inspires, Challenges, and Delights Me

1. Thomas Hart Benton
2. Albert Bierstadt
3. Michelangelo Caravaggio
4. Marc Chagall
5. Frederic Edwin Church
6. Thomas Cole

7. John Constable
8. Salvador Dali
9. Albrecht Dürer
10. Makoto Fujimura
11. Giotto di Bondone
12. Vincent van Gogh
13. George Inness
14. Wassily Kandinsky
15. René Magritte
16. Claude Monet
17. Georgia O'Keeffe
18. Pablo Picasso
19. Jackson Pollock
20. Raphael
21. Rembrandt van Rijn
22. Mark Rothko
23. Henry Ossawa Tanner
24. Jan van Eyck
25. Johannes Vermeer

Twenty Must-See Art Museums (A Lifetime Bucket List)

1. Accademia Art Gallery (Venice)
2. Art Gallery of the Old Masters (Dresden)
3. The Art Institute of Chicago (Chicago)
4. Borghese Gallery (Rome)
5. Boston Museum of Fine Arts (Boston)
6. The Hermitage (St. Petersburg)
7. Kunsthistorische Museum (Vienna)
8. The Louvre (Paris)
9. Metropolitan Museum of Art (New York)
10. Museum of Modern Art (New York)
11. Musée d'Orsay (Paris)
12. The National Gallery (London)
13. National Gallery of Art (Washington, DC)
14. Philadelphia Museum of Art (Philadelphia)
15. The Prado (Madrid)
16. Rijksmuseum (Amsterdam)

17. Tate Britain (London)
18. The Uffizi Galleries (Florence)
19. The Van Gogh Museum (Amsterdam)
20. The Vatican Museums (Rome)

I hope this book has inspired you to take a closer look at the impact the arts can have on your life and faith, or that it has deepened the love of the arts that you already had. There is more great art out there awaiting you than you can probably enjoy in one lifetime, but you'll find the search for new unexpected treasures is part of the joy. While this book has focused mostly on the classics, there are living artists who are creating great work and deserve your attention and support. Instead of buying a print from a favorite dead artist, you might consider purchasing a work that moves you from an unknown living artist. Nothing beats an original! And take in some live concerts. There is nothing like hearing music performed live, and this is where most musicians earn their living. So, indulge.

May what you discover in the arts help you both grow as a person and draw you closer to the Great Artist who is ultimately responsible for all the teeming profusion of beauty and mystery in this world of ours. Amen.

ACKNOWLEDGMENTS

I'd like to thank the team at Moody Publishers, who were a delight to work with. Special thanks to Duane Sherman, who caught the vision for what I wanted to do in this book and was a wonderful advocate at every stage. His enthusiasm helped me at each step of the process. And to Mackenzie Conway, whose editorial skill and eye for details kept me from embarrassing myself. It was a pleasure working with you. Also, to Connor Sterchi for managing the process, Erik Peterson and Matt Smartt for the lovely interior design, Jeremy Slager for help with promotions, and Randall Payleitner for overseeing everything. You folks are amazing.

This is a much better book than it would have been thanks to the insights of my dear friend Carolyn McCready, who read each chapter and provided so much helpful insight and criticism. She encouraged me to tell my stories and not get too bogged down in the academic details. When I followed her advice, I found myself enjoying the process of writing more than I ever have before. I owe you a Starbucks coffee or two or twenty.

And thanks to all the many friends (far too many to list, but you know who you are) with whom I've shared the joys of watching films, discussing books, attending lectures and concerts, exploring museums, and being enraptured at the beauty of God's world. I'm always up for another artistic adventure!

NOTES

Chapter 1 • The Arts and Spiritual Disciplines: Two Paths to a Deeper Faith

1. Francis Schaeffer, "Art and the Bible," in *The Complete Works of Francis Schaeffer: A Christian Worldview*, vol. 2 (Westchester, IL: Crossway Books), 378 (emphasis added).
2. Philip Schaff and Henry Wace, *The Nicene and Post-Nicene Fathers: Second Series,* vol. 8 (Grand Rapids, MI: Eerdmans, 1969), 23.
3. Robin Margaret Jensen, *Understanding Early Christian Art* (New York: Routledge, 2000), 181.
4. Kurt J. Eggert, "Martin Luther, God's Music Man." Lecture, Wisconsin Lutheran Seminary, November 10, 1983.
5. Ibid.
6. Robert Wuthnow, *All in Sync* (Berkeley, CA: University of California Press, 2003), 108.

Chapter 2 • Coming Awake: Teaching Us to Pay Attention

1. M. H. Abrams, *Natural Supernaturalism: Tradition and Revolution in Romantic Literature* (New York: W. W. Norton, 1971), 379.
2. In Mary Oliver, *House of Light* (Boston: Beacon Press, 1990), 60.
3. Alain de Botton and John Armstrong, *Art as Therapy* (London: Phaidon Press, 2013), 11.
4. Dirk deVries, *Contemplative Vision: Photography as a Spiritual Practice* (New York: Church Publishing, 2019), 4. This helpful book not only discusses photography as a spiritual practice, but also provides numerous practical exercises and photographic tips for being more intentional in this kind of photographic endeavor.
5. Mary Oliver, *Upstream: Selected Essays* (London: Penguin Press, 2016), 8.
6. See his book *The Sacrament of the Present Moment*, trans. Kitty Muggeridge (San Francisco: Harper and Row, 1982).
7. C. S. Lewis, *Letters to Malcolm* (New York: Harcourt Brace & Co., 1964), 75.
8. Frederick Buechner, *Now and Then: A Memoir of Vocation* (San Francisco: Harper and Row, 1983), 87.

Chapter 3 • The Eyes of a Child: Rediscovering a Sense of Wonder

1. Barbara Kingsolver, *High Tide in Tucson* (New York: HarperCollins, 2009), 179.
2. G. K. Chesterton, *Orthodoxy* (Wheaton, IL: Harold Shaw, 1994), 61.
3. Antonio Machado, *Times Alone: Selected Poems of Antonio Machado* (Middletown, CT: Wesleyan University Press), 45.
4. Brendan of Birr, quoted in David Adam, *The Open Gate: Celtic Prayers for Growing Spiritually*, 2nd ed. (London: SPCK, 2006), 2.
5. G. K. Chesterton, *Robert Browning* (London: Macmillan, 1903), 158.
6. Asher Durand, "Letters on Landscape Painting," in *The Crayon* (January 3, 1855).
7. Letter from Jasper Francis Cropsey to Maria Cooley, July 4, 1846. NCF Transcripts.
8. Dacher Keltner, quoted in Paula Spencer Scott, "Feeling Awe May Be the Secret to Health and Happiness," *Parade*, October 7, 2016, https://parade.com/513786/paulaspencer/feeling-awe-may-be-the-secret-to-health-and-happiness/.

9. John Constable, quoted in William Vaughan, *Tate British Artists: John Constable* (London: Tate Publishing, 2015), 9.
10. Ibid., 75.
11. Vincent van Gogh, *Letters of Vincent van Gogh*, September 28, 1888.
12. Ibid., January 26, 1885.
13. Gerard Manley Hopkins, *Poems and Prose* (New York: Penguin Books, 1953), 30.
14. Abraham Joshua Heschel, *The Wisdom of Heschel* (New York: Farrar, Straus and Giroux, 1970), 205.

Chapter 4 • The Mystery Dance: Digging for Deeper Meanings

1. *The American Heritage Dictionary of the English Language* (Boston: Houghton Mifflin Co., 1976), 1344. This use of Blake's poem was suggested by Malcolm Guite in *Faith, Hope, and Poetry: Theology and the Poetic Imagination* (London: Routledge Press, 2016), 1. I have found Guite's insights to be particularly helpful for the topic of faith and poetry, and highly recommend his book.
2. William Blake, *The Penguin Poets: William Blake* (New York: Penguin Books, 1958), 49–50.
3. William Shakespeare, *Hamlet*, Act III, Scene 2, line 24.
4. C. S. Lewis, *Surprised by Joy: The Shape of My Early Life* (New York: Harcourt, 1955), 170.
5. Sir John Davies, *The Poems of John Davies* (Oxford: Oxford University Press, 1975), 20.
6. Guite, 1.
7. C. S. Lewis, *Voyage of the Dawn Treader* (New York: HarperCollins, 1952), 226.
8. C. S. Lewis, *Miracles* (New York: Harper One, 1947), 212.
9. Guite, 5.
10. Sallie McFague, *Speaking in Parables: A Study in Metaphor and Theology* (Philadelphia: Fortress Press, 1975), 29.
11. Fleming Rutledge, *The Crucifixion: Understanding the Death of Jesus Christ* (Grand Rapids, MI: Eerdmans, 2015).
12. Marc Chagall, *Chagall by Chagall* (New York: New English Library, 1979), 199.
13. Frederick Buechner, *Wishful Thinking: A Seeker's ABC* (San Francisco: Harper San Francisco, 1993), 76.
14. Ibid.
15. Rainer Maria Rilke, *Letters to a Young Poet / The Possibility of Being* (New York: MJF Books, 2000), 35.
16. Phillip Salim Francis, *When Art Disrupts Religion: Aesthetic Experience and the Evangelical Mind* (Oxford: Oxford University Press, 2017)
17. William Shakespeare, *Hamlet*, Act 1, Scene 5, lines 167–68.
18. See his brilliant books, *The Sacred Canopy: Elements of a Sociological Theory of Religion* (New York: Doubleday, 1967), *A Rumor of Angels: Modern Society and the Rediscovery of the Supernatural* (New York: Doubleday, 1969), and *The Heretical Imperative: Contemporary Possibilities of Religious Affirmation* (New York: Doubleday, 1979).
19. C. S. Lewis, *The Great Divorce* (New York: Harper One, 1946), 40.
20. Charles Taylor, *A Secular Age* (Cambridge: Harvard University Press, 2007).
21. Flannery O'Connor, *The Habit of Being: Letters of Flannery O'Connor* (New York: Random House, 1979), 349.
22. Julian Barnes, *Nothing to Be Frightened Of* (New York: Vintage, 2009), 5.

Chapter 5 • A Bigger Picture: Bringing the Scriptures to Life

1. The Midrash: Avot 5:26
2. Francis Wade, *Biblical Fracking: Midrash for the Modern Christian* (Eugene, OR: Wipf and Stock, 2019), 2.
3. Rachel Held Evans, *Inspired: Slaying Giants, Walking on Water, and Loving the Bible Again* (Nashville: Nelson Books, 2018), xx.
4. Kenneth Pople, *Stanley Spencer: A Biography* (New York: HarperCollins, 1991), 309.
5. For a discussion of this painting, see my book: Terry Glaspey, *75 Masterpieces Every Christian Should Know: The Fascinating Stories Behind Great Works of Art, Literature, Music and Film* (Chicago: Moody Publishers, 2021).
6. Ron O'Grady, ed., *Christ for All People: Celebrating a World of Christian Art* (Maryknoll, NY: Orbis Books, 2001).
7. Patricia C. Pongracz, Volker Küster, and John Wesley Cook, *The Christian Story: Five Asian Artists Today* (New York: Museum of Biblical Art, 2007).
8. Anne Pyle, *Printing the Word: The Art of Watanabe Sadao* (New York: American Bible Society, 2000), 25.
9. Robert Atwan and Laurance Weider, eds., *Chapters into Verse: Poetry in English Inspired by the Bible*, 2 vols. (Oxford: Oxford University Press, 1993).
10. D. S. Martin, *Adam, Eve, and the Riders of the Apocalypse: 39 Contemporary Poets on the Characters of the Bible* (Eugene, OR: Cascade Books, 2017).

Chapter 6 • The Best Kind of Heartbreak: Helping Us Deal with Our Emotions

1. William Congreve, *The Mourning Bride*, Act One, Scene One.
2. Aristotle, *Nicomachean Ethics*, 1109a25.
3. Daniel Goleman, *Emotional Intelligence: Why It Can Matter More than IQ* (New York: Bantam Books, 2005), 56.
4. William James, *The Principles of Psychology*, vol. 2 (New York: Henry Holt and Co., 1890), 462–63.
5. Goleman suggests that IQ only contributes about 20% to the factors that determine our success in life, leaving 80% determined by other factors. Among the most powerful of these other factors is emotional intelligence.
6. Goleman, *Emotional Intelligence*, 54.
7. This story was shared with me by one of the curators at the Denver Art Museum during a visit.
8. Molly Guptill Manning, *When Books Went to War: The Stories That Helped Us Win World War II* (Boston: Houghton Mifflin Harcourt, 2014), xi–xii.

Chapter 7 • We Are Not Alone: Finding Comfort and Discovering Courage

1. Quoted in Matthew Fox, *Creativity: Where the Divine and Human Meet* (New York: Penguin, 2004), 195.
2. Ibid., 45.
3. Michka Assayas, *Bono on Bono: Conversations with Michka Assayas* (New York: Riverhead Books, 2006), 204.
4. C. S. Lewis, *God in the Dock* (Grand Rapids, MI: William B. Eerdmans, 1970), 52.
5. Wendell Berry, *Standing by Words: Essays* (San Francisco: North Point Press, 1983), 201.
6. Quoted in Patrick J. Keane, *Emily Dickinson's Approving God: Divine Design and the Problem of Suffering* (Columbia, MO: University of Missouri Press, 2008), 179.
7. Emily Dickinson, "Some Keep the Sabbath Going to Church," *The Complete Poems of Emily Dickinson* (New York: Little, Brown, 1976), 153.
8. As quoted in Norman Sherry, *The Life of Graham Greene*, vol. 3, 1955–1991 (London: Jonathan Cape, 2004), 188.

9. Henri J. M. Nouwen, *The Return of the Prodigal Son: A Story of Homecoming* (New York: Doubleday Image, 1994), 5, 15.
10. Frederick Buechner, *Wishful Thinking: A Theological ABC* (New York: Harper and Row, 1973), 34.

Chapter 8 • A World Bigger Than Me: Making Us More Empathetic

1. C. S. Lewis, *An Experiment in Criticism* (Cambridge: Cambridge University Press, 1961), 140.
2. Ibid., 141.
3. William A. Dyrness, *Rouault: A Vision of Suffering and Salvation* (Grand Rapids, MI: William B. Eerdmans, 1971), 79.
4. José Maria Faerna, *Rouault* (New York: Cameo-Abrams, 1997), 28.
5. Julian Barnes, "Julian Barnes: My Life as a Bibliophile," *The Guardian,* June 2012.
6. Quoted in *The New York Times*, October 3, 2013.
7. Quoted in the excellent documentary film about Roger Ebert, *Life Itself* (2014).
8. Roger Ebert, "Ebert's Walk of Fame Remarks," RogerEbert.com, June 24, 2005, https://www.rogerebert.com/roger-ebert/eberts-walk-of-fame-remarks.

Chapter 9 • Prophetic Voices: Awakening a Passion for Justice

1. Abraham J. Heschel, *The Prophets* (New York: Harper Perennial, 1962), 250.
2. Walter Brueggemann, *Interrupting Silence: God's Command to Speak Out* (Louisville, KY: John Knox Press, 2018), 25.
3. Heschel, *The Prophets*, 365.
4. William Blake, *A Selection of Poems and Letters* (New York: Penguin, 1958), 162.
5. Helena Kelly, *Jane Austen: The Secret Radical* (New York: Alfred Knopf, 2017), 33.
6. Walker Percy, *Signposts in a Strange Land* (New York: Farrar, Straus, and Giroux, 1991), 378.
7. Ibid., 206.
8. Ibid., 180.
9. Ralph Ellison, *Living with Music: Ralph Ellison's Jazz Writings*, ed. Robert G. O'Meally (New York: Modern Library, 2001), 129.
10. W. E. B. Du Bois, *The Souls of Black Folk* (Columbia, MO: University of Missouri Press, 2003), 12.
11. James H. Cone, *The Spirituals and the Blues: An Interpretation* (New York: Seabury Press, 1972).
12. Ralph Basui Watkins, *Hip-Hop Redemption: Finding God in the Rhythm and the Rhyme* (Grand Rapids, MI: Baker Academic, 2011), 41. This is an extremely helpful book for understanding this musical genre from a Christian perspective.
13. For the backstory on this song, see Dorian Lynskey, *33 Revolutions Per Minute: A History of Protest Songs, from Billie Holiday to Green Day* (New York: Ecco Books, 2011), 429–46.
14. Ibid., 57.
15. Bob Dylan, *Chronicles: Volume One* (New York: Simon and Schuster, 2004), 54.

Chapter 10 • Quiet Places: Assisting Us in Prayer and Contemplatoin

1. George Herbert, *The Country Parson, The Temple* (New York: Paulist Press, 1981), 165–66.
2. Martin Laird, *Into the Silent Land: A Guide to the Christian Practice of Contemplation* (New York: Oxford University Press, 2006), 15.
3. Robert Hudson, *The Art of the Almost Said: A Christian Writer's Guide to Writing Poetry* (Friendswood, TX: Bold Vision Books, 2019), 46.

4. Makoto Fujimura, *River Grace* (New York: Poiema Press, 2007), 3.
5. Ibid., 16.
6. Makoto Fujimura, "How to 'See' My Painting," February 12, 2015, https://www.makotofujimura.com/writings/how-to-see-my-painting.
7. John Drury, *Painting the Word: Christian Pictures and Their Meanings* (New Haven, CT: Yale University Press, 1999), xiii.
8. Terry Glaspey, *Beautiful Prayers to Inspire Your Soul* (Eugene, OR: Harvest House Publishers, 2016).
9. Thomas Merton, *Thoughts in Solitude* (New York: Farrar, Straus, and Giroux, 1958), 79.
10. Herbert, *The Country Parson, The Temple*, 281.
11. John Donne, *Selected Poems* (New York: Dover Publications, 1993), 64.
12. *The Book of Common Prayer* (New York: Seabury Press, 1979), 77.
13. T. S. Eliot, *Four Quartets* (New York: Harvest Books, 1943), 19.
14. John Leclercq, *The Love of Learning and the Desire for God* (London: SPCK, 1974), 257.
15. William Law and Alexander Whyte, *Characters and Characteristics of William Law: Nonjuror and Mystic* (London: Hodder & Stoughton, 1893), 159.
16. Henry Ward Beecher, *Yale Lectures on Preaching* (New York: Fords, Howard & Hulbert, 1900), 118–19.
17. John Cassian, *The Conferences* (New York: Paulist Press, 1997), 384.
18. See C. S. Lewis, *Reflections on the Psalms* (New York: Harcourt Brace Jovanovich, 1958), and Dietrich Bonhoeffer, *Psalms: The Prayer Book of the Bible* (Minneapolis: Augsburg, 1970).

Chapter 11 • Soul Food: Resources for Your Spiritual Journey

1. I also highly recommend Greenberg's entertaining and informative series of audio and DVD courses on music and opera available from The Great Courses.
2. Cousins has also produced an enlightening series (available on DVD) of the same name, focusing on the history of cinema around the world, and has also created a series focusing on the work of women filmmakers. Both are highly recommended.

(continued from page 2)

In *Discovering God through the Arts*, Terry Glaspey masterfully weaves the magnificence of great works of art with the beauty of our Christian faith. His lively descriptions, captivating stories, and conversational tone will expand not only your understanding of creativity, but of your Creator.

MELISSA MAIMONE, acclaimed speaker and author of *The Radiant Midnight: Depression, Grace, and the Gifts of a Dark Place*

In *Discovering God through the Arts*, Terry Glaspey thoughtfully and joyfully ushers us into a world of wonder. A world of creative endeavor God intends for us to observe, enjoy, and participate in. Carefully researched and illustrated, the chapters prove readable and informative for anyone: from the arts novice to the experienced creative to the seasoned historian. This book is a gift!

JUDITH COUCHMAN, art historian and author, *The Art of Faith*

Living in a world full of beauty, too often we ignore it, downplay its importance, or think of it only as something to be used for our own purposes. We become hardened and blind. Terry Glaspey wants to teach us to see again. *Discovering God through the Arts* invites us to bask in the wonder of God's gifts of art, story, and music, heightening our appreciation and at the same time refreshing our spirits and enhancing our worship.

GINA DALFONZO, author of *Dorothy and Jack: The Transforming Friendship of Dorothy L. Sayers* and C. S. Lewis and editor of *The Gospel in Dickens: Selections from His Works*

LET YOUR FAITH BE MOVED BY THE MASTERPIECES

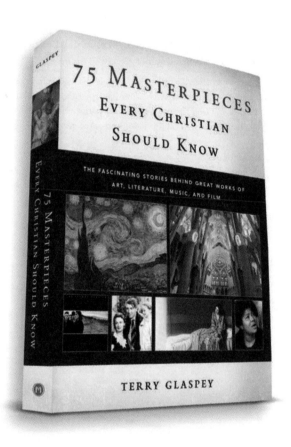

MOODY
Publishers®

From the Word to Life®

75 Masterpieces Every Christian Should Know anthologizes some of humanity's most influential and renowned works of art that examine the realities of the human condition and Christian truth. Through engaging these masterpieces, Christians today can enrich their own faith with the creativity of history's brilliant artists.

978-0-8024-2087-9 | also available as an eBook